Edward Williams

Antipaedobaptism Examined

A strict and impartial inquiry into the nature and design, subjects and mode of

baptism - Vol. 1

Edward Williams

Antipaedobaptism Examined

A strict and impartial inquiry into the nature and design, subjects and mode of baptism - Vol. 1

ISBN/EAN: 9783337368791

Printed in Europe, USA, Canada, Australia, Japan

Cover: Foto ©Lupo / pixelio.de

More available books at **www.hansebooks.com**

Antipædobaptism Examined:
OR,
A STRICT AND IMPARTIAL
INQUIRY
INTO THE
NATURE AND DESIGN, SUBJECTS AND MODE
OF
BAPTISM.
INCLUDING, ALSO,
AN INVESTIGATION OF THE NATURE OF
POSITIVE INSTITUTIONS
IN GENERAL, AND
OCCASIONAL STRICTURES ON HUMAN
CEREMONIES IN MATTERS OF RELIGION.
CONTAINING, IN PARTICULAR,
A FULL REPLY TO
Mr. BOOTH's Pœdobaptism Examined.

By EDWARD WILLIAMS.

WHEN I HAD WAITED—I SAID, I WILL ANSWER ALSO MY PART, I ALSO WILL SHEW MINE OPINION. ELIHU.

VOL. I.

SHREWSBURY:
PRINTED AND SOLD BY J. AND W. EDDOWES;
SOLD ALSO BY T. LONGMAN AND J. BUCKLAND, PATER-NOSTER-ROW; C. DILLY, IN THE POULTRY, LONDON
AND W. BROWNE, BRISTOL.
MDCCLXXXIX.

PREFACE.

THE following work is not intended *merely* as an answer to Mr. BOOTH's *Pædobaptism Examined*; the author, as occasion offered, has taken notice of what appeared to him the most plausible arguments and objections contained in Dr. STENNETT's Answer to Dr. ADDINGTON, Dr. GALE's Reflections on Dr. WALL's History, and some others; and therefore, he has ventured to give the result of his inquiries the title of *Antipædobaptism Examined*; not so much as a counter-title to that of Mr. BOOTH's publication, as that the *Antipædobaptist System* at large, is made the subject of inquiry. This extent of design will, in some measure, account for the largeness of the work; to which I must add another reason, viz. That I was desirous my principles may be thoroughly understood by every reader, if possible, without hazard of mistake; and this appeared the most effectual method—to set them in different positions—and to shew their connection with the several branches of dispute, and their genuine practical tendency. Whence arises, eventually, a double advantage to the inquisitive reader; he not only must needs perceive clearly what the principles are, but also has an opportunity to judge of their *truth*, by observing the universality of their application.

At different intervals of relaxation from more important engagements, the subject of these volumes had attracted the Author's attention for some years; but he did not resolve to write and publish, till some time after Mr. Booth's *Pædobaptism Examined* made its appearance: nor was it his design, when he began to write, to handle the several branches of controversy in so extensive a manner. But, in his progress, the more he considered his leading ideas, in their various application to the different parts, the more he was induced to extend his plan.

When I read Mr. Booth's Preface to the *second edition* of his work, which came out after the former part of mine was sent into the press, my curiosity was not a little gratified with the following paragraph: "Should this examination of Pœdobaptism have the honour of being regarded as deserving an answer, and should any of our opposers write against me, it will not avail to refute some particular parts of the work, detached from the general principles

PREFACE.

ples on which I proceed. No; the *data*, the *principal grounds* of reasoning, which are adopted from Pœdobaptists themselves, must be constantly kept in view; or nothing to the honour of infant sprinkling will be effected. For as the grand principles on which my argumentation proceeds, and whence my general conclusions are drawn, are those of Protestants when contending with Papists, and those of Non-conformists when disputing with English Episcopalians; it will be incumbent on such opposer to shew, either that the *principles themselves are false*, or that my *reasoning upon them is inconclusive*. Now as I do not perceive how any Protestant can give up those principles, without virtually admitting the superstitions of Popery; nor how they can be deserted by any Dissenter, without implicitly renouncing his Non-conformity; so I conclude, that the whole force of any opponent must be employed in endeavouring to prove, that I have reasoned inconsequentially from those principles. That this might be easily proved, I am not at present convinced: and whether any of our Pœdobaptist Brethren will consider this publication as of sufficient importance to excite such an attempt, is to me uncertain*."

* p. 19, 20.

The data, the principal grounds of reasoning must be kept in view. Well, I reflected, here is my task fairly pointed out; and I am not a little pleased to observe, that what is here prescribed is precisely the same as what I had from the first imposed upon myself: that is, not to nibble at some of the branches of his stately tree, but to lay the axe of opposite principles to the root of it; not to uncover a little here and there of his building, to find a few faults in quotations, translations, and the like, but to undermine the foundation. The *principal grounds* of reasoning I have endeavoured constantly to keep in view; and my aim is throughout to shew that the *principles* of Protestants and Nonconformists, taken in their only true sense and force, are either misunderstood or *misrepresented* by my opponent, and consequently his reasoning upon them, which derives all its plausibility from that misrepresentation, is *inconclusive*. His conduct in applying their maxims to his cause, may be compared to that of a Judge who should produce, from the best writers, definitions of Justice in the abstract, and then arbitrarily tack these to any cause, right or wrong, according to his humour. But will such an arbitrary application of a definition, formed abstractedly,

PREFACE. vii

stractedly, make a cause more or less just in itself? Should not the circumstances of the point in litigation be first attended to, and the facts be accurately ascertained, in order to infer the *quantum* of justice or injustice in the whole aggregate? So far were the most eminent of the Protestants and Non-conformists from discarding the use of right reason and scripture analogy in their investigations of gospel worship and institutions, that sometimes they were not a little offended with insinuations to the contrary. The following words of Dr. JOHN OWEN may be fairly deemed a proper specimen of their thoughts upon the matter: " I have of late been much surprised with the plea of some for the *use of reason* in religion and sacred things; not at all that such a *plea is insisted* on, but that it is by them built expressly on a supposition, that it is by others, whom they reflect upon, *denied*; whereas some, probably intended in those reflections, have pleaded for it *against the Papists* (to speak within the bounds of sobriety) with as much reason, and no less effectually, than any amongst themselves*."

IN fact, the christian church has been shamefully abused by extravagant opinions and superstitious

* On the Sabbath, Exercit. I. § 8.

stitious ceremonies, which may well raise the indignation of a mind in love with the sacred authority of scripture, and rational devotion; and this has occasioned some, in the height of their antipathy and pious zeal, to fly into the opposite extreme of adhering to the *mere letter* of divine laws, to the neglect of their *true spirit*. But this is not all; what was designed as a preventive to the former disease, becomes itself, in common with it, the occasion (or, shall I say, the culpable cause?) of a malady far more dangerous. " Among other prejudices," — says a shrewd observer, who, hiding himself behind the scene, attentively watched their motions—"among other prejudices there is one of a particular nature, which you must have observed to be one of the greatest causes of modern irreligion.— Whilst some *opinions and rites* are carried to such an *immoderate height*, as exposes the absurdity of them to the view of almost every body but them who raise them, not only gentlemen of the *belles lettres*, but even men of common sense, many times see thro' them; and then out of indignation and an excessive renitence, not *separating* that which is true from that which is false, they come to deny both, and fall back into the contrary extreme, a contempt of all religion in general *."

* WOLLAST. Relig. of Nat. p. 60, 61. Edit. 1725.

PREFACE.

I SHOULD be very sorry if what is advanced in the following Examination, should in any measure violate the sacred bond of christian charity and friendship that subsists between me and, in this instance, my differing brethren; with several of whom I wish to preserve and cultivate a fraternal affection. And those of them who bear the ministerial character, with whom I agree in weightier points of evangelical truth, are welcome to my pulpit, my house, and my heart; and none would be more so, according to my present views, than the author of the *Reign of Grace*, and *Pædobaptism Examined*.

I NOW submit the performance to the impartial judgment of the candid public, and implore the blessing of God on every grain of truth contained in it, for the reader's real benefit; earnestly wishing that evangelical knowledge may increase, and that all our acquaintance with God's word, covenant, institutions, and all the means of grace, may be reduced to experience and useful practice, to the glory of God, the Father, the Son, and the Holy Ghost. *Amen*.

OSWESTRY, Dec. 9, 1788.

ERRATA.

Vol. I. p.	7	line 1. Note, for	Treatise on,	read, History of.
	89	10	(§)	(§ 4.)
	95	29	negatives	negative
	137	26	Rom.	1 Cor.
	184	4	Corrollary	corollary
	198	ult.	corolaries	corollaries
	200	23	shall	should
	217	8	promisor	promiser
	224	12	fants	infants
	283	17	were	where
	——	ult.	Grotius	Grotium.
	286	15	dele as	
	298	2 Note,	state	happiness
	311	11	31	39
	356	33	παιζαι	παιςιχι
	386	penult.	their	your
	395	penult.	dele bad	
Vol. II. p.	3	17	catechresis	catachresis
	63	18	tincturat	tinctura
	120	13	let	led
	199	1	cafe	cause
	210	25	παιδιαν	παιδιων
	211	12	fail	feal
	213	4	dele *as* after *well*	
	——	—	major	magis
	268	28	his word	God's word
	288	4	see it	see to it.
	382	18	* Blackst. Comm. Introd. § 2.	

CONTENTS.

Volume the First.

Introduction. *Containing some preliminary Remarks* —— *p.* 1—20

Chap. I. *Of positive Institutions and analogical Reasoning* —— *p.* 21—98

Chap. II. *Of the nature and design of Baptism* —— —— *p.* 99—197

Chap. III. *Of the proper subjects of Baptism* *p.* 198—412

Volume the Second.

Chap. IV. *Of the signification of the terms baptize and baptism* —— *p.* 1—189

Chap. V. *Objections and Evasions of Antipædobaptists answered* —— *p.* 190—266

Chap. VI. *Practical Reflections* *p.* 267—350

Appendix —— *p.* 351—417

Intended to be published, as soon as the Author's other Engagements will permit,

AN

ESSAY

ON THE

EQUITY OF DIVINE GOVERNMENT,

AND THE

SOVEREIGNTY OF DIVINE GRACE.

Wherein, particularly, The

LATITUDINARIAN HYPOTHESIS OF INDETERMINATE REDEMPTION,

AND THE

ANTINOMIAN NOTION of the DIVINE DECREES being the rule of ministerial conduct, are carefully examined.

By EDWARD WILLIAMS.

SHALL not the Judge of all the earth do right? Gen. xviii. 25.

AND he doth according to his will in the army of Heaven, and among the inhabitants of the earth. Dan. iv. 35.

WHY doth he yet find fault? for who hath resisted his will? Nay but, O man, who art thou that repliest against God? Shall the thing formed say unto him that formed it, Why hast thou made me thus? Rom. ix. 19, 20.

THE secret things belong to the Lord our God; but those things which are revealed belong unto us and to our children for ever. Deut. xxix. 29.

ANTIPÆDOBAPTISM EXAMINED.

INTRODUCTION,

Containing some Preliminary Remarks.

§ 1. *The importance of the subject.* § 2. *The advantages of a strict and impartial inquiry into it.* § 3. *Preliminary Remarks.* § 4. (1) *Of the kind of evidence required in this debate.* § 5. (2) *Concerning the main hinge of the controversy.* § 6. (3) *Of defining and explaining the principal terms.* § 7. (4) *Of human authority and opinion.*

§ 1. THAT the subject investigated in the following pages is of a nature considerably important, will hardly be questioned by any who reflect, that *no person* professing christianity can lawfully exempt himself from paying it at least a practical attention; for, if he imagine (as the *Quakers*, and some of the followers of Socinus do) that he is under no obligation to espouse

espouse the practice of water baptism, as a *standing ordinance* in the christian church, surely he ought to have substantial reasons for that determination, or else must incur the censure of precipitate rashness and irreligion. It concerns him impartially to judge, whether or not the arguments adduced in favour of this christian practice be of *superior force* to those insisted on to justify an absolute neglect of it. If the ordinance be from heaven, a law once enacted by the Great Head of the church; is our evidence for its repeal stronger than any we have for its continuance? If not, the neglect must be highly criminal, as implying an impeachment of the divine wisdom, and a contempt of the divine authority*. But if it be an evident truth, that this ordinance is of *perpetual obligation*, no sincere christian can hesitate a moment from inferring, that it is of some importance to know, how he may *best* discharge any duty that relates to it? To say, that it is of no consequence *who* is baptized, or immaterial *how* the rite is to be performed, *without*

due

---

* The notion, " that this institution doth not extend to the descendants of professing christians; being neither suitable to their circumstances, nor intended to bind them," is justly stiled, by a Gentleman who has lately published on the subject, a *new idea* concerning baptism, as appropriate to *present times*; which he refutes by shewing — that there is nothing in the nature of any particular *command*, or any *circumstance* in the injunction that renders it peculiarly proper, or any ways limits it to the persons and times then present, or which immediately succeeded — and that there is nothing in the rite of baptism, in its meaning and *design*, that indicates its being founded on *partial* considerations. See Toulmin's *Essay on Baptism, passim.*

due examination, is incompatible with christian sincerity. Whatever bears the stamp of divine authority has an undisputed claim on our reverential regards. I may further add; the consideration of its frequent occurrence—that most gospel ministers have reiterated calls to determine about the subjects and circumstances of it—that there are innumerable families who have repeated occasions to decide upon the case—and, in a word, that no parent of a living child in the whole christian world, ought to reckon this ordinance as a matter of mere indifference—these considerations, I say, and others that might be mentioned, are concurring reasons at once to justify a strict and impartial inquiry into this controverted subject, and thereby an attempt to ascertain its comparative importance.

THUS far, therefore, I have the pleasure to agree with the respectable Author whose publication I more professedly examine, when he says, " Some persons affect to represent all disputes about the mode and subjects of baptism as not only stale and unimportant, but as unworthy the character of any who profess a warm regard for the Person, the atonement, and the grace of Jesus Christ. It must, indeed, be acknowledged, that church order, positive rites, and external forms of worship, are not of *equal* importance with those doctrines which immediately respect the object of our worship, as rational creatures; the ground of our hope, as criminals deserving to perish; or the source of our blessedness, as intended

tended for an immortal exiftence.—But is this a fufficient reafon for treating the law of baptifm as if it were of little or no importance—as if it were *obfolete*, or as if our Great Legiflator had *no meaning* when he enacted it?—Are we not required to *contend earneftly*, but with virtuous difpofitions, *for* every branch of *that faith which was once delivered to the faints?* If, therefore, infants be folemnly fprinkled by divine right, it muft be the *indifpenfible duty* of Pædobaptifts to contend for it*"—efpecially when *attacked*. To this I would add, if the baptizing of infants be *at all* a duty, it *muft* be an *important* one, for it is to be obferved, as Bp. BUTLER has done before, " That all chriftians are commanded to contribute, by their profeffion of chriftianity, to preferve it in the world; for it is the very fcheme of the gofpel that each chriftian fhould, in his degree, contribute towards continuing and carrying it on; all by uniting in the publick profeffion and external practice of chriftianity †," which cannot properly be done without duly attending to the introductory rite to fuch a profeffion.

§ 2. A FAIR inveftigation of the fubject before us, in its full extent, and the *general principles* on which the weight of the controverfy depends, may be attended alfo with fome confiderable advantages. A liberal, yet modeft, inquiry after truth, efpecially in matters of duty and

---

* Mr. BOOTH's Pædobaptifm Examined. Preface, p. 7.
† BUTLER's Analogy, Part II, Ch. 1. p. 219. 2d. Edit.

and practice, cannot fail of being immediately advantageous to the inquirer, and, when attended with fuccefs, muft be greatly beneficial in its confequences. For, to difcover truth, and the *evidence* of truth, muft needs afford more fubftantial profit, and a more generous pleafure, than can be expected in the mazes of falfehood and error, ignorance and prejudice. We may reft affured that the valuable gem, TRUTH, will lofe nothing of its luftre or worth by a thorough examination. If what has appeared to us, in the femblance of a precious jewel, turn out on a clofer fearch to be no better than a worthlefs pebble, it muft be weak and prepofterous ftill to retain and prize it as moft valuable. But if long efteemed as of real worth, and pronounced genuine by many able judges, proportionable caution is neceffary; we fhould turn and view it on every fide, avail ourfelves of the beft light, and every proper advantage, left, gulled by the artful, ourfelves and our families fuftain an important lofs. If Pædobaptifm be in reality what its oppofers of the prefent day pronounce it to be, namely, " *abfurd* and *unfcriptural**," to refign it will be no lofs, but real gain. But if it be of God, it is a *truth*; and if it be a truth, there is *attainable evidence* for its being fo; for, I confefs, I have no high opinion of what Mr. B. calls a wonderful fecret—*truth without evidence*—tho' it were difcovered by a right reverend

* STENNET's Anfwer to ADDINGTON, p. 234.

verend prelate †. But I would not have Mr. B. be transported with joy at the idea of his possessing " greatly preponderating evidence on his side," till he has better justified the *principles* on which he argues; left while he is endeavouring to demolish the labours of others, and pleased,
" greatly

† Bp. TAYLOR's Liberty of Prophesying. This prelate, whom Mr. B. so often quotes, wrote the treatise here referred to in the times of the rebellion in England; in which he undertakes to shew, with a view to moderate the rigor of the parliamentarian party, *how much* might be said of two sorts of Dissenters, the Antipædobaptists and the Papists.—And in his plea for the former, tho' he there declares himself well satisfied with the principles of Pædobaptism, of which he gives a summary account, and says, that he takes the other opinion to be an *error*; yet under pretence of reciting what may be said for this error, he draws up so elaborate a system of arguments against infant baptism, and sets them forth to such advantage, that he is judged to have said more for the Antipædobaptists than they were ever before able to say for themselves. And Dr. HAMMOND says (Six Queries, Infant Baptism, § 49.) It is the most diligent collection and the most exact scheme of the arguments against Infant Baptism that he had ever met with. Therefore the Dr. wrote an answer to this piece, solving each objection particularly; towards the conclusion of which (§ 139.) he observes, " I have " passed thro' all the several heads of arguments that are here proposed, " and considered them as nicely as I could, so as not to let fall one " word that seemed to me to have any shew of validity in it, or in " the consequence of it, and must consent to the truth of the author's " [the Bishop's] observations, " that the Anabaptists have been en- " couraged in their error more by the accidental advantages given them " by the weakness of those arguments that have been brought against ", them, than by any truth of their cause." And afterwards Bp. TAYLOR himself, having premised that he was sorry if any one had been so weak as to be misled by such objections, and that he counted it great condescension in Dr. HAMMOND to bestow an answer on them, wrote also his own answers to his own objections, and inserted them in a latter edition of the said treatise. (See WALL's
Treatise

"greatly pleased," with the thought, his own foundation be undermined. Nor would I have him be so "greatly discouraged," as he professes to be, in respect of an issue to the present controversy, while he thinks that the Baptists *alone* "will plead preponderating evidence, and firmly insist upon it as a maxim of logical prudence, that our *assent* should always be proportioned to the *degree of evidence.*" Sir, let not this discourage you; surely the Pædobaptists will think better of it than to reject so excellent a rule in pleading their cause. For my own part, I have the pleasure to assure you, that I feel no reluctance at all to appeal, on every occasion, to so equitable a maxim, be the consequence what it may. "Nor have I any apprehension (to borrow the words of an opposite writer) that this trial will at all injure the cause I am defending; on the contrary, I am well persuaded it

---

Treatise on Infant Baptism, Part II. Chap. 2. § 6.)—After all, tho' there be nothing which we can pronounce to be truth without suitable evidence, yet in a qualified sense I question whether the Bishop's remark—" I think there is so much to be pretended against that [Pædobaptism] which I believe to be the truth, that there is much more *truth* than *evidence* on our side"—deserves all that severity of satire which Mr. B. bestows on it. For by *evidence*, I presume, he intends a particular *kind* of evidence, an *express* command, *totidem verbis*, or, demonstrable scriptural example: and by *truth*, a conclusion fairly drawn from *other* premises. Nor will Mr. B. deny, that there are many things of a religious nature demonstrably *true*, or in matters of practice absolute *duty*, the *evidence* whereof does not arise from express revelation. Whether this remark will apply to the subject in question, will be further examined.

it will serve it. It is the part of error, not of truth, to elude inquiry: and he who would establish a point in debate, if he is satisfied of the goodness of his cause, will know how even to avail himself of the objections of his opponents. Truth is always perfectly consistent with itself: and however collateral circumstances may be so disguised, or placed in such a point of light by skilful management, as, for a time, to weaken and confound the plainest evidence of a real fact; yet, when those circumstances come to be thoroughly looked into, they will not only cease to have their effect, but will corroborate and brighten that evidence to which they before proved so unfriendly.*"

§ 3. It is no uncommon thing in controversial matters for the contending parties to misunderstand one another on their first setting out; either some ambiguous terms are not explained, on which, notwithstanding, considerable stress is laid; or something is much insisted on which has only a remote reference, but is far from being essential, to the subject in hand; or a multitude of arguments are produced in proof of a point, when most, if not all, would have not the least plausibility but from begging the question in debate. This method may, indeed, dazzle and confound the weak, but is ill calculated to convince the judicious. This being the case, and perhaps never more so than in disputes about baptism,

* Stennet's Answer to A, p. 213.

baptifm, it may be proper to make a few *Preliminary Remarks*.

§ 4. (1) I BEGIN then, with a pertinent obfervation of an ingenious Antipædobaptift, which he afterwards exprefsly applies to baptifm. " No theological fubject (fays he) requires more accurate inveftigation than the article of *evidence*. Evidence is that which *demonftrates*. Now there are various kinds and degrees of evidence, and it would very much contribute to clear a point in debate, were difputants firft of all to agree on certain data, or *what* fhould be allowed evidence in the cafe in queftion. In law this is a matter of great confequence, and when divines proceed in the methods ufed in our courts of law, they gain infinite advantage — They do, as it were, fwear the witneffes before they admit them as evidence*."

IT is ftrongly infinuated by Mr. B. that whatever has been faid in vindication of Pædobaptifm is fit only to deceive " fuperficial obfervers." Take his own words. " It is manifeft that nothwithftanding the number of evidences ufually fubpœnaed againft us, when the validity of infant fprinkling is to be *publickly* tried; and notwithftanding the formidable appearance they frequently make, in the eye of a fuperficial obferver; yet, when thefe very evidences are impartially examined by Pædobaptifts in *private*, without being perplexed with captious queries, they have not *a word* to fay for infant fprinkling; but all their

* ROBINSON's Notes on CLAUDE's Effay, Vol. II. p. 247.

their depositions are directed to prove doctrines and facts of a quite different nature †." Surely this is very astonishing if true. What! are *all* the conclusions of *every* Pædobaptist disputant so naked, so arbitrary, so irrational, that not *one principle* is found which, as a faithful evidence, and unsuborned, will stand uniform in its depositions, unmoved, and unawed by cross-examination? I would now only beg of the reader to admit, that it is at least *possible* Mr. B. is misled by too hasty and partial a judgment. Is he sure, has he *demonstrated*, not only that the witnesses give evidence in his favour, but that, in Mr. Robinson's phrase, they are " sworn before they are admitted?" I am not a little suspicious that his *principal* witness, nay the *only* one in which he seems to place any confidence, is not *legally* introduced.

To be a little more explicit; I apprehend the Antipædobaptists build on the following *supposition* as their chief corner stone, confide in it as their great palladium, and refer to it as the standard of all their arguments, namely, " That the law of baptism in the New Testament is of a nature *intirely positive*, as to the subject and mode of it;" and, if I understand them right, they are willing that their cause should stand or fall with it. Thus Mr. B. when animadverting on the conduct of one of his brethren for occasionally quitting that fort, " Except it be maintained, that *positive* ordinances are to be

intirely

† Idem p. 449.

intirely governed by *positive law* and primitive example, it is *impossible* for him to stand his ground by *fair argument* in various cases, when disputing with Pædobaptists as such *." " All who pretend, (says a Gentleman before quoted) to defend infant sprinkling, do but trifle, except they go to the *true ground* of the debate, and either prove —that infant sprinkling is somewhere appointed by Christ our Legislator—or that the authority of Christ is not necessary to the establishment of a *positive institute*—or that some person has since appeared vested with such authority as Christ himself exercised †." A dire dilemma! But, upon recollection, to ease myself a little of this tripple perplexity, I beg leave to return the *third* part of the difficulty to the author himself and the pretended successors of St. Peter, to be amicably settled between them. The two former I shall not *trifle* with, but shall endeavour fairly to answer them. For as our opponents seem willing to hazard the reputation and existence of their cause with the strength of the aforesaid maxim, " Baptism is a merely positive rite;"—and concluding it to be *divine*, they in their turn, " in the language of self-gratulation, repeat the old ευρηκα of ARCHIMEDES, *I have found it! I have found it!*"—it will be necessary, and it shall be the leading part of this work, to examine its pretensions with strictness. Thus I, also, shall attempt, on proper occasions, to ascertain the *kinds* and *degrees* of evidence, and

" swear

* p. 462. † ROBINSON's Notes, Vol. II. p. 423.

"Iſwear the witneſſes." Nor am I diſcouraged at the proſpect of " proving, that infant baptiſm IS SOMEWHERE *appointed* by Chriſt our Legiſlator."

§ 5. (2) I PROCEED to obſerve, that it appears to me extremely deſirable, in controverſial debates, that the diſputants ſhould be peculiarly ſolicitous to fix upon the *main hinge* of the difference between them, as that not only tends to reduce it in bulk, but would alſo ſuperſede much impertinence, altercation, and falſe reaſoning; hereby a fairer opportunity would be afforded for a cloſe encounter, the combatants would ſtand, as it were, upon even ground, and thus we may hope the one party might avoid the charge laid againſt it by the other, *viz.* That it no ſooner fixes upon a ſpot for the engagement, than it finds it neceſſary or expedient to quit that for another.

BUT how ſhall a man know what this turning point is? Mr. ROBINSON aſſures us that " Abraham's covenant, greek particles, and a thouſand more ſuch topicks, no more regard the ſubject than the firſt verſe of the firſt book of Chronicles, Adam, Sheth, Enoſh *!" Dreadful ſcythe! And no mean mower, to cut ſo much at one ſtroke!

——Dr. S. with more moderation, expreſſes himſelf as follows, " This queſtion, ſays he,— WHETHER BAPTISM IS A MEAN OF FAITH AND REPENTANCE?—I take to be the *main hinge* upon which the diſpute between us and the Pædobaptiſts

* Notes on CLAUDE, Vol. II. p. 423.

dobaptifts turns †." I am at a lofs, however, how to reconcile this declaration with what he fays elfewhere; for inftance, where he reprefents the fuppofed " JOINT INTEREST OF PARENTS AND THEIR CHILDREN IN THE COVENANT, as that upon which the *whole fuperftructure* of infant baptifm ftands," adding, " What pity then our brethren will not yield to the force of this plain truth, that pofitive inftitutions muft in their own nature derive their authority, not from the uncertain deductions of analogy, but, from the clear and exprefs declarations of God's word!" And what would follow? Why, " yielding to this propofition, they would at once find themfelves obliged to lay afide infant baptifm*." Certainly then, the faid propofition muft be no mean hinge, if not the main one. But has the Dr. or any one elfe, fairly proved not only that the propofition itfelf is true, but alfo *applicable* to the ordinance of baptifm, and confequently that this " Yielding" is our *duty*. Ah, *hic labor, hoc opus eft*, this, this is the main *difficulty*. What a pity the Pædobaptifts fhould be fo importuned to yield *without evidence!*—I alfo will fhew mine opinion refpecting the queftion to be decided, and it is this, WHETHER IT IS THE WILL OF CHRIST THAT THE INFANTS OF BELIEVING PARENTS SHOULD BE BAPTIZED? It certainly is his will that all who are proper fubjects of baptifm fhould be baptized; we contend that the infants of believing parents are fuch; and therefore fhould be

† Anfwer to A. p. 34.   * Idem p. 174.

be baptized. If they are proved to be *proper* subjects, that is, such as come within Christ's *intention* when he instituted the ordinance, it must follow that it is HIS WILL and pleasure they should be baptized.—I say the infants of *believing* parents, for it is not essential to the controversy to include any others; what may be said of *others* is only a circumstance which does not affect the argument. For the Antipædobaptists' arguments are intended to conclude against *all children* alike, and it must be as conclusive against their system to prove it to be the *will of Christ* that any *one* infant whatever should be baptized, as if *all* were included in the reasoning.

HENCE another question arises, namely, How MAY WE KNOW WHAT IS THE WILL OF CHRIST IN THIS MATTER? Mr. B. replies; " Seeing baptism is as really and intirely a positive institution, as any that were given to the chosen tribes; we cannot with safety infer either the mode or the subject of it, from any thing short of a *precept*, or a *precedent*, recorded in scripture, and relating to that very ordinance ∥." He frequently expresses himself to the same purpose, as do all the writers of note on that side of the question. We see that Mr. B. intends that this declaration should be applied not only to the mode but also to the *subject* of baptism, that is, in other words, to this question, " WHO is to be baptized?" Now, independent of the *fact*, that the

∥ p. 13.

the right of infants is or is not supported by a revealed exprefs precept or precedent, nay, on *suppofition* that there is in fcripture *neither*, I maintain that the infants of believers are intitled to the ordinance, and of courfe that the rule he works by is a falfe one. It proves too much, and is reducible, on his own principles, to a downright contradiction. This affertion I hope to make good againft our author in the following pages, notwithftanding what he fays about " pofitive laws implying their negatives †."

What our oppofing friends fay about *pofitive rites, precepts, precedents,* " and a thoufand more fuch topicks," are to no good purpofe, until they demonftrate that the faithful dictates of the law of our nature, of right reafon and common fenfe, are no part of Christ's will to his people and minifters, when thefe dictates are not *exprefsly* controuled and fuppreffed.

It is not a little furprifing to obferve how ftrenuoufly they oppofe moral and analogical reafonings on this *one fubject* of baptifm, while they juftly affume the fame liberty with us on other fubjects *equally pofitive*. I do not wifh to fee any, whom Chrift has made free, wear the galling yoke of thofe ceremonies which he did not *intend* fhould continue, tho' *commanded* by himfelf, and *practifed* by his primitive difciples. Therefore, this liberty, I fay, they *juftly* take in all New Teftament inftitutions, this of baptifm *alone* excepted; and this liberty we affert is the right

† p. 187.

right of us *all*, and without exception of *any* inftitution. The Antipædobaptifts are guilty of a great piece of *inconfiftence* in making fuch a diftinction where there is no apparent ground of difference, and fo in pronouncing judgment without fuitable *evidence*; but we confiftently claim a right of appealing to reafon, analogy, and common fenfe, in connexion with the *nature* and *defign* of the inftitution, and the moft apparent *intention* of our Lawgiver. Nor is it in their power to maintain the *perpetuity* of this ordinance, againft the Quakers and others, the obligation of minifters to baptize thofe who are *taught*, &c. but by thofe very aids which they would fain deny us.

§ 6. (3) INAUSPICIOUS to this controverfy, above moft others, *terms* of ambiguous import, and unexplained, have been bandied about by both parties, on which, however, confiderable ftrefs has been laid; and thus, much confufion and little profit have often attended very laboured arguments. For inftance, the term INFANT SPRINKLING has been fubftituted for *infant baptifm*, not indeed always by way of contempt, but often improperly, becaufe thereby is conveyed the fecondary idea of a neceffary connexion between the mode *fprinkling* and the baptifm of an infant. Whereas thoufands are *dipped* in infancy as well as fprinkled, in the chriftian world, and fome even in England. So that, upon our opponents' own principles, thofe infants who
are

Preliminary Remarks. 17

are dipped in the name of the Sacred Three, by a Minister of Christ, in obedience to HIS WILL, ought to be reckoned as BAPTIZED: for since they maintain that baptizing and dipping are synonymous terms, it follows that those are baptized who are thus dipped. Not to insist upon the absurd consequence of substituting the one term for the other; for then it would also follow, that there are *many baptisms* to which the *same person* ought often to submit for his health's sake; that as often as a child is dipped it is baptized; that as often as any person in the world, Christian, Jew, Turk, or Heathen, is plunged, on any occasion whatever, he is baptized; yea, that as often as *any thing* is plunged, according to them, it is baptized; whereas I know of no Pædobaptists who wish to make sprinkling, or indeed any other *particular mode* of using water, synonymous with baptism.

BESIDES, the question is not, whether scripture expresly enjoins *infant baptism*, by a direct specification, but whether it enjoins *baptism* to all *proper* subjects, and whether the administrator, who has a discretionary right of judging about qualifications, has sufficient reasons to conclude, or such evidence as the nature of the case requires, that infants are such as are included within our Lord's *intention*, when he instituted the ordinance. If infants possess, as I am persuaded they do, the essential qualifications of proper subjects, then it was not only needless
but

but would have been *impertinent* to specify them. When therefore I speak of the mode, it is on supposition of agreement about the subject; and when I speak of the subject, it is on supposition of agreement about the mode.

The remark already made on the abuse of terms, is notoriously exemplified in the word COVENANT, without adding any more instances. It must be acknowledged that many Pædobaptist writers have been extremely unguarded in this particular, which has afforded no small handle to the opposite party. But our opponents are not free of blame on this head, and I am not a little surprised to find a person of Dr. S.'s circumspection and polemical acumen prolong an argument to above thirty pages, which has no force at all but in proportion as the word *covenant* is taken in a sense which, I am persuaded, most Pædobaptists reject. And this conduct is the less excuseable in this ingenious and worthy writer, because he professedly " lays down all the *possible senses* in which persons may be said to be in a covenant*." The Doctor, surely, need but to be *reminded* of this matter, for his own sagacity must have *informed* him how inconclusive his reasoning is, had he taken all the *possible* senses of being in a covenant.

§ 7. (4) The numerous *quotations* in Mr. B.'s *Pædobaptism Examined* make, indeed, a formidable

* Answer to A, Letter II, and III,

midable appearance, and the rather becaufe there are among them, as he juftly obferves, " fome of the moft eminent Pædobaptifts that ever filled the profeffor's chair, or that ever adorned the proteftant pulpit." But my judgment intirely fails me if a *very great number* of thefe quotations are not perfectly *confiftent* with the practice of the perfons quoted, and therefore improperly introduced as evidences againft themfelves.

But fuppofing that all the paffages our author employs were directly in his favour, and unexceptionably tranfcribed or tranflated; nay, were they an hundred times more numerous and large, and ftill more favourable to the caufe for which he pleads, it is evident from his own declaration, that he ought not to confider " either the number or weight of fuch quotations, as conftituting *any part* of the ground on which the diftinguifhing conduct of the party proceeds," or on which the caufe depends. That many great and learned men have entertained different and even contradictory fentiments on the fubject, does not affect it. That one fhould give up a topick in the debate, which another thought valid, is immaterial. It is of little confequence, in point of argument in the prefent cafe, to urge what is the *opinion* of good and wife men upon the matter; whereas it is of effential importance to inquire whether what is pleaded for be defenfible or indefenfible. *Amicus Socrates, amicus Plato; fed major amica* VERITAS. It is certainly

very

very becoming, that the sentiments and testimonies of respectable authors should be treated with modesty and decorum, but I must beg leave to discard all human *authority*, or human *opinion*, singly or collectively taken, from bearing any part of the *principal* evidence; for I would appeal to the *case itself*, and not to the number or manner of its defenders or opposers.

CHAP. I.

Of the nature and obligation of positive laws and institutions in general, together with the use of inferential and analogical reasoning, with relation to the ordinance of baptism.

§ 1. *Of law in general.* § 2. *Positive laws and institutions defined and explained.* § 3. *Positive precepts distinguished from moral ones.* § 4. *Their comparative obligations.* § 5. *The importance of positive institutions.* § 6. *They are necessarily of an external nature.* § 7. *They presuppose the dictates of reason and revelation.* § 8. *All the institutions of christianity are of a mixed nature.* § 9. *As appears* (1) *from the false principle on which the contrary opinion is founded.* § 10. (2) *From the concessions of opponents, as to the nature of positive institutions.* § 11—14. (3) *From incontestible facts.* § 15. *How to determine what is positive and what is moral in a mixed law.* § 16. *The importance of analogical reasoning.* § 17, 18. *To deny the use of it in our inquiries about baptism, leads to absurd consequences.* (1) *Without it, we can know nothing about the ordinance.* § 19—22. (2) *Our opponents cannot prove their authority to administer, and the validity*

validity of the action. § 23—26. (3) *Nor to determine who is a proper subject.* § 27. (4) *Other ridiculous consequences.* § 28, 29. (5) *Transubstantiation retorted.* § 30. *Extremes of different kinds.* § 31—34. *Objections answered.* § 35. *Recapitulation.*

§ 1. LAW, in its most general and comprehensive import, signifies a *rule of action,* dictated by some superior. And man, considered as a creature, must necessarily be subject to the Laws of his Creator, as to disposition and conduct; and is bound, from the very idea of his absolute dependence, to regulate his actions and behaviour according to the intimations of his sovereign pleasure.—The WILL OF GOD is the grand law of our nature. But this will is discoverable principally two ways; either by *human sagacity*—including that intuitive perception whereby we discern what is most conducive to our own welfare, which welfare the will of our Maker ever supposes, and the exertions of right reason—or by *direct revelation.* " If our reason (says an eminent writer) were always as in our first ancestor before his transgression, clear and perfect, unruffled by passions, unclouded by prejudice, unimpaired by disease and intemperance, the task of discovering what the *law of nature* directs in every circumstance of life would be pleasant and easy; we should need no other guide but this. But every man now finds the contrary in his own experience; that his reason

is

is corrupt, and his underſtanding full of ignorance and error. This has given manifold occaſion for the benign interpoſition of divine providence; which, in compaſſion to the frailty, the imperfection, and the blindneſs of human reaſon, hath been pleaſed, at ſundry times and in divers manners, to diſcover and enforce its laws by an immediate and direct revelation. The doctrines thus delivered, we call the revealed or divine law, and they are to be found only in the holy ſcriptures. Theſe precepts when revealed, are found upon compariſon to be really a part of the original law of nature, as they tend in their conſequences to man's felicity*."

IT is to be carefully noticed, that revelation, as referring to human actions, performs a double part; it either renders more authentick and indubitable, what human ſagacity perceived as probable, or elſe enjoins duties which mere reaſon could never have diſcovered. Hence ariſes the obvious diſtinction of moral and poſitive laws.

§ 2. BY *poſitive laws* I underſtand, ſuch laws as do not appear to us obligatory, except upon the *mere authority* † of the Divine Legiſlator. And for

---

* BLACKSTONE's Commentaries, Vol. I. Introd. § 2.

† WHEN I ſay that the obligation of poſitive laws reſts upon the *mere authority* of the Legiſlator, let the reader obſerve, that this is not to be confounded with an *arbitrary diſpoſition* in the Deity. This diſtinction is well deſcribed by an elegant and philoſophic pen: "When ſome ſpeak of the *Will of God* as the "*Rule of Duty*, they do not certainly mean a blind arbitrary "principle of action, but ſuch a principle as is *directed* by reaſon,

this authority is sufficiently and absolutely binding from the consideration of our being previously assured of the wisdom, justice, and goodness of God, who enacts the law. *Positive institutions*, strictly taken, are a species of positive laws, and differ as a *law* differs from an *institution*. The former *may* be transient, but the latter is, at least for a term, of standing obligation. The command given Abraham to sacrifice his son, was a positive *law*, but not properly speaking an institution; and the right of circumcision was a positive *institution* as well as a law. Jesus commanding Peter to walk on the water, was a transient law, but his command to go and baptize proper subjects of all nations, is a permanent institution. " And altho' no laws but positive be mutable, yet all are not mutable which be positive. Positive laws are either permanent or else changeable, according

---

" son, and *governed* by wisdom, or a regard to certain ends in *preference*
" to others. Unless we suppose some principle in the Deity analogous
" to our sense of obligation, some antecedent affection, or determi-
" nation of his nature, to prefer some ends before others, we
" cannot assign any sufficient, or indeed any possible reason, why he
" should will one thing more than another, or have any election
" at all. Whatever therefore is the *ground* of his *choice* or will
" must be the *ground* of obligation, and not the choice or will
" itself.—That this is so, appears farther from the common dis-
" tinction which divines and philosophers make between *moral*
" and *positive* commands and duties. The *former* they think *obli-*
" *gatory*, antecedent to will, or at least to any declaration of it;
" the *latter* obligatory only in consequence of a positive appoint-
" ment of the divine will. But what foundation can there be for
" this distinction, if all duty and obligation be equally the result
" of *mere will?*" FORDYCE's Elements of Moral Philosophy,
B. I. Sect. 3.

cording as the *matter itſelf* is, concerning which they were firſt made †."

§ 3. It is evident, upon the leaſt reflection, that poſitive laws are no further binding than the authority by which they are enjoined is *diſcerni-ble*. And it is equally evident, that there is no poſſible method of diſcerning the Lawgiver's authority and will, relative to theſe laws, but by his own expreſs declarations; for if they are diſcernible any other way, they are no longer poſitive. The *difference*, therefore, between poſitive and moral commands is clear and obvious. " Moral precepts, (as Biſhop Butler well obſerves) are precepts the reaſons of which we ſee: poſitive precepts, are precepts, the reaſons of which we do not ſee." But I would further obſerve, with the ſame ſagacious author, that " this is the diſtinction between moral and poſitive precepts, conſidered reſpectively *as ſuch*.— Moral and poſitive precepts are in ſome reſpects alike, in other reſpects different. So far as they are alike, we diſcern the reaſons of both: ſo far as they are different, we diſcern the reaſons of the former, but not of the latter. And, moral duties ariſe out of the nature of the caſe itſelf, prior to external command: poſitive duties do not ariſe out of the nature of the caſe, but from external command: nor would they be duties at all, were it not for ſuch command, received from him whoſe creatures and ſubjects we are.—Care, then, is to be taken, when a comparison

‡ Hooker's Eccles. Polit. B. I. § 15.

comparison is made between positive and moral duties, that they be compared no farther than they are different: no farther than as the former are positive, or arise out of mere external command, the reasons of which we are not acquainted with; and as the latter are moral, or arise out of the apparent reason of the case, without such external command. *Unless this caution be observed, we shall run to endless confusion* *." Whether Mr. B. is sufficiently *cautious* in observing this necessary distinction, will appear, I presume, in the sequel of this treatise.

§ 4. THE following remarks from the above mentioned author, concerning our *comparative obligations* to obey positive and moral commands, appear just and pertinent. " Suppose two standing precepts injoined by the same authority; that, in certain conjunctions, it is impossible to obey both; that the former is moral, i. e. a precept of which we see the reasons, and that they hold in the particular case before us; but that the latter is positive, i. e. a precept of which we do not see the reasons; it is indisputable that our obligations are to obey the *former*; because there is an apparent reason for this preference, and none against it. Farther, positive institutions, I suppose all those which christianity enjoins, are *means* to a moral end; and the *end* must be acknowledged more excellent than the means. Nor is the observance of these institutions any religious obedience at all, or of any value, otherwise

* BUTLER's Analogy, Part II. Chap. I. p. 227.

wife than as it proceeds from a moral principle. I add, that the whole moral law is as much matter of revealed command as positive institutions are; for the scripture injoins every moral virtue. In this respect then they are both upon a level. But the moral law is, moreover, written upon our hearts; interwoven into our very nature. And this is a plain intimation of the author of it, which is to be preferred when they interfere.——Upon occasion of mentioning together positive and moral duties, the scripture always puts the stress of religion upon the latter, and never upon the former: which, tho' no sort of allowance to neglect the former, when they do not interfere with the latter; yet is a plain intimation, that when they do, the latter are to be preferred.—Our Lord himself, from whose command alone the obligation of positive institutions arises, has taken occasion to make the comparison between them and moral precepts; when the Pharisees censured him, for *eating with publicans and sinners*; and also when they censured his disciples, for plucking the ears of corn on the sabbath day. Upon this comparison he has determined expresly, and in form, which shall have the preference when they interfere. And by delivering his authoritative determination in a proverbial manner of expression, he has made it general: *I will have mercy and not sacrifice*. For the sense and the very literal words of our Lord's answer, are as applicable to *any other* institution, on a comparison between positive and moral duties,

duties, as to this upon which they were fpoken. It is remarkable too, that, as the words are a quotation from the Old Teftament, they are introduced, on both the forementioned occafions, with a declaration, that the Pharifees did not underftand the meaning of them. This, I fay, is very remarkable. For fince it is fcarce poffible, for the moft ignorant perfon, not to underftand the literal fenfe of the paffage in the prophet; (Hof. vi.) and fince underftanding the literal fenfe would not have prevented their *condemning the guiltlefs*; (Mat. xii. 7.) it can hardly be doubted, that the thing which our Lord really intended in that declaration, was, that the Pharifees had not learnt from it, as they might, wherein the general fpirit of religion confifts.— Yet it is highly neceffary that we remind ourfelves, how great prefumption it is to *make light* of any inftitutions of divine appointment; that our obligation to obey *all* God's commands whatever, are abfolute and indifpenfable: and that commands merely pofitive, admitted to be [*fuch*, and] from him, lay us under a moral obligation to obey them: an obligation moral in the ftricteft and moft proper fenfe *."

It may here be objected, " Was not Abraham commendable for obeying a pofitive command at the expenfe of a moral one?" I anfwer, Abraham did well to obey the command to facrifice his fon, for it was in perfect confiftence with the *morality* of the fixth command. Which only implies

* Butler's Analogy, *ut fupra.* p. 230—234.

implies that one *man* has no right to take away the life of another *unjuftly*, but by no means intends that God has no right to take away the forfeited life of a finful creature, which is abfolutely at his difpofal, by what methods he pleafes. Whatever excellence there was in Abraham's obedience, muft fpring from a difpofition regarding God's abfolute dominion, power, wifdom, &c. And his facrificing Ifaac was no duty any further than he was *certain* God commanded it. Had he been more forward or particular in that bufinefs than the command was exprefs and circumftantial, he muft have been in that proportion guilty of a prefumptuous crime; inafmuch as the pofitive command required him to offer violence to the natural feelings of humanity. Dr. GROSVENOR well obferves, " Where the evidence is not *fo clear*, the obligation is weakened in proportion; but where the terms are *plainly* binding, and ftrongly commanding, there the obligation is not to be evaded.—When we fee the broad feal of heaven, where there is the divine warrant, *Thus faith the Lord*; it is worfe than trifling, to cavil and fay, It is but an external rite."—But we fhould not forget, that tho' *all* pofitive duties are above the reach of mere reafon, fome may be *more remote* than others; and the nearer thofe duties approach to our natural notions of congruity and expediency, the lefs is the evidence of pofitive authority, and therefore a fmaller degree of it is proportionably binding.

§ 5. NOTWITHSTANDING the indisputable superiority of laws natural and moral to those of a positive nature, whenever they come in competition, the latter are of very great use and consequence. " The very notion of a visible church implies positive institutions, for the *visibility* of the church *consists* in them. Take away every thing of this kind, and you lose the very notion itself. So that if a visible church and an instituted method of education, are advantages, the reason and *importance* of positive institutions in general is most obvious, since without them these advantages could not be secured to the world †."

§ 6. ALL acts of religious worship are either internal or external. All *internal* acts are of *moral* consideration as resulting from certain relations. As soon as these *relations* are discovered, whether by the dictates of reason or pure revelation it matters not, the obligation of duty naturally arises from them, independent of any external command to inforce the same. The propriety of this distinction will easily appear when we observe, that no internal act of religion *can be* our duty but what springs from *relative* considerations, and since no relation subsisting between moral agents can be *ascertained*, but we are immediately, from the nature of the case, laid under every obligation possibly assignable. Hence it follows, that whatever precepts and duties deserve the name of *positive*, must be of an *external* nature. Indeed " a *disposition* to obey divine

† Idem, p. 216, 217.

divine orders, either positive or moral, (as Dr. GROSVENOR justly observes) is part of that *holiness without which no man shall see the Lord*." But then it is equally true, that this very disposition is, in the properest sense, of moral obligation *prior* to any external command, and, therefore, is perfectly distinct in its nature from the *positiveness* of those divine orders. But notwithstanding all positive duties be in their own nature *external*, it does not follow, that all external acts of religious worship are also positive. To elucidate this matter a little I would offer these two remarks:

1. THAT God is to be worshipped *in general*, even in *some external* form, is of *moral* obligation. For, as the obligation of internal worship arises from the relation we stand in to God, without a positive command, so it is clear, from the nature of the case, this internal worship, reverence, gratitude, &c. ought to be externally *manifested* in a manner suited to these emotions. Nor can it be doubted, that there is a natural congruity between such internal emotions and certain *modes* of expressing them in preference to others as less proper; for there are, doubtless, *some postures* and gestures of the body, independent of national custom, or the like circumstances, that may with *more propriety* than others be termed, reverent, humble, modest, decent, devout, &c. and we are under a moral obligation to *prefer* the most becoming, whenever this is not determined by positive command.

2. THAT

2. THAT any *particular* external mode of worſhip is enjoined to men, the reaſon and propriety of which does not appear prior to the external command, is of *poſitive conſideration*. Poſitive precepts may be conſidered as certain *exceptions* from a general rule, but as a general rule and common analogy ought to be quitted *only* where they are incompatible with the exception, and preciſely in that *degree*; ſo we are to recede from moral and analogical reaſoning, in our inquiries after the path of duty, *only* when obliged by a poſitive precept *as ſuch*, or exactly in the proportion it is ſo, and no further. For to do otherwiſe would be to quit a common rule without any apparent neceſſity; and to deviate from a way, which is at leaſt probably the right one, to another which is abſolutely uncertain. To this I would add, that the circumſtances of an action being *naturally convenient*, may and ought to have conſiderable influence in determining what is or is not our duty, in thoſe circumſtances of it that are indeterminate; for this plain reaſon, that we are ſure the law of ſelf-preſervation is the law of God in all thoſe caſes where he has not ſhewn us the contrary. Whatever, therefore, appears to militate againſt life, health, and comfort, without any revealed warrant, may and ought to be avoided, on the principles of natural law and obligation. This is applicable to all the unpreſcribed circumſtances of *poſitive* duties, as well as to thoſe of a moral kind. " This law of nature, (as Sir WILLIAM BLACK-

BLACKSTONE obferves) being coeval with mankind and dictated by God himfelf, is of courfe fuperior in obligation to any other. It is binding over all the Globe, in all countries, and at all times*," when not *exprefsly* countermanded by pofitive interpofition.

§ 7. FROM what has been faid we may further conclude, that a pofitive inftitution is a kind of *ingrafture*, fo to fpeak, upon the law of our nature; the former is the fcyon, the latter is the ftock. The choice of the inftitution depends upon the fovereign pleafure of God. But when this is determined, the law of nature written in our hearts, the principles of reafon and common fenfe, or fome revealed law, are *prefuppofed*, and may be compared to the ftock upon which the ingrafture is made. For as the fcripture itfelf fheweth not with certainty what books are divine; as all acceptable obedience to divine commands prefuppofes a fuitable difpofition; as all arts and fciences have their *præcognita*, and every branch of abftrufe learning prefuppofes firft principles, and even the moft infallible geometrical demonftration its axioms and poftulates; fo all pofitive laws and inftitutions take fome principles for *granted*.

§ 8. ANOTHER confequence that follows naturally from the preceding confiderations is this: That there are *no precepts* now in force, at leaft, of a nature *merely* pofitive. None, I mean, wherein all the *minutiæ* of circumftances neceffary

* Comment, *ut fupra*.

for the discharge of the duty commanded are specified by the Lawgiver; and therefore those institutions of christianity which are commonly termed positive are but *partially* so. The necessity of ascertaining this difference in the present controversy is very apparent; and yet it has somehow hitherto been strangely overlooked, by both contending parties. The Pædobaptists in general have tamely submitted to this position, " *Baptism and the Lord's Supper are positive institutions,*" in its most absolute and undistinguished sense, as a maxim not to be controverted; and the Antipædobaptists are, doubtless, much obliged to us for this piece of complaisance, as it is evidently the main pillar of their cause, and the armour in which they trust. Pertinent to our present purpose is the following remark of Bp. WARBURTON; " When two parties go upon different [principles] they naturally begin with examining one another's, whereby the true being at length settled or discovered, by its aid the controversy is timely determined; but where a *false* principle has the luck (as his Lordship expresses it) to be embraced by *both sides*, they may wrangle for ever, and be, after all, but farther from the truth*." But it may be asked, if we resign the good old maxim, " that the two standing ordinances of christianity, Baptism and the Lord's Supper, are *positive* institutions, and *absolutely* so," and allow that they are of a *mixed* nature, or partly positive and partly moral; how are we to draw the line

of

---

* Bp. WARBURTON's Alliance, B. I. Sect. 1.

of diſtinction? If moral and poſitive precepts thus run into each other, like the ſhades of a painted figure, or the colours of the rainbow, how can we aſcribe to all their due, or determine where the one ends and the other begins? Towards ſolving this difficulty I beg leave to propoſe the following obſervations.

§ 9. (1) IT is utterly abhorrent from ſound divinity, as well as logical preciſion, not to ſay chriſtian modeſty, to determine, *a priori*, with what *degree* of evidence any given particular inſtitution *ought* to have been delivered by the divine Legiſlator, any more than what the inſtitution *itſelf* ſhould be.

FOR, as Bp. BUTLER obſerves, " our principal obligation of ſearching the ſcripture, and to what all our inquiries ought to be directed, is, in order to ſee what the ſcheme of revelation *really is*, inſtead of determining before hand from reaſon, what the reaſon of it *muſt* be *." To *inveſtigate* the degree of evidence from the fact of the inſtitution, and to *infer* the degree of the obligation from the evidence found, is *our* province; but to determine what the nature and degree of the evidence *muſt* be, is the excluſive prerogative of the Inſtitutor himſelf, whoſe will and authority muſt be the ſole and excluſive ground of the inſtitution.

I AM, therefore, not a little ſurpriſed to find the gentleman, whoſe work I am more immediately examining, and for whoſe abilities and diſpoſition

* BUTLER's Analogy, *ut ſupra*.

position I have a real esteem, expressing himself as follows: "Positive institutions originate in the divine pleasure, and derive their whole being from the sovereign will of God.—We *cannot know any thing* about their precise nature, their true design, the proper subjects of them, or the right mode of their administration *further than the scriptures teach.*—It does not appear from the records of the Old Testament, that, when Jehovah appointed any branch of ritual worship, he left either the subject of it, or the mode of administration, to be inferred by the people, either from the relation in which they stood to himself; or from general moral precepts; or from any branch of his moral worship; nor yet from any other well known positive rite: but he gave THEM special directions relating to the very case.——— For as nothing but the divine will can oblige the conscience, and as *that will cannot be known, unless revealed*; so when made known, whether in reference to moral or positive duties, it must oblige. CONSEQUENTLY, SEEING BAPTISM IS AS REALLY AND INTIRELY A POSITIVE INSTITUTION AS ANY THAT WERE GIVEN TO THE CHOSEN TRIBES, we cannot with safety infer either the mode or the subject of it, from any thing short of a precept or precedent, recorded in scripture, and relating to that very ordinance. *It seems natural hence to infer*, that our sovereign Lord MUST HAVE REVEALED HIS WILL concerning the ordinance of baptism in a manner proportional to its obligation and importance.

For,

For, as an appointment of Chrift, it originated in his will, and from a *revelation of that will* the whole of its obligation refults. In proportion, therefore, as we annex the idea of *obfcurity* to what he fays about the mode and the fubject of it, we either fink the idea of obligation to regard it, or *impeach the wifdom, or the goodnefs, or the equity of our divine Legiflator:* for we neither have, *nor can have any acquaintance* with a pofitive inftitution, *farther than it is revealed*. We are, THEREFORE, obliged to conclude that our Lord HAS CLEARLY REVEALED his pleafure, with reference to this appointment, in that code of law, and rule of religious worfhip, which he gave to the church, in the volume of the New Teftament*."

THUS alfo Dr. S. " Here I would obferve then, that all pofitive inftitutions depend *folely* upon the *will* of the inftitutor, and that therefore in every queftion relating to them, we muft be guided by his *exprefs declarations*, or by thofe of perfons he has duly authorized to *fignify his will*. Nor is it to be doubted that a wife legiflator will, *in all matters of this fort*, take care to exprefs his mind *in the moft plain and intelligible manner*. Now baptifm is a pofitive inftitution of Chrift: and, agreeably to his infinite wifdom and goodnefs, he has expreffed himfelf. in *the myft clear and explicit manner* refpecting both the mode and the fubject of it.— And THEREFORE the iffue of this inquiry ought to be refted *alone* upon

* p. 11—13.

upon his own *exprefs declarations*, and thofe of his apoftles and firft minifters *." — And again, " A right to baptifm muft depend, and depend alone, upon the direct exprefs command of the inftitutor; for it is abfurd to talk of analogy and confequence in the matter of pofitive inftitutions †." And again, " As pofitive duties depend folely upon the will of the inftitutor, every queftion refpecting them ought in reafon to be decided by his exprefs declarations; which declarations, *if he be a wife legiflator, will, no doubt, be clear and explicit* ‡." There are other paffages in both thefe writers very much to the fame purpofe.

Not to ftop to examine the truth and propriety of fome things in the above quotations which are taken for granted; fuch as the *abfolute pofitivenefs* of *every branch* of ritual worfhip under the Old Teftament œconomy; wherein *nothing* was to be *inferred* by the people; or to inquire whether it can be *juftly* concluded that *becaufe*, on fuppofition that the Old Teftament rituals were of that kind, thofe of the New Teftament *muft* be fo likewife; both which I believe they would find too difficult to prove: paffing by fuch things, let us attend to the point of immediate confideration;—which is to demonftrate contrary to thefe affertions, that the New Teftament inftitutions ARE NOT of a nature *merely pofitive*; or, in other words, that Baptifm and the Lord's Supper, in their completenefs and comprehenfion, are

* Anfwer to A. p. 3, 5.   † p. 90.   ‡ p. 293.

Ch. 1.   *and Analogical Reasoning.*   39

are inftitutions of a *mixed* nature, that is to fay, partly pofitive and partly moral. And in profecution of this defign I further obferve that,

§ 10. (2) FROM thefe gentlemen's own account, it follows, that the inftitutions of the New Teftament are either of a *mixed* nature or not *at all* pofitive. For according to them, *all matters of this fort* fhould be expreffed in the moft plain and intelligible, the moft clear and explicit manner; and, THEREFORE, feeing baptifm and the Lord's Supper are not IN FACT fo circumftantially defcribed as not to need, or fo minutely exprefs as to prohibit moral reafoning, analogy and confequence; it inevitably follows, that, if thefe inftitutions are not of a *mixed* nature, partly pofitive and partly moral, they are no pofitive inftitutions AT ALL. And as they allow none to be of that fort but thefe two, chriftianity muft be left without any; and fince chriftianity is the laft and unalterable difpenfation of religion among men, it is impoffible there fhould be any to the end of time; and fo all pofitive inftitutions are, on their own fuppofition, fairly and utterly banifhed out of the world.

BESIDES, their anticipated mode of determining the degree of evidence with which a pofitive law *ought to be* enacted, is quite fubverfive of the very nature of fuch a law; for it is allowed on all hands, and by thefe gentlemen in the plaineft terms, that the diftinguifhing nature of pofitive laws confifts in the meafure and the degree of their *inftitution*, and that they derive their

whole

whole being from the *sovereign will* of God. And thus their reasoning is built upon a *petitio principii*, a begging of the question, whereby they first take it for granted, that baptism is an institution merely positive, and then take it further for granted, that being such it *must be* free from all obscurity.

§ 11. (3) BUT if it be contended, that our Lord has, *actually*, been plain and explicit in the institution of this ordinance, and that therefore it is easy to be understood: I might ask, to *whom* is it easy? and what *sense* of it is easy? Is it the honest christian, the judicious divine, the learned critic, or the profound universal scholar to whom the sense is *easy?* But what sense of the institution is so plain and easy? Mr. B. and Dr. S. no doubt, think that their *own* sense bids fair for this character. But here is an extraordinary phenomenon! here are not a few thousands of honest christians; not a few hundreds of judicious divines, learned critics, profound scholars; commentators who have developed the most abstruse parts of holy writ; who yet cannot see this sense of the institution which is so *easy*. Can *that sense* of a passage of scripture, or of the nature and design of an institution, be with any propriety called *plain* and *easy*, *clear*, *explicit* and *most intelligible*, which five men out of twenty contend is the true sense, but which the other fifteen, possessed of an equal share of parts, piety and learning, maintain is the wrong sense? That great numbers should unanimously stand out against some kinds of truth, not very abstruse

struse in their own nature, is a very possible case; either when a truth may not appear to be of so much importance as to engage persons duly qualified to study it with close application; or when it has been a point of mere speculation; or when slavish fear and worldly interest have prevailed over the honest dictates of conscience; but that so many protestant worthies, who have left all to follow Christ; that so many learned commentators and casuists, of unblemished character, of unexceptionable ability, having no interest to serve whereby the judgment should be biassed, or the conscience bribed; calling no man master upon earth, but, with a generous freedom, shaking off the prejudices of education, the shackles of custom, and the influence of different systems; that these, I say, should oppose unanimously the sense of an institution *quite plain* and *easy* to be understood, is a case, I believe, unparallelled and unaccountable. I would rather infer, and with what propriety let the reader judge, that either the Antipædobaptist sense of Christ's institution is *not at all* the true sense, or, at any rate, a sense *very difficult* to come at.

§ 12. But Mr. B. still urges, that " in proportion as we annex the idea of *obscurity* to what is said about the mode or the subject of baptism, we either sink the idea of obligation to regard it, or impeach the wisdom, or the goodness, or the equity of the divine Legislator." That his idea of the institution of baptism, as an ANTIPÆDOBAPTIST, appears to by far the greater number

number of competent judges an *obscure* one, is an inconteſtible *fact*; judges competent, I mean, in a moral as well as natural reſpect. And, therefore, it follows, on his own principles, that their obligation to adopt the Antipædobaptiſt Hypotheſis is *ſunk* in proportion; and that the perſons, ſo qualified, who can ſee *no truth* in it, are under *no obligation* to embrace it; but are obligated to retain the Pædobaptist ſyſtem, as what they ſee *more clearly*.

Allowing, therefore, our annexing the Idea of *obſcurity* to what is ſaid about the ſubject and the mode of baptiſm, in the reſpect now mentioned, to be true, I might be excuſed from vindicating myſelf and my friends from the crime of impeaching the divine wiſdom, goodneſs, and veracity, by adopting the alternative of ſinking the obligation; were it not that Mr. B.'s charges run ſtill higher, when ſpeaking of the ſignification of the terms of the inſtitution. " Nay, ſays he, were the leading term in any human law, to have an ambiguity in it, equal to that for which our Brethren plead with regard to the word *baptiſm*; ſuch law would certainly be conſidered as betraying, either the weakneſs, or the wickedneſs, of the legiſlator; and be condemned, as opening a door to perpetual chicane and painful uncertainty. Far be it, then, from us to ſuppoſe, that our gracious and omniſcient Lord ſhould give a law relating to divine worſhip, and obligatory on the moſt illiterate of his real diſciples, which may be fairly conſtrued to mean,

mean, *this* or *that* or the *other* action—a law which is calculated to excite and perpetuate contention among his wifeſt and ſincereſt followers—a law, that would diſgrace a Britiſh Parliament in reſpect of its *tripple* meaning, as being involved in the dark ambiguity of a Pagan oracle †." What! and is Mr. B. alſo among the analogical, hypothetical, and conſequential reaſoners, upon the matter of a poſitive inſtitution? This mode of reaſoning, on *our* principles, would have ſome plauſibility; on *his* is quite out of character. But what ſignifies ſetting up our own idea of propriety againſt a plain fact; it is a *fact*, that wiſe and good men *cannot* ſee the eſſentiality of dipping in the leading term of this law; while Mr. B. and his friends think they do. It is a *fact*, that wiſe and good men ſincerely believe the law of chriſtian baptiſm extends to infants, and that they are as much included in the very terms as their parents are. But does it from thence follow, that our Divine Legiſlator has leſs wiſdom than a Britiſh Parliament; or deſigns an impoſition like a Pagan oracle?

§ 13. Mr. B.'s argument is, that as the principal terms of all approved human laws are without ambiguity in their meaning, *therefore* much more *ought* the laws of Chriſt relating to divine worſhip to be ſo. But do we forget that poſitive inſtitutions depend intirely on the *ſovereign will* of Heaven, and that we know *nothing* about them further than they are revealed? Allowing

† p. 34.

lowing this; yet, it may be objected, if our all-wife Legiflator *does* enact any law of this kind, we may reafonably prefume that it will be fo *plain* and *eafy* that the moft illiterate of his real difciples cannot miftake its meaning. This is ftill indulging *fuppofition* againft *fact*.

Let us fuppofe, for illuftration' fake, that an ante-diluvian faint had adopted this mode of reafoning.—" It is true, it depends intirely on
" the fovereign will of God whether he will re-
" veal himfelf to my pofterity, whether he will
" give them laws and pofitive inftitutions, to re-
" gulate their lives and prove their obedience;
" but *if he do* fo favour them, I may eafily infer
" from his infinite wifdom, goodnefs and equity;
" from his omnifcience, and grace, that thefe
" laws and inftitutions muft be fo *plain* and *eafy*
" that the moft ignorant of the righteous, cannot
" mifinterpret them. For were I, a finful fhort-
" fighted creature, to form a code of laws for
" my pofterity, they fhould be all of that charac-
" ter, and therefore much more will thofe which
" the Moft High may deliver, be free from all
" ambiguity. Yes, He fees the end from the
" beginning; and as he is capable by reafon of
" his unerring wifdom, fo he is bound by his
" immenfe goodnefs, to prevent all occafion of
" chicane and painful uncertainty. If prophets
" be raifed to addrefs my ruined pofterity, their
" meffage muft be fo *plain* and *eafy* to be un-
" derftood, that none of thofe to whom they are
" delivered can miftake their meaning; their cre-
" dentials

"dentials muſt be of ſuch a nature as to admit,
"of no debate whether they ſhould be credited
"or not. And when the promiſed Saviour ap-
"pears, he will, undoubtedly, deliver himſelf in
"ſuch a manner as to prevent all diſpute among
"his followers, eſpecially concerning matters of
"everlaſting moment. There will be no queſ-
"tion among them whether this Saviour is the
"Creator himſelf in man's nature, or only an
"extraordinary prophet of ſuperior wiſdom and
"holineſs; ſince all this may be prevented by a
"few words out of his own mouth. He will
"put it out of all doubt with all the wiſe and
"pious of his followers, whether he is to be ſerved
"with, or without, a form of devotion in pub-
"lick aſſemblies; whether chriſtian magiſtrates
"ought, or ought not, to form an *alliance* be-
"tween the church and the ſtate; whether or
"not ſome perſon, for the time being, ſhould
"act as his viceroy to the end of time, at the
"head of his univerſal church. And if he ſhould
"inſtitute a rite of initiation into his church, it
"is reaſonable to expect that his wiſdom and
"goodneſs will prevent all painful uncertainty
"reſpecting the *mode* of admiſſion, and who are
"the proper *ſubjects*," eſpecially when we conſider
that "all doubt of the matter might be precluded
by a few plain words." Thus the pious ante-
diluvian might meditate, and reaſon, *a priori*, from
the wiſdom and goodneſs of the Great Supreme;
rejoicing in the proſpect of the halcyon days which
his poſterity ſhould enjoy, when all laborious

ſearch

search, and tedious analogical reasoning, would be utterly precluded by the explicitness and perspicuity with which he would signify his pleasure. All this seems quite reasonable, very desirable, and mighty fine; but yet is attended with one great infelicity, it is a theory which does not agree with FACTS: But shall a benighted sinner exclaim, when *his* views of propriety and wisdom are confronted, deranged, and totally overthrown, "the LORD's ways are not equal!" Rather let me shrink to my proper nothingness, and say, O *the depth of the riches both of the wisdom and knowledge of God, how unsearchable are his counsels, and his ways,* his providence and his various dispensations, *how past finding out!* "Let us appeal (says Dr. S.) to the words of the institution, which no doubt are expressed, *as all laws* OUGHT TO BE, in so *clear* a manner as that he who runs may read." I walk and read, stand and read, meditate and read, pray and read, and yet cannot discern the sense he puts upon the law of the institution. And, what is far more extraordinary, thousands whom it concerns, many of whom are far better qualified to judge than I am, are equally at a loss to discover, what Dr. S. pronounces to be *without doubt,* so *clear* a meaning that he who runs may read it. *

OUR

---

* WHAT the pious Mr. FLAVEL said of himself, is, no doubt, the unfeigned sentiment of numbers not less sincere and upright than he, however superior he was to most divines in ministerial abilities and usefulness; *viz.* " We have a witness in your bosom, " (says he in his reply to Mr. CARY) that the defence of *Christ's* " pure

OUR opponents involve themselves in a glaring inconsistence. They maintain that positive rites depend solely on the pleasure of the Institutor, and then, with the same breath, plead that their evidence *must* be in a certain given degree of explicitness, that is, the superlative degree. For if they are not expressed in the *most* plain and intelligible manner, they are not worthy of a *wise* Legislator. This is to profess *absolute subjection* to the sovereign Lord, and afterwards to *prescribe rules* for him to enact his laws. Thus they insist upon a postulatum on which to erect their system, which it is out of our power to grant them without offering open violence to logical precision and sound Theology.

§ 14. FROM what has been said I conclude — since it is essential to an institution *merely positive*, our opponents themselves being judges, it should be free from all obscurity and ambiguity, relative to mode and subject, and since the institution of baptism does not bear that character, as stubborn facts proclaim — that baptism is an ordinance of a *mixed* nature. And it appears further reasonable to conclude, from the foregoing premises, that, as all allow baptism has *something* in it of a positive nature, " the set-
" ting

" *pure worship and institutions* hath cost us something; and as for
" me, were I convinced by all that you have here said, or any
" of your friends, that in baptizing the infants of believers we did
" really depart from the primitive purity, I would renounce it,
" and turn Anabaptist the same day." FLAVEL's Reply to Mr.
CARY's Solemn Call. *Works*, Vol. II. p. 1005. First Ed.

"ing apart a person apparently a proper subject of the visible church of Christ, by the use of water, in the Name of the Father, of the Son, and of the Holy Ghost, by a teacher of christianity," seems to bid fair for that character. Thus far Pædobaptists and Antipædobaptists generally agree; but whether a total *immersion* of the subject be *essential* to the ordinance, or even the *most proper* mode of admission; and whether some infants are not equally intitled to the privilege as adults; with other questions of inferior consideration, must be necessarily decided by moral and consequential reasoning.

§ 15. LET us now attend to what seems the only remaining method for determining about the degree and proportion of *positiveness* and *morality* in a law or institution commonly termed positive. And here I observe, towards solving this difficulty, the two things following,

1. THAT we ought carefully to distinguish between what is true of a positive institute in its own nature, or simply and *abstractedly* considered, and the same thing attended with its necessary circumstances. It has been shewn, that baptism is an institution which is positive but in part, and, therefore, that such a distinction as is here proposed is necessary. I am willing then to own the propriety of Mr. B.'s reasoning upon the nature and essential properties of positive institutions, *as far as they are such*, but deny that any just consequences from them are favourable to Antipædobaptism. And if we admit,

what

Ch. 1.   *and Analogical Reasoning.*   49

what I hope has been sufficiently proved, and what the following pages will more abundantly demonstrate, that there is no institution of the gospel dispensation so merely positive as not requiring prudential and moral aid to determine about the due performance and proper subjects thereof; and consequently, that the ordinance of baptism does not agree to the *abstract* notion of positive institutions; I venture to assert, as no less true than extraordinary, that there is not ONE of all the quotations from Pædobaptist writers contained in the first part of his *Pædobaptism examined*, concerning the nature of positive institutions, but is PERFECTLY CONSISTENT with Pædobaptist principles! But the specious sophism was supported by arbitralily uniting what were in themselves different; by extending the abstract nature of an institution, to the particular circumstances of it.

2. LAYING aside all preconceived ideas, we should carefully inquire *how far* any institution in question, from an impartial survey of what is recorded of it, *agrees* with the definition of a positive institution in its abstract sense. We all agree that such an institution, as deserves the denomination of positive, is *that*, the reason of which we do not see, yet delivered with such plainness, clearness, and circumstantial evidence, as is liable to no misconstruction from a person of common capacity and religious sincerity. Let us apply this rule to baptism, and we find, that there are *some* things wherein the rule and the

D   ordinance

ordinance agree, and *other* things wherein they disagree. Bp. BUTLER will furnish us with a slight specimen of the manner of applying the above rule. " The most important obligations and privileges signified by baptism are of *moral* consideration.—For instance, if some are commanded *to be baptized in the name of the Father, and of the Son, and of the Holy Ghost*; there are obligations of duty resulting from the command as *positive*, but the *importance* of these duties may be judged of by observing, that they arise not from positive command *merely*, but also from the offices which appear from scripture to belong to those divine persons in the gospel dispensation; or from the *relations*, which, we are there informed, they stand in to us*." This I call a *specimen*, but that the distinction above noticed is applicable to the subject and circumstances of baptism, will be afterwards considered.

§ 16. HENCE we may infer, that analogical and consequential reasoning is not only lawful, but *essential* to this controversy.

WE have seen (§ 12.) that our opponents themselves do occasionally run into this strain, however inconsistent with their favourite maxim; and we have seen that, hitherto, it has done them no service. From their being so extremely reluctant to admit of this sort of argument on the subject of baptism, we may justly suspect that it is proportionably injurious to their tenet. Mr. B. indeed, is very explicit on this head, as before

* BUTLER's Analogy, *ut supra*.

fore obferved; "Except it be maintained (fays he) that pofitive ordinances are to be *intirely* governed by pofitive law and primitive example, it is *impoffible* for the Antipædobaptifts to ftand their ground by *fair argument* in various cafes, when difputing with Pædobaptifts as fuch *." Dr. S. infifts, " that prefumptive proofs are infufficient to eftablifh duties of a pofitive kind ||." And I take the liberty of infifting in my turn, that, as no fuch duty exifts, in his application of the term *pofitive*, prefumptive proofs are very good ones, becaufe they are the very beft that the nature of the cafe can admit of. To argue from what is *certain* in one cafe, the *probability* of a cafe lefs evident, when the latter bears fome ftriking relation or refemblance to the former, has ever been reckoned fair and proper in fubjects of morality and duty; it therefore follows, that, as the duty in queftion is partly founded on *moral* grounds, the fame method of arguing is fair and proper to a certain degree in the prefent cafe. For when the *circumftances* of a duty commonly termed pofitive are left in an indeterminate ftate, and therefore of neceffity muft yield to *moral* confiderations, and when thefe moral confiderations do not arife immediately from the evident relation of the cafe in hand, or are not determined clearly by precept or example; what more rational method of determining thefe circumftances, than by recurring by means of analogy

* p. 462. || p. 293.

to thofe which we are fure met with the divine approbation?

What has been faid already upon this article, might appear, I prefume, quite fufficient, in vindication of a method of defence which our opponents would fain deprive us of, were it not that they are impertinently inimical to it upon every occafion, as might be eafily fhewn by numerous quotations out of their writings, and Mr. B.'s Pædobaptifm Examined in particular. But as their favourite terms, POSITIVE LAW and APOSTOLIC EXAMPLE, as oppofed to *moral* and *analogical* reafoning, are a two-edged fword, which they brandifh with great parade, and with which they pretend to do great execution; let us now fee whether this weapon may not be wrefted out of their hands.

§ 17. That principle, whereby our opponents decry all ufe of analogy in this debate, is reducible to the moft glaring *abfurdities*. For,

(1) It is impoffible that Mr. B. Dr. S. or any one elfe in the prefent day, fhould know any thing about this ordinance without the aids of the very method which they fo much oppofe. This is evident when we reflect, that as fcripture can never be proved to be of divine original, fo neither can any particular part of it be proved to have *this* meaning rather than *that*, but by means of moral and analogical reafoning. The evidence of revelation is either external or internal; its *external* evidence muft depend on the *faithfulnefs* of our predeceffors who have recorded and transfmitted

Ch. 1.   *and Analogical Reasoning.*   53

tranfmitted fuch facts as conftitute the fame; but will any man, *compos mentis,* hefitate a moment refpecting the neceffity of examining the pretenfions and credentials of our fellow-mortals, when they affert they were fent of God to claim the attention, belief, and obedience of mankind? And how can this be decided without the affiftance of moral reafoning? Its *internal* evidence muft be fought by the fame method; for nothing can be of God which is evidently and demonftrably falfe or impious, however recommended by figns and wonders.

Nor will it avail to fay, the moft abftrufe things, indeed, will admit of fuch inveftigation, but fome things are " fo plain and eafy to be underftood that he who runs may read." Such parts of fcripture, then, need only to be propofed, and they appear *felf-evident.* I will not deny but there are many fuch truths in fcripture; inafmuch as fome of the plaineft dictates of common fenfe and reafon are there recorded. And, indeed, this is no fmall part of the glory of revelation, that it is " a republication of natural religion; fo that natural religion, in the words of Bp. BUTLER, feems as much proved by the fcripture revelation, as it would have been, had the defign of revelation been nothing elfe than to prove it *." But it muft amount to an evident contradiction to affert that *pofitive laws* are *felf-evident* in their own nature; for, on the fuppofition, we know nothing about them further than

* BUTLER's Analogy, *ut fupra.*

than they are *revealed*. Nor will it mend the matter to say, that *when* revealed they are self-evident; for, it is likewise granted, that they derive their whole force and being from the sovereign *authority* that enjoins them; which authority itself cannot be self-evident, but must be examined, weighed, compared, and finally determined by some *antecedent* principles; and this is the province of moral reason and analogy.

§ 18. But if it be said, that " tho' we need these aids to ascertain the truth of revelation, yet when that is once done we have no farther need of it:" I answer, this can by no means solve the difficulty; for in order to discover the import of any law or precept of holy writ, we must either take the *literal* and strict meaning of it, or we must have recourse to the *design* of the passage from the most probable intention of the Lawgiver; if the *latter*, the point is given up; if the *former*, the most absurd consequences will immediately follow. For it is evident to a demonstration, that two persons, who would undertake to perform a positive command, may both alike plead the strict *letter* of the law to be on their side, and yet one of them may *commit sin* while so doing, and the other discharge incumbent duty. And I may venture to say, there is not a positive law in all the inspired volume, relating to the mosaic or the christian œconomy, but might furnish an illustration and proof of what I assert. To avoid prolixity I shall insist upon the law of baptism only: on which Mr. B.
thus

Ch. 1. *and Analogical Reasoning.* 55

thus reflects. "It should be well observed, that when our Lord after his resurrection, says, *Go—baptize*; he does not mention baptism by way of allusion, or incidentally. No, he speaks the language of *legiflation*; he delivers DIVINE LAW. He mentions and appoints baptism as an ordinance of God, and as a branch of human duty. Where, then, must we expect precision in the use of terms, if not on such an occasion*?" Where? why, in those parts of revelation where man's everlasting welfare is more immediately concerned. For is it probable that the law of initiation into the visible kingdom of Christ, and an external relation to him and his church, is of more importance, and requiring greater precision in its terms, than that which ascertains their qualification for the kingdom of grace and glory? But supposing, for argument sake, that the law of baptism (Mat. xxviii. 19.) is delivered with greater precision than usual, and let us try—not with a view to impeach the wisdom or the goodness of Christ—let us try, I say, whether moral reasoning and analogy are not necessary for the right observance of it, even upon our author's own principles.

Mr. B. will allow that this law consists of three parts; the action itself, *baptize*; the qualification necessary for the subject previous to baptism, implied in the word *teach*; and the commission given to the administrators, *Go ye*. The first of these ideas will be more professedly examined

* p. 33.

amined hereafter; but by the bye, one would think that the great diverſity of opinions reſpecting this *action*, and the various practices of different nations and churches in performing what they apprehend to be included in it, might lead a modeſt and impartial obſerver to conclude—not that one party of chriſtians excluſively are in the right, while all the others are *eſſentially* wrong, many of whom have ſeriouſly, deliberately and impartially examined the authority and the mind of their divine Lord in the matter, whoſe ſovereign pleaſure is more dear to them than their lives, and whom they would not wilfully offend therein for the world—to conclude, I ſay, either that the precept is not delivered with all that plainneſs and preciſion which our opponents contend for, in favour of *their* manner of performing the *action*, or elſe that it is of ſuch latitude as to include divers manners. I would only remark, that, ſuppoſing (without granting) the excluſive invariable meaning of the term, *baptize*, ſignifies to immerſe, I might, on *that* ſuppoſition ſo fulfil the command *literally*, in plunging a proper ſubject, as that Mr. B. I am perſuaded, would either not admit it to be at all true baptiſm, or would require no ſmall aſſiſtance from that very method of arguing which he oppugns, to prove its validity. But I ſhall obſerve, more particularly, ſome things with reſpect to the commiſſion of the adminiſtrators, which will furniſh a ſecond argument againſt the oppoſers of analogical and moral reaſoning on the ſubject.

§ 19.

§ 19. (2) It is impossible, on the principle I am opposing, for Mr. B. or Dr. S. to prove their right and *authority* to administer the ordinance of baptism to any subject, and of consequence the *validity* of the action. The sentiment I refer to, is, that nothing short of a *precept* or *precedent* will suffice for the due performance of the duty. Now that every action performed by apostles, disciples, or saints, with, or without, the special directions of the Holy Spirit, is not to be regarded as a *precedent*, or an example to be imitated, will, I presume, admit of no debate. It therefore follows that we must either gather from moral considerations, or consequential deductions, whether any particular action is to be imitated by us, or not; or else that there must be a *precept* previously given, whereby any such action receives a special direction and determination to influence our choice. And so it remains that an action, however and by whomsoever performed, can be to us no rule of duty, *no precedent at all*, OF ITSELF. It is therefore absurd to say that we can regard *any action* as a precedent, without the aids of inferential reasoning. We are, now, driven to *precepts* to perform the difficult task. Let us, therefore, attend to that " language of legislation, that divine law where we may expect, we are told, the greatest plainness and precision." Go ye, *therefore, and teach.*—This is the *precept*. But to *whom* is it given? The answer, no doubt, will be, To the *disciples*, and to their *successors* in the gospel

pel miniſtry. Rather, To the diſciples, and, we may juſtly *infer*, to their ſucceſſors in the goſpel miniſtry to the end of time. For our Lord adds, "Lo! I am with you alway, even to the end of the world;" which *more likely* refers to our Lord's authoritative and gracious preſence with all the then future, properly qualified teachers and propagators of the goſpel, than excluſively his immediate ſucceſſors, the apoſtles and diſciples, who ſhould be endowed from above with extraordinary abilities, remarkably owned, and attended with ſigns and wonders for the eſtabliſhment of the chriſtian religion, on the ruins of the jewiſh hierarchy.

BUT ſuppoſing, (without granting) that the former propoſition is ſo ſelf-evident as to preclude all need of inference, or analogy. The queſtion ſtill returns, what conſtitutes a diſciple, and teacher of religion? Chriſtian godly parents are diſciples, and they alſo teach their children and domeſtics the principles of chriſtianity; have *they*, therefore, authority to *baptize* ſuch as they teach? Without analogy and inference how can their pretenſions be diſproved? May they not plead, from the very paſſage in queſtion, that becauſe they may teach, they may likewiſe baptize? It will be ſaid, perhaps, the adminiſtration of goſpel ordinances belongs to *publick* teachers. But publick and private are *relative* terms; and who ſhall draw the line of diſtinction *how far* publick his character and teaching muſt be? May any one run, without being ſent, to teach and baptize?

Does

Does this conftitute a teacher of chriftianity, that he *fancies* he may fet up for one? or is he to be admitted to the difcharge of his minifterial function in fome more regular way? How fhall we judge about the *regularity* of that way? The wearer of the tripple crown afferts an univerfal claim to this right of admiffion, as his fovereign prerogative. With a prieftly nod, with roaring bulls, or with dire anathemas, he excludes all of us, who are of the heretical tribe, from approaching to officiate at the baptifmal font, or the holy altar. And what is extraordinary, he urges *exprefs*, *literal* paffages of fcripture, on which to found his pretenfions.

§ 20. But Proteftants, alfo, talk of the divine right of epifcopacy, and the neceffity of an epifcopal commiffion, for preaching God's word, and for the valid miniftration of the chriftian facraments. And this they attempt to prove from the *holy fcriptures*, as well as the doctrine and practice of the primitive church. Thus the *twenty third* article of the church of England, paraphrafed by a faithful fon and champion; " *It is not lawful* by the law of God *for any man to take upon him the office of publick preaching or miniftering the facraments in the congregation* or church of Chrift *before he be lawfully called* according to the law of God, *and fent to execute the fame. And thofe we ought to judge lawfully called and fent* according to the law of God, *which be chofen and called to this work by men, who* by the law of God *have publick authority given unto them*

them in the congregation or church of Chrift, *to call and fend minifters into the Lord's vineyard.* I have put in the words *according to the law of God,* (fays the Paraphraft,) becaufe it is certain *that* is meant by the word *lawful* in this place. Thefe articles were drawn up by the Bifhops and Clergy in convocation or fynod, who were ever efteemed to be interpreters or expofitors of the law of God, and to have authority to declare what was agreeable to his laws, and what not— Confequently (fays this Doctor of Laws) when they fay, it is not lawful for any man to take upon him the office of publick preaching or miniftering the facraments in the church, they could not mean that it was not lawful in this realm only by virtue of the temporal laws here in force, becaufe they had no authority to declare or expound thofe laws, but that it was *not lawful* according to the LAW OF GOD, and therefore could not be allowed in any realm, in any country, in any church or fociety of *chriftians.* — And in the preface to the forms of ordination, it is faid, that *it is* EVIDENT *to all men diligently reading* HOLY SCRIPTURES, *and ancient authors, that from the apoftles' time, there have been thefe orders of minifters in Chrift's church, bifhops, priefts and deacons, which offices were evermore had in fuch reverend eftimation, that no man by his own private authority, might prefume to execute any of them, except he were firft called, tried, examined and known to have fuch qualities as were requifite for the fame, and alfo by publick prayer, with impofition of hands, approved*

and

and admitted thereunto.—She [the church] also declares these three orders to be of *divine inſtitution,* when she says that *it is evident to all men diligently reading* HOLY SCRIPTURE *that there have been theſe orders of miniſters in Chriſt's church.*— And therefore according to the doctrine of the church of *England,* declared by her ordinal and articles as they expound each other, *it is not lawful for any man to take upon him the office of publick preaching, or miniſtering the ſacraments in the congregation or church of Chriſt, before he be lawfully called and ſent to execute the ſame by ſome* BISHOP; *that is, before he be* EPISCOPALLY ORDAINED; and this by the LAW OF GOD, who by his Holy Spirit has appointed the order of bishops, and *directed* that only those who are of that order should ordain others, conſequently is a law not only obligatory in the church of England, but throughout the whole catholic church. — She further declares, in the *twenty ſixth* article, that *altho' in the viſible church the evil be ever mingled with the good, and ſometime the evil have chief authority in the miniſtration of the word and ſacraments; yet foraſmuch as they do not the ſame in their own name but in Chriſt's, and do miniſter by* HIS COMMISSION *and authority, we may uſe their miniſtry both in hearing the word of God, and in the receiving of the ſacraments. Neither is the effect of Chriſt's ordinance taken away by their wickedneſs, nor the grace of God's gifts diminiſhed from ſuch, as by faith, and rightly do receive the ſacraments miniſtered unto them, which be effectual becauſe of Chriſt's*

Chrift's INSTITUTION *and* PROMISE, *altho'* they be miniftered by evil men. Here the church plainly makes the VALIDITY of the facraments depend intirely upon Chrift's COMMISSION. For the reafon alleged why they may be received from evil minifters, is becaufe fuch minifters have *commiffion and authority* from Chrift, and that facraments fo received are effectual becaufe of Chrift's *inftitution and promife*, which evidently implies that where there is no fuch commiffion there is not the inftitution and promife of Chrift, confequently they are not effectual without the commiffion. Thus the church of *England* moft clearly maintains and afferts both the *divine right of epifcopacy*, and alfo the neceffity of an *epifcopal commiffion* to the VALID adminiftration of the facrament *."

§ 21. THUS the large body of venerable Bifhops, together with their numerous fons and fervants the Clergy, in convocation affembled, as the reprefentatives of millions, deliver their final and permanent fentiments, concerning the *authority* neceffary for minifters to difcharge the duties of their function, and the *validity* of their miniftrations thereon depending. But what is very remarkable is, that their determination appeals, not to the uncertain reports of tradition, to moral, inferential, or analogical reafoning, but to a *pofitive law*; to the *exprefs inftitution* of Chrift. And our expounding Doctor juftifies thefe ecclefiaftical decifions, *on the very fame principles*, by appealing

* Dr. BRETT's Divine Right of Epifcopacy, § 1—4.

appealing to the language of legiflation, the divine pofitive command, to which we firft referred. Thus he fettles his point: " That the *apoftolical* or higheft order, which was appointed to fupply the place of Chrift himfelf after his afcenfion, was intended by him not for a temporary, but a perpetual inftitution, is evident from the commiffion he gave them after his refurrection. For, having fingled out the eleven Apoftles, out of above five hundred, to whom he appeared at once after his refurrection, and appointed them alone to meet him at a mountain in *Galilee*, he fpake unto them, faying, *All power is given unto me in heaven and in earth*. And having thus declared his own power, he commits it to them, and fays, Go *ye therefore*, as my deputies and vicegerents, *and difciple all nations, baptizing them in the Name of the Father, and of the Son, and of the Holy Ghoft, teaching them to obferve all things whatfoever I have commanded you. And lo I am with you alway, even unto the end of the world, Amen*. In which words he *plainly* thews that their office was intended to be continued alway, even unto the end of the world, and he confirms this promife with an *Amen*, thereby teftifying that he would verily and indeed fulfil it. Now it was *plainly* the apoftolical office which our Saviour here promifed he would be alway prefent with, to ratify and confirm their miniftrations. For it was only the eleven difciples or apoftles, whom he had before fent, as he was fent by the Father, to whom he made

the

the promife. And that the promife was made to the *office* or *order* with which he had vefted them, and not to their perfons, is *evident*, becaufe otherwife his promife muft have failed at their deaths, and confequently he was fo far from continuing with *them* to the end of the world in the difcharge of this office, that he did not continue with them an hundred years, for all thefe eleven Apoftles were dead in lefs than that time. But fome pretend that the words which we here tranflate, *the end of the world*, fignify no more than *the end of that age*. But if they are underftood to fignify no more, then the commiffion to difciple by baptifm, and to teach what Chrift had commanded, muft end with that age alfo, and then chriftianity muft have ceafed with that age, fo that ever fince our preaching has been vain, and your faith alfo vain; for it has fince had no promife of Chrift to depend upon, if this promife is to be extended to no longer time; and that is not *faith*, but *prefumption*, which is not founded upon any promife. But if the promife is to be extended to the end of the world, and that it muft be, or there can be no chriftianity in the world, then muft the office, the *apoftolical office* or order, to which it was made, continue fo long. For Chrift did not fay, *I am alway prefent to ratify and confirm thefe miniftrations by whomfoever performed*, but *I am with you alway*; with *you* whom I have fent, as I was fent by the Father, with *you* whom I have appointed to difciple all nations by bap-

tifm

tifm, with *you* whom I have appointed to teach all things which I have commanded and will ratify and confirm what *you* do in thefe miniftrations, that is, *you* who are commiffioned for that purpofe. Therefore the office, *the apoftolical office*, to which this commiffion was given, muft continue for the miniftry of thefe ordinances, or there is no promife that thefe ordinances fhall be effectual to any after the death of thofe perfons to whom this commiffion was particularly given. But if the ordinances continue, then the commiffion alfo is continued, for the promife is not made to the ordinances, but to the commiffioners in the miniftration of thofe ordinances; and therefore if thofe who have not the commiffion undertake to adminifter them, there is no word of promife to make fuch miniftrations effectual.

" Now whence do the facraments receive their *validity?* Certainly not from any thing that is naturally intrinfick to the outward vifible fign, but from the *inftitution* of Jefus Chrift. But then it is not every kind of baptifm, or of wafhing with water, that will have effect: it muft be done according to *his inftitution*, or it is not the facrament which he has ordained. Now when Chrift ordered baptifm to be adminiftered to all nations, when he appointed that all fhould eat of that bread and drink of that cup, he did not only ordain in what manner, or with what form of words thefe facraments fhould be celebrated, but likewife directed what particular *perfons*

fhould

should celebrate them. Thus when he ordered all nations should be made disciples by baptism, he did not indiscriminately command *all persons* that should know how to recite the form of words with which baptism was to be administered, to baptize, but the *Apostles* only, whom he chose out of a vast multitude of his disciples, and to them particularly, as I have before observed, he gave commission to *go and disciple all nations, baptizing them*. So also when he instituted the holy eucharist, he did not commit the ministration of it to all his disciples, but only to *the twelve*. And to them only he said THIS DO, that is, consecrate bread and wine, and distribute it, as I have now done, in remembrance of me.—The Apostles on neither of these occasions met our Saviour by accident, but by appointment. Whereas if he had intended to have commissioned *more* for either of these purposes, he could as easily have ordered more to have attended him upon either of these occasions. But by not requiring their attendance, and at the same time requiring that of the Apostles, he *plainly excluded* all the rest.—I know it is objected, that a bare omission in this case does not amount to a prohibition, and therefore since our Saviour only forebore to command, but did not prohibit his other disciples to administer his sacraments, we have no ground from scripture to say that none but *Bishops*, as *Successors* to the Apostles, may minister them, or that if any others do it, they are invalid, and of no effect

what-

whatsoever. But we answer, that *an omission in this case does amount to a prohibition.* For wherever a commission is necessary to authorize an act, whosoever is *left out* of the commission, is unauthorized, and therefore cannot perform that act so as to make it *valid.*—I never could understand that a prince when he granted a commission to levy, or any other commission whatsoever, did expresly or in direct terms forbid any other to do what he authorized those to do whom he did commission. For a commission is always given to authorize a man to do that, which without such commission neither he nor any one else has otherwise a right to do.—There was therefore no occasion for our Saviour to prohibit others from administering his sacraments, since the authorizing some and not others was itself in the nature of the thing as full a prohibition, as if he had forbid them to do these things in express words.—Now the promises of God with relation to the sacraments, at least to the sacrament of *baptism,* are not made to the act itself, but to the persons by whom that sacrament is ordered to be administered. For Christ does not say, I am with the act of baptizing, or washing in the name of the Father, &c.—But he says, *Lo, I am with* YOU *alway, with* YOU *my Apostles, with* YOU *whom I have commissioned to minister baptism, and with* YOUR *Successors to the end of the world.* The promise being therefore not made to the bare baptism or washing with water, but to the Apostles,

and

and their Succeffors, who were commiffioned to minifter that facrament, thofe that are not baptized by perfons fo commiffioned, have no promife to depend upon, that they have received Chrift's baptifm; and therefore for any to believe that they have received it, is not *faith* but *prefumption*, and being *not of faith* St. Paul tells us *it is fin*. It is fin in the perfon who pretends to *adminifter* it, for he takes upon him an office unto which God has not called him, he acts without authority, and prefumptuoufly fuppofes God will ratify that which he has given him no commiffion to do: it is alfo *fin* in the perfon who *receives* it from one whom he knows to have no commiffion to give it, for he alfo is prefumptuous, and expects a bleffing where God has made no promife of any.—Any pretended baptifm therefore miniftered by fuch as have no commiffion, is deftitute of this promife, and being fo, is of no effect or validity, for it is not *Chrift's baptifm*, but a baptifm of *human invention* *."

§ 22. THE attentive reader will eafily obferve, that Dr. BRETT, when he wrote the above, was on his road to *Rome*; taking, however, *pofitive precepts*, which always imply their negative, for his guide. And had he compleated his journey, he and his *principles* would have met with the moft cordial welcome. For by fuch principles the papal chair is fupported, and the whole ftructure of the holy catholic church can boaft

* Ibid. § 9. 25—28.

boast of a similar foundation. "Yes, whether it be an assembly of presbyters, or a council of prelates; whether it be the injunction of a pope, or the mandate of a prince, by which the inventions of men are incorporated with the appointments of God; they admit of the *same kind* of defence." How Mr. B. would answer the above pretended apostolical succession, I will not take upon me to determine; but for my own part, since my Maker and Judge has given me eyes to see and ears to hear, I would attend to what the Spirit of truth saith unto the churches; I would diligently and with diffidence search my bible, and especially those parts that seem more immediately to refer to these matters; seek light and direction from the Father of lights, who liberally imparts wisdom, and prudence profitable to direct; I would examine, reason, *moralize, analogize*, and use ALL the means and methods which a gracious God has furnished me with; and, finally, I would shew that the Doctor's foundation, notwithstanding his appeal upon every turn to positive appointment and apostolic practice, is contrary to the genius of the gospel dispensation, and reducible to manifold *absurdities*, which can never be a part of the divine will.

§ 23. (3) BUT supposing, for argument' sake, these gentlemen could extricate themselves from the above entangling difficulty; it would prove but a temporary relief, for another still greater awaits them. I assert, therefore, in the next place, That it is impossible, on their own avowed

prin-

principles, whereby they discard from their system all use of *moral* considerations, inference and analogy, to determine in practice who is a proper *subject* of baptism among adults and who is not; and if so, are not only *liable* to commit sin instead of performing duty, but as often as they perform the action of baptism they *inevitably* plunge themselves into sin.

LET us not lose sight of that " divine law," where, *if at all*, we may expect precision with respect to the *qualifications* of the subject. Go — TEACH — *baptize*"— As " this instructive text, says Mr. B. is the first appointment of baptism for the use of the *gentiles*, and as it is the law of administration to the end of time, so it cannot but require the most submissive regard. For Jesus Christ, on this occasion, expressly claims *all authority in heaven and on earth*. He plainly appears as King of Zion, and Sovereign of the world. His language, here, is not a mere *allusion* to baptism, — but it is the *institution* of that ordinance, it is DIVINE LAW; and therefore the expressions contained in it, must be understood in their natural and obvious meaning, *except any absurdity* would follow such a construction of the sacred statute. — As to any *absurdity* following upon it, our opponents pretend none, but what implies a begging of the question disputed*."— Overlooking a great piece of inconsistency observable in the above paragraph, where it is said that " this text is the *first appointment* of baptism,

for

* p. 322.

for the use of the Gentiles," implying that it was before appointed *for the use of the Jews,* which is the real fact; tho' that *first institution* is not mentioned in the evangelic history: and where it is also said, " that this is not a mere *allusion* to baptism, but is *the institution* of that ordinance;" which, if it has any determinate meaning, must imply, by the opposition intended, that it *was not before instituted,* which involves a contradiction. It was not a mere allusion, but *the institution itself,* of what was *before instituted.* Passing by this, what, pray, is that disputed question which the Pædobaptists *beg* at the hands of their brethren? Is it the *favour* of disputing about the *qualifications* of subjects on *moral* grounds? They have no need to *beg* that; it is their *native right,* as the preceding pages, I presume, do evince; and as the following will further establish. Or is it that the *natural* and *primary* signification of the greek term, μαθητευσατε, is to *disciple* rather than to *teach?* At present I only observe, that, whatever advantage would accrue to the cause for which I am pleading, from such a *grant* in its favour, Mr. B. and his friends will be no great gainers by a peaceful *possession* of what they so highly esteem. My present argument does not require a professed examination of the above question, and therefore let it be now supposed that the word is properly rendered, TEACH. I will also grant that Mr. B. is in the properest sense a qualified person to execute Christ's commission, as properly qualified

as

as those to whom the commission was originally given. After all, I insist it is not in his power to perform his appointed work, to *teach* in order to baptism, but by the aids of moral and analogical reasoning. Without this he will be at a loss about the *kind* and the *degree* of teaching. The word *teach* is vague and indeterminate, because it is not only of various kinds, about which however we will suppose no misunderstanding, but admits of endless *degrees*. How much teaching is sufficient? The *qualification* of the *taught* is by no means to be measured by the time, the pains, or the abilities employed by the teacher. Some are ever learning without ever coming to the knowledge of the truth; and few gospel teachers but have occasion to make the mournful observation. No given degree whatever of skill, of faithfulness, or of laborious diligence in the discharge of his high commission, can enable a teacher to decide who is fit for baptism and who is not. Were a teacher to come to this determination, that each catechumen should be sufficiently qualified when able to recite the Lord's prayer, the ten commandments, and a certain short creed; all this, and much more, may be taught a person, while he has not a grain of religion; nay, continuing openly irreligious. And should *such* be baptized? Besides, by what authority could he fix upon such a standard? The object and the end of this teaching, then, is the *moral improvement* of the instructed, of which the teacher is the appointed judge.

judge †. But what *positive* precept or example can enable him to do this? *Positive* institutions are of an *external* nature, as before shewn, (§ 6.) and are perfectly distinct in their nature from all *moral* considerations.

§ 24. Mr. B. very frequently refers us to the Mosaic ritual as of a *similar* nature with baptism: or, in other words, finds an *analogy* between baptism and those antiquated rites, to which he is fond of referring us. And on a certain occasion, when speaking of the signification of terms, he throws down the gauntlet; and, *feeling the ground on which he treads*, exclaims, "We may safely challenge our opposers to produce an instance of this kind out of the Mosaic ritual*." Before we accept the challenge, I would fain learn, upon what principle Mr. B. draws a *comparison* between baptism and the Jewish ceremonies? How the law that enacts the former, *ought* to have any thing in it *analogous* to those inforcing the latter? It seems he makes it *requisite* that there should be an *analogy* between these laws; " the whole *being* of which, and all their legitimate connections, depend on the sovereign pleasure of God ‡."

But, instead of acceding to this proposal of producing an instance out of the Mosaic ritual enjoined in a manner *similar* to what we conceive

† " Admission to baptism lies *solely* in the breast of the *Administrator*, who is the *only judge* of qualifications for it, and has the *sole power* of receiving to it, and of rejecting from it." Gill's Body of Divinity, Vol. III. B. III. Chap. I.

* p. 33.   ‡ p. 460.

ceive the latter to be; I beg leave to demand ONE INSTANCE out of all the numerous precepts, which Mr. B. calls positive, delivered by Moses to the chosen tribes, that required in the subject a discriminating *moral qualification?* An institution *merely positive*, in regard to the subject, necessarily requires distinguishing marks in him of an *external* nature; a distinction that is sensible, circumstantial, not liable to misconstructions, and, in a word, infallibly characterized; otherwise, the choice of the subject, to whom the rite is to be applied, depends not upon *positive* rules, but *prudential* maxims, and *moral* considerations. Hence we may observe, that *those* rites were awfully guarded with temporal visible *penal sanctions*, which baptism is not. *He that believeth and is baptized shall be saved, but he that* BELIEVETH NOT, or rejects the Redeemer and his salvation, *shall be* DAMNED. The neglect of baptism, in proportion as it is a duty, is sinful; but it is guarded with no penal sanction. There appears another important reason why the Mosaic ritual was connected with external characters, as distinguished from moral ones, and also their being guarded by penal threats, and that is, their being *typical* of future blessings under the Messiah; but no gospel ordinance, strictly speaking, is a type. — On the whole, then, we may observe this remarkable difference between the institutions of the Old Testament and those of the New; the *former* referred, for instance, to persons of such a *sex* and *age*, as circumcision; to persons who

had

Ch. 1. *and Analogical Reasoning.* 75

had certain *marks* on their bodies, as the cure of the leprosy; to persons who *touched* any thing declared to be unclean; to persons who *uttered* certain words, as the blasphemer; to persons who committed certain *actions*, as the manslayer; &c. —but the *latter* refer to *moral* qualities, to certain *dispositions* of mind, to persons in such *circumstances* as are answerable to the *end* and *design* of the institutions, according to the judgment of the Administrator. Mr. B.'s reasoning, therefore, is of no force when he argues, that because the terms of the Mosaic ritual left nothing to be *inferred*, respecting the qualifications of the *subject*, therefore the same must hold in baptism; and his challenge is impertinent. To discard moral grounds from this controversy, leads to this absurdity, for it is the same as to say, that Christ gave a command to his ministers, in executing which, no *reasoning* or *inference* is at all necessary, and yet without this they are liable to perpetual mistakes. It is like a sovereign giving his representative a *discretionary* commission to treat with a foreign power, but every word of the treaty, he is told, is written and unalterably *fixed*, and must be taken in its strictest meaning. Which is the same as to say, The nature of your commission necessarily requires some liberty and latitude, some discretionary power of determining certain points, which cannot possibly be included in these rules and this treaty, and yet you must not recede a hair's breadth from the particulars therein contained.

E 2. § 25.

§ 25. If it be objected, (what indeed seems to me to be the only objection of any plausibility that can be urged) " that tho' our Lord has drawn no line in the command to determine *what degree* of instruction is necessary, yet according to the letter of the command *some degree* is requisite;" To this I reply, that *teaching*, in the present case, is of no further use than a *mean* to a moral end. Its *only use* seems to be to discover, produce, or promote a *moral qualification*. This is evident when we consider that if this important *end* is attained, the other is of course superseded; for whether the subject, on our opponents' principle, has been *taught* by another, or has profited, in a solitary way, by prayer and reading, &c. as a pre-requisite qualification, is quite immaterial. The subject *has already* attained to what is a necessary qualification, in the Antipædobaptist sense, and therefore teaching for *that end* is unnecessary. Which sufficiently shews the weakness and futility of forming an absolute and indispensible connexion between *teaching* and baptizing. The objection, therefore, is of no force, but on supposition that human teaching is a *necessary* mean, without which there can be no moral qualification, which is contrary to fact; for it is demonstrable from the concessions of our opponents, that many of the human race are *actually* in possession of that end, to attain which is the sole use of the teaching intended, who yet are not beholden to its aid. Nor can it be denied, that there are *other* means

of

Ch. 1.   *and Analogical Reasoning.*   77

of information *beside* what arise from the circumstance of teaching, whereby we may conclude with *sufficient* certainty, that is, with a certainty *equal* to what teaching can afford us, or equal to any *profession* whatever, that certain persons are in the *state* of which a profession, as the effect of teaching, is only an indication; except it be maintained that profession is an *infallible* sign, which is absurd.

But should any one still insist, that a competent knowledge of christian principles, and a credible profession are necessary; I ask, what is the standard of this *competency* or *credibility?* What positive rule can answer this purpose? And again, I ask, *necessary for what?* If the reply be, to answer the nature and design of the institution—it is evident this is only begging the question, as I shall fully shew in the next chapter; where I hope also to demonstrate, that there is nothing in the nature and design of baptism, but is equally applicable to the infant child of a believer as to himself, however eminent he may be in faith and piety. Upon the whole it appears, that teaching cannot be any way an *essential* qualification for baptism, and therefore is required in certain *circumstances* only.

§ 26. From what has been said it follows, that our opponents, if they act upon their avowed principles, are not only *liable* to commit sin by baptizing an unqualified person, but do *inevitably* commit sin, by renouncing and deserting the real and only guide left to conduct us in the
path

path of duty. To baptize the *inſtructed* would be no duty, without attending to the *moral* circumſtances of the inſtruction; and to perform what is *materially* right without an adequate rule, is *morally* an evil, or ſinful. It is the obſervance of the deſign and reaſon, the moral purpoſes of the command, as it refers to teaching, and not the mere letter of it, that conſtitutes a teacher's duty. For of two miniſters, keeping to the letter of the precept, in a manner equally ſtrict, one may be performing the intention of the Lawgiver, and the other committing a ſin. The office of teaching, therefore, is a diſcretionary office, to be meaſured by the *moral* deſign of the inſtitution to which it refers. How abſurd to argue thus: OMAI the ſavage is *taught*—the *Paternoſter*—the ten commandments—the apoſtles' creed—therefore he ſhould be baptized; however deſtitute of chriſtian virtue and religion. Yet, on the principle I am oppoſing, this muſt be good logic. — Now, if we ought to *reject* ſome candidates for baptiſm who yet are taught, becauſe not in a ſtate that ſeems to comport with the deſign of the inſtitution; we are at liberty, for the ſame reaſon, to *admit* others who appear in a condition ſuited to that deſign, tho' not taught, if upon inquiry any ſuch ſhould be found. Whether infants be of that number, will be conſidered in its proper place.

§ 27. (4) WHAT innumerable other abſurdities would follow from that mode of interpreting ſcripture which Mr. B. contends for, even in

reference

reference to the very commiffion in queftion! For inftance, Whofoever believeth and is baptized, fhall be faved; Simon the forcerer believed and was baptized; therefore he is faved. He that believeth not fhall be damned; infants believe not; therefore *(horribile dictu!)* they fhall be damned. And *thefe figns* fhall follow them that believe: in my name they fhall caft out devils; they fhall fpeak with new tongues; they fhall take up ferpents; and if they drink any deadly thing, it fhall not hurt them; they fhall lay hands on the fick, and they fhall recover: but *thefe figns* have not followed for many ages back; therefore, during all that time, none have believed. Or, on the other hand, many have believed without *thefe figns* following; therefore, Chrift is not true to his word.—Again, Jefus fpake nothing but in parables; but he fpake the commiffion to preach the gofpel and to baptize; therefore this commiffion is a *parable*. The command is not only *teach all nations*, but preach the gofpel to *every creature*; (the latter being laft written explaining the former;) but four-footed beafts, fowls, and fifhes, &c. are creatures; therefore it behoved the difciples to preach to *thefe*. Again, *Paul* was not fent to baptize, but to preach the gofpel; but he baptized *Crifpus* and *Gaius*, and the houfhold of *Stephanus*; therefore he did that which he was not fent to do, or acted contrary to his commiffion, and was blameworthy in baptizing them. How can fuch a ridiculous mode of reasoning be confuted without *inferential* reasoning?

§ 28. WILL any say, that there is no danger of running into such ridiculous inconsistencies; that a very moderate share of common sense, a little sober reason, a small attention to the scope of a passage, and the analogy of faith, would prove a sufficient barrier against the apprehended danger? Very true; this is all we desire. But this is the very barrier which the Antipædobaptists would fain demolish. When Dr. S. professedly inquires by what kind of proof we are to be determined in this controversy, he says, " Here I would observe then, that all positive institutions depend solely upon the will of the institutor, and therefore *in every question relating to them* we are to be guided by his express declarations, or by those of persons he has duly authorized to signify his will. — Now this principle granted, I might very properly be excused considering the much greater part of Mr. A.'s book, which consists of analogical reasoning; — because a *matter of this importance* in its own nature *requires* an express positive declaration*." And Mr. ROBINSON is so well satisfied and pleased with this principle, (however repugnant in its genuine consequences to that freedom of inquiry which on other occasions he professes and adopts, and for which he is reprehended by Mr. B. as inconsistent with himself †) that he looks upon it as a most formidable weapon employed against the

* Answer to A. p. 3, 6.   † p. 462, Note.

the Pædobaptists; and publickly compliments his reverend brother, when he says, " Dr. STENNETT has given the *death wound* to Mr. A——'s arguments for infant baptism by this method §." But Mr. R. need not be informed that the warlike *Achilles* was not *invulnerable*, any more than the vaunting *Goliah*. And I am fully persuaded that the *merely positive system*, whatever gigantic and formidable appearance it hath made in the eyes of its votaries, and however loud and strong its defiance, must fall at the feet of sound reason and genuine analogy.—Mr. B. we may be sure, is otherwise minded; " This maxim, says he, [of adhering to precepts and precedents] is a firm barrier against encroachments on the government of Christ, by princely domination, priestly pride, and popular unsteadiness. It guards the throne of our ascended sovereign, and secures his honour as legislator in his own kingdom. This maxim duly observed, his disciples treat, with equal contempt, the mandates of a pope and the edicts of a prince, the canons of a council and the statutes of a parliament, whenever they presume to appoint rites of divine worship, or to *alter those which Christ ordained.*" In reading this paragraph and some others of the same complexion, I could not help smiling at the thought, how well it would suit *(mutatis mutandis)* a popish doctor in defending—*transubstantiation!* In vain do Protestants wage war against this first-born of absurdities, while it is defended

§ Notes on CLAUDE, Vol. II. p. 247.

defended by such a *firm barrier*. Entrenched in this *camp*, the catholics are secure; having *this* for their *guard*, no arguments can approach them; planting in front this *positive canon*, they defy every assault. In vain do we oppose to their maxim, common sense, the use of reason, moral considerations, the assistance of analogy; &c. for what has all this to do with a positive institution? " Let the subject of inquiry be *moral* truth,
" or *moral* duty, may popish advocates reply, and
" we admit inferential proof in as large an ex-
" tent as any of our opposers; concluding, that
" a *genuine* inference from a moral principle,
" and relating to things of a moral nature, has
" all the certainty of the principle itself. — But,
" when a *positive* duty is under our notice;—
" the case is greatly altered. For the inquiry
" being intirely conversant about the *sovereign*
" *pleasure* of God, concerning an article of hu-
" man faith or duty, which absolutely depends
" on a *manifestation* of the divine will; the na-
" ture of the case forbids our expecting any
" intelligence relating to it, except what arises
" from divine revelation, precept, or scriptural
" precedent. Such is the ordinance of the eu-
" charist; such was the system of ritual appoint-
" ments in former times; and such is the mystery
" of *transubstantiation*, which is *essential* to the
" aforesaid ordinance, as it is founded upon the
" *plain words of institution*, THIS IS MY BODY.
" Methinks they need but be read, and they must
" produce conviction, if taken in their plain and
                                          " *proper*

" *proper* fenfe. And that they are to be taken
" in their *proper* fenfe, in oppofition to one that
" is figurative, is apparent hence, for furely Chrift
" would fpeak in the *plaineft* manner to his dif-
" ciples, while his language is the *inftitution* of
" that ordinance; it is DIVINE LAW. And what
" is very remarkable, St. PAUL received of the
" Lord Jefus, now afcended to glory, what he
" was to communicate to the churches as of
" ftanding obligation till the Lord come, a con-
" firmation of the inftitution in the felf fame
" words, *This* IS *my body*; whereby the cavils
" of heretics are for ever confounded. 'Tis true,
" *before* the confecration it *was bread*; but *after*
" that it was *his body*. And as to any *abfur-*
" *dity* attending our interpretation, none can
" be pretended by thofe who admit, that the
" Divine WORD *was made* FLESH; and other
" gofpel myfteries equally remote from human
" comprehenfion."

§ 29. MR. B. after quoting a paffage from AINSWORTH'S *Arrow againft Idolatry*, remarks; " By this abftract of the mafterly mock apology which the famous Puritan makes for the conduct of Jeroboam—it appears—that the moft deteftable corruptions of ritual worfhip admit of a plaufible defence, when managed by perfons of genius, if you do but allow them the privilege of arguing on *general* principles, as diftinguifhed from pofitive laws, and on fuch paffages of facred writ as are *foreign* to the fubject in queftion. It certainly behoves us, therefore, to be
exceed-

exceedingly careful of deserting *positive law* and primitive example, when a ritual ordinance is under consideration; seeing this apology for Jeroboam defies the art of man to confute it, on any other ground *." What! cannot *Idolatry*, that superlatively detestable *moral evil*, be condemned on *moral* grounds? Would this abomination, this spiritual whoredom, this root of all evil, be an *innocent* thing, then, were it not *positively* prohibited? *Credat Judeus.* While the masterly pen of AINSWORTH describes *in mockery* the conduct of the idolatrous Jeroboam, on *general* grounds; the learned and eloquent pens of a numerous train of Romish doctors vindicate *in earnest* the doctrine of transubstantiation on POSITIVE ground; and I may with the greatest propriety add, " their apology defies the art of man to confute it," without the aids of inferential and moral reasoning; and that in the case of an institution *confessedly positive*.

A CERTAIN anonymous writer, who professes himself an enemy to the corruptions of Popery, after an appeal to *antiquity* and *universality*, to early *Fathers*, *Councils*, and *Liturgies*, in evidence that the practice of the church respecting the *eucharistick cup*, was to OFFER WINE MIXED WITH WATER, as best agreeing with the *original institution*; and having observed, that this is not the only *essential defect* the church of England is to be charged with in the commemoration of this great mystery, writes to his learned friend as follows: " Give me leave therefore to ask you in what

* P. 472.

what tolerable fenfe we may be faid to retain this inftitution of our Lord's, when we obferve neither the *matter* nor the *form* of it? If it be anfwered, that we do retain the inftitution, tho' maimed in fome parts of it; I afk again, whether, in a POSITIVE INSTITUTION, every part of it be not *equally neceffary* to be obferved, efpecially when there is nothing in the nature of the things themfelves which can produce the effects, but all the benefits we receive thereby are derived to us upon account of our *exact conformity* to the will of him that inftituted them? But again, if every part of a *pofitive inftitution* be equally neceffary, where is the power that can difpenfe with our non-obfervance of the foregoing particulars? If there be fuch a power, that power may difpenfe with as many more particulars, and fo on till the whole be taken away, and then it will follow, that *our Saviour inftituted fomething for a continual remembrance of his death, which might lawfully be taken away before his coming again.*" The reader fhould obferve, that the writer of the above, and the perfon addreffed, both ftood on the *merely pofitive ground*, and accordingly the *latter* fo felt the force of the *former's* reafoning on their common principle, that he made the following ingenuous acknowledgment: " To this long objection &c. I muft confefs *I know not how to return a fatisfactory anfwer* †." Here is a man honeftly fubmitting to the ftrength and evidence of his own avowed principle, however

† BRETT's Divine Right, &c. Appendix. p. 189—191.

ever repugnant to *found analogy* and the *genuine spirit* of the chriftian difpenfation.

§ 30. THE real fact is, that the path of truth is daily tranfgreffed on either fide. Some leave the line of duty fo flack and entangled, that it proves of little or no ufe to guide; others draw it to fuch a *pofitive tightnefs*, that it breaks; they furely are beft off who cautioufly obferve the golden mean.

THERE is, no doubt, in the divine difpenfations, an admirable *analogy* obfervable, an analogy eftablifhed and confirmed by uncontefted *facts*; nor fhould we quit the clue afforded by the former, in theological as well as philofophical fubjects, but when obliged to do fo by the latter. The Supreme Being obferves in the works of creation and providence, in the revolutions of ftates, the rife and fall of empires, and the fucceffive difpenfations of religion, refpectively, a wonderful *proportion*; and who can deny that a due attention to the fame, as explained by facts, eminently diftinguifhes a wife politician from a weak patriot, or a judicious chriftian from an enthufiaftick bigot. Among the extravagancies of the latter, of which the chriftian world furnifhes too many inftances, not a few are eftablifhed and fupported by the pretended aids of analogical reafoning, while others are beholden to the abufed patronage of pofitive laws. But the real parent of the former is not fober and juft *analogy*, but rather a kind of *anomaly*; and that of the latter *anomy* of lawlefs breed.

§ 31.

Ch. 1.   *and Analogical Reasoning.*   87

§ 31. (1) BEFORE I close this part of my subject, I shall take notice of some *objections* that may be made, beside those already anticipated, to what has been delivered in the preceding pages, whether in itself or in its consequences. And, first, it may be objected, " If the preceding account be true, that baptism is not an institution *merely positive*, as much so as any enacted under the Mosaic dispensation, then the present œconomy hath no institutions at all of that kind." This objection supposes,

1. THAT precepts of a positive nature under the Mosaic dispensation, were absolutely so in all their circumstances; so as not to leave any thing to be inferred by the person or persons concerned, in the discharge of the duty enjoined.—But if these things were so, if the Jewish ritual was so express as to leave nothing to be determined by inference, one might well wonder whence could spring so many *Targums* and *Talmuds*, so many voluminous works intended to explain and illustrate the various circumstances attending the performance of these *positive duties* among others. Are not these *unprescribed circumstances* of ritual worship, and other positive injunctions, what in a great degree swell the interpretations of the *Rabbins?*—The truth is, that there were many precepts under the Jewish œconomy positive in a *considerable degree*, relative to the *subject* as well as the mode of an institute, and respecting the former, it was sometimes particularly scrupulous, for reasons already assigned (§ 24.); but it does

not

not follow that ANY ONE of thefe were fo ftrictly pofitive, as not to take fome things for *granted* refpecting the circumftances of the duty, fuch as national cuftom, the common dictates of fenfe and reafon, traditionary knowledge, the general principles of the law of nature, &c. And it fhould not be forgotten, that the adminiftration of the Jewifh rites had the fubjects diftinguifhed and characterized in a *fenfible manner*, which qualification was to be determined by the fame fort of evidence as any *facts* in common life; but the adminiftrator of the Chriftian rites has no fuch grounds to proceed on; his commiffion is of a *difcretionary* nature, arifing from the nature and defign of the inftitutions themfelves, as before fhewn (§ 23.)

2. THE objection again fuppofes, that there is fome *excellency* in an inftitution being merely and abfolutely pofitive, more than in one of a mixed nature. But this fuppofition is vain and erroneous. For what conceivable fuperior excellency can there be in any precept or duty on account of its *pofitivenefs?* Were there any force in the objection, it would imply that the Chriftian difpenfation is *lefs excellent* than the Mofaic; as having fewer pofitive rites, and their proportion of pofitivenefs being alfo fmaller. And it would alfo imply, that the reafonable duties of prayer and praife, as founded on the law of nature, as well as more fully enjoined by revelation, were *lefs excellent* than baptifm and the Lord's fupper; and it would follow, that the fervices of the church

church triumphant are in their own nature *less excellent* than those of the church militant; which are consequences from the force of the objection equally genuine and absurd. Our Lord's answer respecting the first and great commandment, shews at once that what is the most *important* duty, is also the most *natural*, and therefore the most remote from what is merely positive; and that is the *love of God.* This matter has been fully shewn before. (§   ) In one word, the spirit of the objection is truly pharisaic.

§ 32. (2) Some may perhaps object, " that this has been always admitted as true, that baptism and the Lord's supper are positive institutions of the New Testament; and that many Pædobaptists have availed themselves of this sort, in ascertaining the nature and enforcing the obligation of the latter, and particularly Bp. HOADLY. And as his Lordship's principle, in his *Plain Account of the Sacrament of the Lord's Supper,* has been deemed unanswerable, Mr. . Foot, Dr. STENNETT, and others, have taken. but the same method in treating about baptism." To this I reply,

THAT, as principles taken upon trust, dignified titles, and lawn sleeves, are light as a feather in the scale of argument ; so, on the other hand, I am satisfied the Bishop of Winchester's positions, taken in a sound sense, nay, the *only* consistent sense in which they can be taken, are evidently true and important. The sum is this; " That all positive duties, or duties made such by
                                              institution

institution alone, depend intirely upon the will and declaration of the person who institutes or ordains them, with respect to the real design and end of them, and consequently, to the due manner of performing them." This is strictly true, *in the degree that any duties are positive*, but no further. And to denominate a precept or duty *positive*, tho' but *partially* so, I have no objection, for the sake of distinguishing them from such as are merely moral, and evidently founded on the reason and nature of things. " Except we observe this caution," as Bp. BUTLER observes, " we shall be in danger of running into endless confusion."

§ 33. (3) It may be said, " If we resign this maxim, that a positive precept or duty excludes all moral reasoning, analogy and inference, we open a door to numberless innovations, and deprive ourselves of a necessary barrier against the encroachments of popery, &c. *" In reply to this specious objection let it be observed,

1. That this maxim, whatever confidence our opponents place in it, is a very *insufficient* barrier for the defence of truth, if the objection implies, that it is calculated to defend truth against error, and not error against truth as well. For it is notorious, that there is hardly any extravagance, in the whole compass of the distinguishing peculiarities of religious practice, that is not barricadoed by this very maxim. If *Protestants* use it against Papists, *Papists* in their turn use it against Protestants.

* Thus Mr. B. p. 190, 443, &c.

Proteſtants. If the Quakers are purſued and foiled when they occaſionally quit this fort, they ſoon rally their controverſial forces, and, entrenching themſelves behind the ſtrength of this maxim, the *warleſs race* becomes again *victorious.* Whence paſſive obedience and non-reſiſtance? Whence an oppoſition to all *forenſic* ſwearing, in common with profane? Whence the Quakers' nonconformity to what other ſerious chriſtians conſider as lawful? Their peculiar mode of ſalutation and addreſs? Their method of conducting religious worſhip? The little ſtreſs they lay on the obſervance of the chriſtian Sabbath? &c. Whence the popiſh abſurd figment of tranſubſtantiation *, apoſtolical ſucceſſion †, extreme unction? &c.——On the contrary,

2. Nor to diſtinguiſh between the *poſitiveneſs* and *morality* of a precept, ordinance or duty, and not to aſcertain their reſpective *degrees*; and to deny that the *latter* diſtinction admits of moral reaſoning, inference and analogy, open a wide door to *bigotry*, and numberleſs glaring abuſes of the ſacred oracles. By rejecting the analogy of faith and the *deſign* of ſcripture herein, we give the moſt effectual encouragement to every ſenſeleſs intruſion. And what is ſtill more re-markable is, that the *more firmly* any one adheres to the undiſtinguiſhing poſitive ſcheme, in reference to any chriſtian ordinance whatever, the more cloſely will he be allied to the intereſt of genuine bigotry. For it has a direct tendency

---

* See § 28.   † See § 21.

dency to make the unprescribed circumstances of a positive rite, *essential* to the rite itself, and consequently to make that necessary and essential which the institutor has not made so. How far this is applicable to the Antipædobaptist's cause, will be further considered.—The doctrine that teaches the propriety of yielding our reason to positive institutions *as such*, or in the *degree* they are so, is just and proper, as founded on the sovereign, absolute and manifest authority of the Supreme Legislator; and in this view it has been of singular service in refuting the cavils of deistical impiety. But to carry the principle any further, tends to betray the cause of christianity into the hands of infidels, and to breed unhallowed party zeal and uncharitable animosities among its sincerest professors. " For who are most likely to put weapons into the hands of *infidels*; they, who seem to discard *reason* in the investigation of truth, or they, whose researches are founded on her most vigorous exertions, and most rational decisions?—They, who make scripture bow to their preconceived notions, in direct opposition to the dictates of reason and common sense, or they, whose arguments are founded on a *coalition* of scripture and right reason †?". Once more,

3. THE objection, as it includes Mr. B.'s favourite maxim, and tends to oppose the distinction above stated, involves a great inconsistence with itself. For on what principle, except what they

† DE COURCY's Rejoinder, p. 252.

they affect to difcard, do our opponents retain *fome* of the pofitive rites of the New Teftament and reject *others?* Why regard *baptifm* and the *euchariſt* as of ſtanding obligation; while the *pedilavium* and *feaſts of charity* (the *former* injoined exprefsly by our Lord, and *both* practifed by the difciples of the apoftolic age, fee John xiii. 14, 15. 1 Tim. v. 10. Jude 12.) are judged unworthy of continuance? Why receive *females* to communion, or adopt the *firſt* day of the week for the chriftian fabbath? How can they juftify their conduct in thefe matters, thefe circumftances of *poſitive* inftitutions, without undermining their own avowed hypothefis? With regard to the fabbath, indeed, the Antipædobaptifts are divided among themfelves; while fome are content with the *firſt* day of the week, others obferve the *feventh*. On this point Dr. S. is very open and ingenuous; Mr. ADDINGTON appeals to an objecting Antipædobaptift, " whether he does not think himfelf fufficiently authorized to keep the chriftian fabbath, tho' Chrift has no where faid in fo many words, *Remember the firſt day of the week to keep it holy* ‖?" To this the Dr. replies, " There is, I acknowledge, fome weight in this " objection: and all I can fay to it is, that not " having yet met with any paffage in the New " Teftament that appears to me to have re-
" pealed the fourth commandment, and to have
" required the obfervation of the firſt day, I
" cannot think myfelf fufficiently authorized to
" renounce

‖ The Chriftian Minifter's Reafons, &c. p. 143.

"renounce that, and to keep this †." If the Doctor is professedly an observer of the Jewish sabbath, he is consistent with himself, however different from so great a part of the christian world; if *not*, he and his tenet are at variance; analogy and inferential reasoning have got the better of the positive system, which nevertheless must not be resigned, for fear of worse consequences.

§ 34. (4) ANOTHER objection much insisted on is, "If our Lord has left any thing to be *inferred* relative to the *subject* and *mode* of baptism, being a positive institute; or if he has not delivered himself *expressly* and *clearly* in every thing, respecting the question *who* are to be baptized, and the manner *how*; it implies a reflexion on his wisdom and goodness." But this objection is impertinent on different accounts. For,

1. Its force is derived from the supposition that the Institutor was somehow *obliged* to make his will known to men by *one* method only. But is the Great Supreme under any such obligations to his absolutely dependent creatures? What should we say of a philosopher, who, having to judge of any important phenomenon in physicks, should quarrel with the author of nature, because he had not confined his method of information to *one* source only, to the exclusion of all others? That his evidence, for instance, was not confined to the information of *sense*, to the exclusion of *reason* and *analogy*?

† Answer to A. p. 177.

Ch. 1.   *and Analogical Reasoning.*   95

analogy? Or what should we say of a person, who having to decide on the truth and reality of a miracle, should impeach the wisdom and goodness of his Maker, because he did not appeal to *one* sense only of his dependent and unworthy creatures, that, of *seeing*, for instance, to the exclusion of that of *hearing?* The answer is plain, and the application easy.

2. The objection is guilty of another impertinence, nearly allied to the former: it unreasonably requires *positive* evidence for what is discoverable by *other* means. It is demonstrable, and I think has been demonstrated, that the qualifications of the subjects of baptism (the *mode* also will be examined in its place) is what cannot possibly be determined by any positive rule whatever as such, but must be resolved to the *discretionary* nature of the commission, or the supposed *wisdom* and *prudence* of the administrators, in common with other parts of the same commission, such as the choice of an *audience*, the choice of a concionatory *subject*, &c. Preach the *gospel* to *every creature*, is a part of the commission, but the execution has no *positive* rule. Nor does this commission of preaching the *gospel* prohibit preaching the *law*, for a lawful use, or any branch of natural religion, notwithstanding Mr. B.'s excluding standard, that " positive laws imply their negatives." In like manner, the commission to baptize *believers*, and the *taught*, we contend and prove, does not mean to include *all sorts* of believers and taught persons,

persons, but such of them as the administrators judge fit, according to the rules of christian prudence and discretion. And we further insist, as shall be more fully shewn hereafter, that the terms of the commission, *believers* and *taught*, stand *opposed*, not to *non-believers* and *untaught*, but to *unbelievers* and persons *perversely ignorant*. What, therefore, falls *necessarily* to the province of inferential reasoning, is impertinently referred to a positive standard.

3. THE objection implies an *ungrateful* reflexion on the Institutor's wisdom and goodness, contrary to what it pretends to avoid. And this it does, by counteracting and vilifying those natural dictates of reason, prudence and common sense, that our all-wise and beneficent Creator has given us — his *goodness*, in not suspending their operations, but leaving them in full force, as to these circumstances of positive duties — his *wisdom*, in grafting what is positive of his laws on these common principles — and, finally, the favourable circumstance of his diminishing the degree of positiveness in New Testament institutions, as well as their number.

§ 35. LET us now recapitulate what has been said in this chapter. — From an investigation of the *nature* of positive precepts and duties, as distinguished from *moral* ones, together with their *comparative* obligations and importance, we have seen, that, in any case of supposed competition, the *latter* claims an undoubted *preference*. We have also seen, that nothing but absolute, deci-

Ch. 1. *and Analogical Reasoning.* 97

five, *discernible authority* can turn the scale in favour of the *former*, or, indeed, place any law or duty in the rank of POSITIVE. Moreover, it has been shewn, that every duty resulting from any discernible *moral relation*, must needs be classed among *moral duties*; that some things appertaining to the very *essence* of baptism, on our opponents' own principles, are of moral consideration; particularly the qualifications of proper subjects; consequently, that baptism is an ordinance of a *mixed nature*, partly positive and partly moral. Of all which an unavoidable consequence is, that our opponents' outcry against all *moral* and *analogical reasons* in our inquiries respecting the subjects and mode of baptism, is impertinent and absurd, and to a demonstration contradictory to their own avowed principles.—The most material, I believe, of the *objections* that may be urged against my principles, have been answered. And this I can sincerely aver, that I have not intentionally concealed one objection, that has been or may be advanced, on account of any apprehended force therein. On the contrary, I have purposely and studiously sought out what appeared to me the *most forcible*. And I am satisfied that no objection, *can be* fairly made, which is not capable of a fair and full answer, and which will not eventually contribute to illustrate and establish what I here contend for.

HAVING now fixed upon the spot, cleared

the rubbish, and laid the foundation, I proceed to the superstructure, and first of all to investigate the *Nature and Design* of the baptismal rite.

CHAP.

CHAP. II.

Of the Nature and Design of baptism; containing an account of the facts, blessings, and obligations represented by it, impartially deduced from all the passages in the New Testament relating to it.

§ 1. *The best method to find the nature and design of baptism.* § 2—7. (1) *Those passages of scripture that speak of baptism in direct terms.* § 8. (2) *Those that are supposed to allude to this ordinance.* § 9. *Axioms of interpretation.* § 10 —12. (1) *The difference between the baptism of John and that of Christ.* § 13. (2) *Their agreement.* § 14. *The general nature of baptism.* § 15—17. (1) *The blessings exhibited by it.* § 18—21. (2) *Obligations resulting from it.* § 22. *General conclusions;* (1.) *baptism obliges to some duties, and exhibits some benefits not expressly mentioned in scripture; benefits and obligations being correlates.* § 23—35. (2) *The propriety of denominating baptism a seal of the covenant.* § 36. *And of consequence the Lord's Supper.* § 37. (3) *The unworthiness of minister or subject does not nullify the ordinance.* § 38. (4) *To renounce infant baptism, as such, by a desire of rebaptizing, militates against the very*

nature

nature and design of the ordinance. § 39. (5) *It is not necessarily attended with spiritual communications.* § 40—42. (6) *The death, burial, and resurrection of Christ, not the principal facts represented by baptism.*

§ 1. THO' I have said so much in vindication of inferential proof and just analogy, in controversial debates about institutions *partially* positive, as baptism is shewn to be; I am far from desiring to evade the force of *any thing* recorded in the New Testament relative to this ordinance: on the contrary, the rules laid down in the preceding chapter require that we should very carefully attend to *revealed facts* before all other considerations, as all reasonings that may contradict these must needs be false and impertinent. It would be ridiculous to borrow the aids of analogy, while investigating any subject whatever, in *opposition* to plain facts. For as an hypothesis in philosophy is justly exploded, when the system-maker, in whose brain it was fabricated, forcibly drags all phenomena into its vortex, in defiance of well attested observations and experiments; so that system in divinity, whether it comprehends the whole body of it, or any particular part, must needs be precarious and vain when it *contradicts* revealed incontestible facts. And it is no less evident, that the pretensions of any hypothesis must be equally futile in proportion as it is *inconsistent* with itself. To avoid these inconveniences

ences I know of no better method, in general, than that which an ingenious writer on this subject has adopted, in a small treatise which he calls; *A Plain Account of the Ordinance of Baptism* *; and that is, to lay together all the texts in the *New Testament* relating to it; that from these, as so many *data*, we may deduce the nature and design of the institution, and learn every thing else that the institutor hath been pleased to *reveal* concerning it. And this method I the rather adopt, not only because it is proper and rational in itself, but likewise cannot be objected to consistently by any of our opponents. The Author of the *Plain Account* produces *first* the passages concerning John's baptism, and *secondly* those that refer to Christ's baptism; and inserts promiscuously those passages that only *allude* to the baptismal rite. I shall attempt, however, a slight improvement of his arrangement, by placing *first* all the passages in the *New Testament* that speak of BAPTISM in direct terms and in whatever connection; and *secondly* those texts that are supposed to *allude* to the institution. This I think is less exceptionable, since the classing of the texts in the manner he does, seems to imply an essential difference between the baptism of John and that of Christ, as a circumstance taken for granted, before the inquiry is made.

F 3 § 2. (1)

* Anonymous, but generally ascribed to Mr. FOOT, of Bristol; addressed to Bp. HOADLEY, in a series of Letters.

§ 2. (1) LET us begin with thofe paffages that fpeak of BAPTISM in direct terms and in whatever connection. Mat. iii. 5—7. Then went out to him Jerufalem and all Judea, and all the region round about Jordan, and were *baptized* of him in Jordan, confeffing their fins. But when he faw many of the Pharifees and Sadducees come to his *baptifm* he faid unto them, O generation of vipers, who hath warned you to flee from the wrath to come?—*v.* 11. I indeed *baptize* you with water unto repentance; but he that cometh after me is mightier than I, whofe fhoes I am not worthy to bear; he fhall *baptize* you with the Holy Ghoft and with fire.—*v.* 13—16. Then cometh Jefus from Galilee to Jordan unto John, to be *baptized* of him. But John forbad him faying, I have need to be *baptized* of thee, and comeft thou to me? And Jefus anfwering faid unto him, fuffer it to be fo now; for thus it becometh us to fulfil all righteoufnefs. Then he fuffered him. And Jefus when he was *baptized* went up ftraightway out of the water; and lo, the heavens were opened unto him, and he faw the Spirit of God defcending like a dove and lighting upon him.— Chap. xx. 22, 23. But Jefus anfwered and faid, Ye know not what ye afk. Are ye able to drink of the cup that I fhall drink of, and to be *baptized* with the *baptifm* that I am *baptized* with? They faid unto him, We are able. And he faith unto them, Ye fhall indeed drink of my cup, and be *baptized* with the *baptifm* that I am am *baptized* with; but to fit on my right hand and on my left is not mine to give, but it shall be given to them for whom it is prepared of my father.—Chap. xxi. 25. The *baptifm* of John, whence was it? from heaven, or of men? And they reasoned with themselves, saying, If we shall say, From heaven; he will say unto us, Why did ye not then believe him?—Chap. xxviii. 19. Go ye therefore and teach all nations, *baptizing* them in the Name of the Father, and of the Son, and of the Holy Ghost.

§ 3. MARK i. 4, 5. John did *baptize* in the wildernefs, and preach the *baptifm* of repentance for the remiffion of fins. And there went out unto him all the land of Judea, and they of Jerufalem, and were all *baptized* of him in the river of Jordan confeffing their fins.—*v.* 8—10. I indeed have *baptized* you with water; but he shall *baptize* you with the Holy Ghoft. And it came to pafs in thofe days, that Jefus came from Nazareth of Galilee, and was *baptized* of John in Jordan. And ftraightway coming up out of the water, he faw the heavens opened, and the Spirit like a dove defcending upon him.—Chap. vii. 4. And when they come from the market, except they wafh, [Greek, *baptize*,] they eat not; and many other things there be which they have received to hold, as the wafhing [Greek, *baptizing*,] of cups and pots, and of brafen veffels and tables.—Chap. xi. 30. The *baptifm* of John, was it from heaven or of men? anfwer me.—Chap. xvi. 15, 16. And he faid unto

unto them, go ye into all the world, and preach the gospel to every creature; he that believeth and is *baptized* shall be saved.

§ 4. LUKE iii. 3. And he came into all the country about Jordan, preaching the *baptism* of repentance for the remiffion of fins.—*v*. 7, 8. Then faid he to the multitude that came forth to be *baptized* of him, O generation of vipers, who hath warned you to flee from the wrath to come?— *v*. 12—14. Then came alfo publicans to be *baptized*, and faid unto him, Mafter, what fhall we do? And he faid unto them, Exact no more than that which is appointed you. And the foldiers likewife demanded of him, faying; And what fhall we do? And he faid unto them, Do violence to no man, neither accufe any falfely; and be content with your wages.—*v*. 16. John anfwered, faying to them all, I indeed *baptize* you with water; but one mightier than I cometh, the latchet of whofe fhoes I am not worthy to unloofe; he fhall *baptize* you with the Holy Ghoft and with fire.—*v*. 21, 22. Now when all the people were *baptized*, it came to pafs that Jefus alfo being *baptized*, and praying, the heaven was opened, and the Holy Ghoft defcended in a bodily fhape like a dove upon him, and a voice came from heaven which faid, Thou art my beloved Son; in thee I am well pleafed.— Chap. vii. 29, 30. And all the people that heard him, and the publicans, juftified God, being *baptized* with the *baptism* of John. But the Pharifees and lawyers rejected the counfel of

God

God againſt themſelves, being not *baptized* of him. — Chap xi. 38. And when the Phariſee ſaw it, he marvelled that he had not firſt waſhed [Gr. *baptized*] before dinner. — Chap. xii. 50. But I have a *baptiſm* to be *baptized* with, and how am I ſtraitened till it be accompliſhed! — Chap. xx. 4. The *baptiſm* of John, was it from heaven or of men?

§ 5. JOHN i. 25, 26. And they aſked him, and ſent unto him, Why *baptizeſt* thou then, if thou be not that Chriſt, nor Elias, neither that prophet? John anſwered them, ſaying, I *baptize* with water. — v. 28. Theſe things were done in Bethabara beyond Jordan, where John was *baptizing* — v. 31. And I knew him not; but that he ſhould be made manifeſt to Iſrael, therefore am I come *baptizing* with water. — v. 33. — He that ſent me to *baptize* with water, the ſame ſaid unto me, upon whom thou ſhalt ſee the Spirit deſcending and remaining on him, the ſame is he which *baptizeth* with the Holy Ghoſt. — Chap. iii. 22, 23. After theſe things came Jeſus and his diſciples into the land of Judea; and there he tarried with them and *baptized*. And John alſo was *baptizing* in Enon, near to Salim; becauſe there was much water there; and they came and were *baptized*. — v. 26. And they came unto John and ſaid unto him, Rabbi, he that was with thee beyond Jordan, to whom thou bareſt witneſs, behold the ſame *baptizeth*, and all men come to him. — Chap. iv. 1, 2. When therefore the Lord knew how the Phariſees had heard that Jeſus made and *baptized* more diſciples than John, (tho' Jeſus himſelf

baptized

baptized not, but his disciples).—Chap. x. 40. And went away again beyond Jordan, into the place where John at first *baptized*; and there he abode.

§ 6. ACTS i. 5. For John truly *baptized* with water; but ye shall be *baptized* with the Holy Ghost not many days hence.—*v.* 22. Beginning from the *baptism* of John, unto that same day that he was taken up from us.— Chap. ii. 38, 39. Then Peter said unto them, Repent and be *baptized* every one of you in the name of Jesus Christ for the remission of sins, and ye shall receive the gift of the Holy Ghost. For the promise is unto you, and to your children, and to all that are afar off, even as many as the Lord our God shall call.—*v.* 41. Then they that gladly received his word were *baptized*; and the same day there were added unto them about three thousand souls.—Chap. viii. 12—17. But when they believed Philip, preaching the things concerning the Kingdom of God, and the name of Jesus Christ, they were *baptized* both men and women. Then Simon himself believed also; and when he was *baptized*, he continued with Philip, and wondered, beholding the miracles and signs that were done. Now when the Apostles which were at Jerusalem heard that Samaria had received the word of God, they sent unto them Peter and John: Who, when they were come down, prayed for them that they might receive the Holy Ghost. For as yet he was fallen upon none of them; only they were
baptized

baptized in the name of the Lord Jefus. Then laid they their hands on them, and they received the Holy Ghoft.—*v.* 36—38. And as they went on their way they came unto a certain water. And the Eunuch faid, See, here is water; what doth hinder me to be *baptized?* And Philip faid, If thou believeft with all thine heart, thou mayeft. And he anfwered and faid, I believe that Jefus Chrift is the Son of God. And he commanded the chariot to ftand ftill. And they went down both into the water, both Philip and the Eunuch, and he *baptized* him.—Chap. ix. 18. And immediately there fell from his eyes as it had been fcales; and he received fight forthwith, and arofe and was *baptized.* Chap. x. 37, 38.—That word (I fay) you know, which was publifhed throughout all Judea, and began from Galilee, after the *baptifm* which John preached; How God anointed Jefus of Nazareth with the Holy Ghoft, &c.—*v.* 47, 48. Can any man forbid water, that thefe fhould not be *baptized*, which have received the Holy Ghoft, as well as we? And he commanded them to be *baptized* in the name of the Lord.—Chap. xi. 15, 16. And as I began to fpeak, the Holy Ghoft fell on them, as on us at the beginning. Then remembered I the word of the Lord, how that he faid, John indeed *baptized* with water; but ye fhall be *baptized* with the Holy Ghoft.—Chap. xiii. 23—25. Of this man's feed hath God, according to his promife, raifed unto Ifrael a Saviour, Jefus: When John had firft preached before

before his coming, the *baptifm* of repentance to all the people of Ifrael. And as John fulfilled his courfe, he faid, Whom think ye that I am? I am not he. — Chap. xvi. 15. And when fhe [Lydia] was *baptized*, and her houfehold, fhe befought us, &c. — v. 33. And he [the jailor] took them the fame hour of the night, and wafhed their ftripes; and was *baptized*, he and all his, ftraightway. — Chap. xviii. 8. And Crifpus the chief ruler of the fynagogue, believed on the Lord with all his houfe; and many of the Corinthians hearing, believed, and were *baptized*. — v. 25. — He [Apollos] fpake and taught diligently the things of the Lord, knowing only the *baptifm* of John. — Chap. xix. 3—5. And he faid unto them, Unto what then were ye *baptized*? And they faid, Unto John's *baptifm*. Then faid Paul, John verily *baptized* with the *baptifm* of repentance, faying unto the people, that they fhould believe on him which fhould come after him, that is, on Chrift Jefus. When they heard this, they were *baptized* in the name of the Lord Jefus. — Chap. xxii. 16. And now why tarrieft thou? Arife and be *baptized*, and wafh away thy fins, calling on the name of the Lord.

§ 7. Rom. vi. 3, 4. Know ye not, that fo many of us as were *baptized* into Jefus Chrift, were *baptized* into his death? Therefore we are buried with him by *baptifm* into death; that like as Chrift was raifed up from the dead by the glory of the Father, even fo we alfo fhould walk

in

in newness of life.—1 Cor. i. 13—17. Were ye *baptized* in the name of Paul? I thank God that I *baptized* none of you, but Crispus and Gaius; left any should say, that I had *baptized* in mine own name. And I *baptized* also the houshold of Stephanas; besides, I know not whether I *baptized* any other; for Christ sent me not to *baptize*, but to preach the gospel.—Chap. x. 2. And were all *baptized* unto Moses in the cloud and in the sea.—Chap. xii. 13. For by one Spirit are we all *baptized* into one body, whether we be Jews or Gentiles, whether we be bond or free; and have been all made to drink into one spirit.—Chap. xv. 29. Else what shall they do, that are *baptized* for the dead, if the dead rise not at all? Why are they then *baptized* for the dead?—Gal. iii. 27. For as many of you as have been *baptized* into Christ, have put on Christ.—Ephes. iv. 5. One *baptism*. —Col. ii. 12. Buried with him in *baptism*, wherein also ye are risen with him.—Heb. vi. 2. The doctrine of *baptisms*.—Chap. ix. 10. Which stood only in meats, and drinks, and divers washings [Greek *baptisms*] and carnal ordinances imposed on them until the time of reformation.—1 Pet. iii. 21. The like figure whereunto, even *baptism*, doth also now save us (not the putting away the filth of the flesh, but the answer of a good conscience towards God) by the resurrection of Jesus Christ.—Rev. xix. 13. And he was clothed with a vesture dipt in [Gr. *baptized* in or with] blood.

§ 8.

§ 8. (2) I SHALL now produce thofe paffages that are fuppofed to *allude* to the ordinance of baptifm, tho' the *term* be not ufed. John iii. 5. Except a man be born of *water* and of the fpirit, he cannot enter into the kingdom of God. —*v.* 25. Then there arofe a queftion between fome of John's difciples and the Jews, about *purifying.*—2 Cor. vi. 11. But ye are *wafhed.*— Eph. v. 26. That he might fanctify and cleanfe it, with the *wafhing of water*, by the word.—Tit. iii. 5. According to his mercy he faved us, by the *wafhing* of regeneration, and renewing of the Holy Ghoft.—Heb. x. 22. Our bodies *wafhed* with pure water.—1 Pet. i. 9. And hath forgotten that he was *purged* from his old fins.— Rev. i. 5.—Unto him that loved us, and *wafhed* us from our fins in his own blood.——— Perhaps the following texts, and fome others, allude to the chriftian purification. Tit. ii. 14.—And *purify* to himfelf a peculiar people.—James iv. 8. —Cleanfe your hands, ye finners, and *purify* your hearts, ye double minded.—1 Pet. i. 22.—Seeing ye have *purified* your fouls in obeying.—2 Cor. vii. 1.—Let us *cleanfe* ourfelves from all filthinefs of flefh and fpirit.—1 John i. 7. The blood of Jefus Chrift *cleanfeth* us from all fin. *v.* 9.—To *cleanfe* us from all unrighteoufnefs. —May I not add? Acts ii. 33.—Having received of the Father the promife of the Holy Ghoft, he hath *fhed* forth this, which ye now fee and hear.—Rom. v. 5. The love of God is *fhed* in your hearts by the Holy Ghoft.—Tit. iii. 6.

iii. 6. Which he *shed* on us abundantly thro' Jesus Christ our Lord.—Acts x. 45.—On the Gentiles also was *poured* out the gift of the Holy Ghost. &c.

§ 9. BEFORE I proceed to consider these passages, I would propose the following remarks as axioms of interpretation.

1. EVERY one of these texts, seperately, considered in its proper connection, must have one principal design and determinate meaning.

2. As they all proceed from the same infallible source, they must have one general meaning, collectively, in which they all agree.

3. THAT cannot be the design and meaning of any particular text which is *contrary* to this general design, or even contrary to any other passage which is more evident than itself.

4. THAT is to be deemed the general meaning of these passages, and their true interpretation, which most unexceptionably harmonizes with the whole revealed will of God, which is ever consistent with itself.

5. As the law of nature, viz. That rule of action which derives its being from the *nature* of God and man, and the *relation* thence arising, was never superseded as useless under any dispensation of religion; but on the contrary always remained in force, and ever will remain; no interpretation of these texts, or indeed any other, should be admitted as true, which *seems* to offer violence to this law of nature, otherwise called the moral law, except it be supported by

the

the clear, indubitable, positive authority of God. The reason is evident; for as this law of nature is always binding in every part of the globe, and thro' every period of time; whatever appears to be *probably* conformable to it, or a faithful dictate of it, every man is laid under a proportionable obligation to obey its voice; until an infallible authority interposes, ushered in with *stronger evidence* against the former supposed probability, from whose decisive verdict there lies no appeal. This I the rather insist upon, because it may serve to explain the genuine meaning of a maxim on which Mr. B. lays considerable stress, viz. " Positive laws imply their negative*." Positive duties as far as, or in the respect that they are *positive*, that is, having no apparent reason to recommend them but the *mere authority* of the Lawgiver, imply their negatives, for this reason, that no law whatever, on the supposition, enjoins these negatives. Not the *natural* or moral law, for then they would not be ranked among positive duties: not any *positive* law, for then the term *negative* would be inapplicable. On the contrary, whatever appears, upon the whole, a *moral* duty, cannot with any propriety be termed the *negative* of any positive duty.

§ 10. (1) I SHALL now make some observations on the foregoing texts. And it is obvious, in the first place, that there is some *difference* between the baptism of John and that of Christ and his Apostles.

1. THE

* p. 187.

Ch. 2. *Design of Baptism.* 113

1. THE immediate *Institutor* of John's baptism was God the *Father*. John i. 33. HE that sent me to baptize with water, the SAME said unto me, Upon whom thou shalt see the *Spirit* descending and remaining on him, the same is he which baptizeth with the Holy Ghost. Here we see that He who sent John to baptize was a divine Person distinct from the Son and Spirit; who must be therefore the Father.—But the immediate *Institutor* of the Christian baptism, which is of perpetual obligation, is Christ the *Son* of God. John iii. 22. After these things came Jesus and his disciples into the land of Judea; and there he tarried with them and baptized. *v.* 26. And they came unto John and said unto him, Rabbi, he that was with thee beyond Jordan to whom thou barest witness, behold the same baptizeth, and all men come to him; &c. Mat. xxviii. 19. Go ye, therefore, and teach all nations, baptizing them &c. From these passages we observe, that Christ was the *Institutor* of baptism *before* his death; and more explicitly before his ascension.

2. JOHN's baptism was a *preparatory* rite, referring the subjects to Christ, who was about to confer upon them spiritual blessings. Mat. iii. 11. I indeed baptize you with water unto repentance; but he that cometh after me is mightier than I, whose shoes I am not worthy to bear; he shall baptize you with the Holy Ghost and with fire. Mark i. 8. I indeed have baptized you with water; but he shall baptize you with

the

the Holy Ghoſt. Luke iii. 16. John anſwered, ſaying to them all, I indeed baptize you with water; but one mightier than I cometh, the latchet of whoſe ſhoes I am not worthy to unlooſe; he ſhall baptize you with the Holy Ghoſt and with fire. John i. 31. And I knew him not, but that he ſhould be made manifeſt to Iſrael, *therefore* am I come baptizing with water. Acts i. 5. For John truly baptized with water, but ye ſhall be baptized with the Holy Ghoſt not many days hence. Chap. xix. 4. Then ſaid Paul, John verily baptized with the baptiſm of repentance, ſaying unto the people, that they ſhould believe on him which ſhould come after him, that is, on Chriſt Jeſus, &c.—The Chriſtian baptiſm was an actual *initiation* into the Meſſiah's viſible kingdom. Acts ii. 41. Then they that gladly received his word, were baptized; and the ſame day there were ADDED unto them about three thouſand ſouls.—This *addition* was to the number of the *diſciples*, and *ſubjects* of Chriſt; for *then*, when they were *baptized*, were they reckoned among his followers.—The baptiſm of John did not actually introduce any into the goſpel kingdom, or make them diſciples of Chriſt; but thoſe whom John baptized were properly his own diſciples, and expectants of the Meſſiah's bleſſings. Whereas thoſe whom Jeſus ordered to be baptized, were ſtrictly *his* diſciples, and were taught to expect the promiſe of the Spirit, in his various gifts and graces.

3. IT

Design of Baptism.

3. It appears from the texts first recited, that the baptism of John was confined to the *Jews*, and temporary; Mat. iii. 5—7. &c.—But the Christian baptism was common to *Jews* and *Gentiles*, and of standing obligation. John iii. 26. The same baptizeth, and *all men* come unto him. Mat. xxviii. 19. Mark xvi. 15, 16. &c.

4. It does not appear that John had any *formula* of administration; nor, indeed, have we any account of his *commission*, but what may be inferred from what he says John i. 33. He that SENT me to baptize with water. And we may further infer that his baptism was FROM HEAVEN, from what our Lord says to the chief priests and elders of the people, Mat. xxi. 25. &c.— Whence it appears that he was *divinely* authorized, and, as before observed, that the *Father* was the Institutor.—But the Christian baptism has a *formula* of administration. Mat. xxviii. 19. IN THE NAME OF THE FATHER, AND OF THE SON, AND OF THE HOLY GHOST.—And still shorter, Acts ii. 31. Be baptized every one of you IN THE NAME OF JESUS CHRIST. Also Chap. x. 38. IN THE NAME OF THE LORD.

5. It may be added, that the baptism of John was the concluding scene of the *legal* dispensation, and in fact part of it. Hence the least in the kingdom of God, *viz.* the gospel kingdom, was greater than he. It may be considered as a final and general purification, performed by John as the last priest. That he discharged his office as a purifying priest to the thousands

thousands of Israel, see Acts xiii. 23—25. Thus John went before Jesus in the spirit and power of Elias (as promised Mal. iv. 5.) to turn the hearts of the fathers with the children to him, and the disobedient to the wisdom of the just; to make ready a people prepared for the Lord. See Luke i. 17.—Christian baptism is the regular entrance into and is a part of the *evangelical* dispensation. Gal. iii. 27. For as many of you as have been baptized into Christ, have put on Christ, &c.

6. It does not appear from the inspired narrative (however probable from inferential reasoning) that any but John *himself* was engaged as operator in his baptism; whereas Christ himself baptized none, but his *disciples* by his authority and in his name. John iv. 2.

§ 11. Some have supposed another distinction between the baptism of John and that of Christ, viz. That the *latter* had an immediate reference to the *Holy Spirit*, requiring of the baptized faith in him as a divine Person, and an expectation of his promised influence; that the *former* had no respect *at all* to that divine Person, nor supposed any information concerning him; in proof of which they urge, Acts xix. 2.—That Christian baptism has an immediate relation to the promise of the Spirit exhibited in the gospel dispensation, I grant and maintain, but that any baptized by John (or even his disciples) should be so grosly ignorant as not to know any thing about the Holy Ghost, or never

to

to have heard of him, is highly improbable. There is nothing upon the subject more expressly and emphatically noticed by the evangelists, than that John directed those whom he baptized to Christ, *as one who would baptize with the Holy Ghost* and with fire. It appears probable, therefore, the disciples at Ephesus meant by their answer, That they had not been informed that the Holy Ghost, in his miraculous influence, had been actually conferred on any of the disciples of John or of the Messiah as yet. As if they had said, We have not so much as heard whether there be any Holy Ghost, miraculously communicated, much less have been made partakers of the same.—If this be not the import of their strange answer, what must we infer? Were they baptized by John in their *infancy*, about thirty years before? Were they children of parents who were so ignorant or so careless as not to inform them of this very important part of John's ministry? Could they be baptized by this popular reformer, or have any connection with those whom he discipled, and not be informed of that extraordinary fact, the descent of the Holy Ghost upon Jesus at his baptism? And was not the appellation *familiar* to John and his followers? Whether we consider these twelve men as natives of Ephesus or foreigners, as Jews or converted Gentiles, whether baptized with their parents in infancy, or when adults; attending the one interpretation there remains insuperable difficulties,

difficulties, according to the other none at all. See Acts x. 37; 38.

§ 12. THE baptism of John, therefore, was a rite appertaining to the legal dispensation, instituted by God the Father for the use of the Jews alone, for a short time, to prepare them for the kingdom of the Messiah then approaching, as by an extraordinary general purification*, attended with suitable instructions and exhortations to the people, and performed by John himself.—And Christian baptism, as far as it has been considered, is an evangelical rite, instituted by Christ, the Son of God, for the use of Jews and Gentiles, to the end of time, to be administered in the name of the Lord Jesus Christ, or, more fully and properly, in the name of the Father, Son, and Holy Ghost, performed by Christ's disciples.

THUS John's ministry and baptism were, in a manner, the voice of the FATHER crying by him in the wilderness to prepare the thousands of Israel for a suitable reception of his divine Son.

---

* John's baptism is to be considered as one of those " divers washings," in use among the Jews on many occasions; for he did not attempt to make any alterations in the Jewish religion as settled by the Mosaic law, any more than to erect a new dispensation. And as these washings were intended not only for " the purifying of the flesh," but to be signs and symbols of moral purity; so the rite of baptism was, in this view, very suitable to the doctrine of repentance, which John preached. JENNINGS's *Jewish Antiquities*, B. I. chap. iii. Art. Proselytes. —And the same Author concludes, from a passage in Josephus, that the latter makes John's baptism to be of the nature of the Jewish purifications or ceremonial washings.

Son. BEHOLD THE LAMB OF GOD! Let your attention be drawn from all legal sacrifices, as about to cease; and let it be directed to HIM in whom all the law and the prophets have their accomplishment, and who is shortly, in a wonderful manner, to bear away the sin of the world!—And lo, a voice from heaven, saying, THIS IS MY BELOVED SON, IN WHOM I AM WELL PLEASED!—*Hear ye him.*—— But the Christian baptism is the institution of the SON, proclaiming the necessity, and directing to the influences of the divine Spirit; and these influences poured upon the disciples of Jesus is the baptism of the SPIRIT. And thus we are led with wonder and gratitude to contemplate the *love* and provident care of the *Father*, the *mediation* and grace of the *Son*, and the efficacious and everlasting *operations* of the *Holy Ghost*. These three are one; and they concur in bearing record to the truth and glory of the blessed gospel. See 1 John v. 6—8. And those who are baptized in the name of Jesus, or the sacred Three-One, should incessantly breathe after the spirit of grace, to which the ordinance refers us. Jesus, our divine Master and Lord, is able and ready to baptize us with the Holy Ghost and with fire: not by conferring *miraculous* gifts, but, what is infinitely more important to us, *sanctifying* graces, whereby we may be purified and made meet for his heavenly kingdom.

§ 13. (2) IT must be allowed, in the next place, that between the baptism of John and that of Chrift, there is an *agreement* in fome particulars. And

1. THEY were both from heaven, or of *divine* inftitution. The one inftituted by the *Father*, the other by the *Son*, but both alike by the higheft authority.

2. THERE appears no mark of difference, in the two inftitutions, as to the *action* of baptizing; we may, therefore, conclude, for aught the different accounts fay to the contrary, that it was the fame. Pure water was the common element, but the nature and mode of the action itfelf will be confidered in its proper place.

3. THE fame may be faid concerning the qualifications of their refpective *fubjects*; which qualifications and the grounds thereof, will be examined at large in the fubfequent part of this treatife.

4. THERE was an agreement refpecting fome of the *bleffings fignified* and exhibited; particularly the *remiffion of fins*. Mark i. 4. Luke iii. 3. and Acts ii. 38.—They both referred to *Chrift* as the *fovereign difpenfer* of the influences of the Spirit, the one indeed in a fenfe more *remote*, and the other *directly*. See Mat. iii. 11. &c. and Acts ii. 38. &c.

5. SOME *obligations* were alfo fimilar; efpecially that of *repentance*. See Mat. iii. 11. Acts xxii. 16.—Alfo that they fhould *believe on Chrift*. Acts xix. 3—5. and chap. viii. 37.—Both required a fuitable *reformation* of life and conduct.

§ 14. I AM led by an attentive and impartial furvey

Ch. 2. *Design of Baptism.* 121

survey of those sacred passages that have any reference to the baptismal rite, to consider it in its most *general nature*, as " the instituted ordi-
" nance of a *regular admission into the visible king-*
" *dom* of Christ, or, as it is sometimes called, the
" kingdom of heaven; wherein the *minister* so-
" lemnly *recognizes the fitness* of the baptized to
" be a subject of that kingdom."

1. It is the instituted ordinance of a *regular* admission. See Acts ii. 41. Charity, and the nature of the case, compel me to conclude, that there are many whom we should deem subjects of Christ's kingdom, even in its visible form, who were never admitted into it *ministerially* by baptism. Among whom we may reckon at least the *promising* (not to say the *infant*) offspring of Antipædobaptists; many well meaning tho' erroneous disciples of Fox and Barkley, &c. Nor should this concession seem at all strange to those who disclaim the pretended *infallibility* of a visible church. But however willing we may be to embrace these in the arms of christian charity, as fellow subjects of Christ's kingdom, yet as they were never initiated into it by the solemn right of baptism, we cannot consider them as *regular* subjects.

2. It is an ordinance of admission into the *visible* kingdom of Christ. Compare Acts viii. 13. x. 47, 48. The Redeemer's kingdom is to be considered in two respects; as to its *spiritual form*, and its *external administration*. Many, no
G doubt,

doubt, belong to the *former*, who have no *regular* connection with the *latter*; and many, it is equally certain, are introduced to the Meffiah's kingdom thro' the baptifmal ceremony, (even in adult age,) who are not the fubjects of his fpiritual government. It is highly probable this was the cafe with great numbers of difciples who followed Chrift but for a feafon, and then forfook him; we might alfo inftance in Judas, Simon the forcerer, &c. And many will fay at laft, We have eaten and drunk in thy prefence, who yet will be difowned. However *regular* the admiffion, and however unimpeachable the *external* allegiance of fome perfons, they may be, notwithftanding, effentially deficient in a *fpiritual* view, and be at laft tranflated into the kingdom of darknefs.

3. It is a folemn *recognition* of the fitnefs of the baptized to be a fubject of that kingdom. See Mat. xxviii. 19. The *qualifications* of the fubjects muft be of a moral nature, as before fhewn, and baptifm does not *produce* thefe but *fuppofe* them. So far is it, therefore, from faving a foul, *ex opere operato*, that it does not even *conftitute* a vifible fubject or member, but only *recognize* one; and fo far from *making* the baptized a child of God, a member of Chrift, and an inheritor of the kingdom of heaven, in the proper fenfe of thefe terms, that it is only *declarative* of his fitnefs to be a fubject of the external adminiftration of that kingdom. Acts viii. 13.

4. The

4. The person whose right it is to determine this fitness is the *minister* who does solemnly recognize it. See Mat. xxviii. 19. Whatever extravagant notions have obtained respecting the power of the keys, in admitting into the kingdom of heaven or shutting out of it, there is, however, a sound sense in which this power is assigned to ministers. They are the appointed guardians of the institution, and have a negative voice in opposition to all claims. If they abuse this power, as *fallible* persons may, to their own Master they stand or fall. Their Sovereign and Judge is at hand.

§ 15. (1) Let us next inquire, by scripture evidence, into the things represented by this significant rite. Passages of information relating to this particular are very numerous; but if I mistake not, there is not one but is naturally reducible to these two heads, viz. *blessings exhibited* by it, and *obligations resulting* from it. I shall begin with the former.

1. One of the important blessings exhibited in the ordinance of christian baptism, as in a bright mirror, is the *remission of sins*. Acts ii. 38. In this, as observed before, the baptism of Christ agreed with that of John, and I may add, with the divers baptisms under the law (Heb. ix. 10.) Indeed it is not easy to conceive how there could be a dispensation of grace, or exhibition of mercy to fallen man, in any period of time, without including this blessing as an *essential* part of it.

2. It exhibits *salvation thro' Christ.* Mark xvi. 16. 1 Pet. iii. 21. The display of *salvation*, simply considered, is not *peculiar* to the christian œconomy, more than the remission of sins; but the peculiarity of the one and the other blessing under the gospel dispensation is, that they are proposed thro' the mediation and atonement of the Messiah *actually come.* Now, in this last most perfect and unshaken establishment of religion, the initiatory rite of it, baptism, exhibits salvation and life eternal to its highly favoured subjects, as not only procured by the *merits*, but also conferred by the *hands* of its divine Founder.

3. In christian baptism is exhibited *union* and *communion* with Christ and with his body the church. 1 Cor. xii. 13. Rom. vi. 3, 4, &c. Col. ii. 11—13. Under every œconomical publication of mercy to the apostate race of Adam, *communion with God* was a privilege singularly important. This Enoch, Noah, Abraham, and indeed all the faithful, enjoyed in every age, more or less; and the subjects of those dispensations, respectively, were favoured with the *exhibition* of it. But it is our distinguished lot, as subjects of the gospel kingdom, to have communion with Jehovah as our God and Father *in Christ*, with whose meritorious sufferings and perfect righteousness he is well pleased, displayed to us in the most explicit and endearing terms, and particularly in the significant institution of baptism. But *communion with Christ* the Son of God,

God, is of a nature still more discriminating. For this supposes not only an access to him for spiritual blessings, and a reception out of his fulness of a liberal supply, but also a twofold union; the one *federal*, the other *mystical*. He exhibits himself, therefore, as a complete *covenant* head, to his visible church, and therewith a correspondent communion; and in virtue of which *general* exhibition, a foundation of hope and encouragement is administered to all without exception. And whenever the ordinance of baptism is duly administered, this glorious truth is represented and signified. Christ is also a head of *influence*; this truth, equally glorious and important, he also exhibits in the same general way; wherever the gospel and its ordinances come, a proclamation is made, that Christ is the head of influence, that there is a most precious endearing communion between him and his people, that he regards them in point of nearness and tender love, *members of his body, of his flesh, and of his bones**. And as Christ is thus the head, all quickened by his vital influence, are members in particular. Hence arises the communion of saints. *For as the body is one, and hath many members, and all the members of that one body, being many, are one body; so also is Christ* and his Church; *For by one Spirit are we all baptized into one body.* See also 1 John i. 3.

4. It exhibits Christ as our spiritual *covering* and complete righteousness. Gal. iii. 27. Remarkable

* Eph. v. 30.

markable. to this purpose are the words of Mr. LOCKE — "So that to God, now looking upon " them, there appears nothing but Christ. They " are as it were covered all over with him, as " a man is with the clothes he hath put on. " And hence he says in the next verse, that " they are all one in Christ Jesus, as if there " were but that one person †." In every instance of baptizing into Christ, an exhibition is made of him in this illustrious view: He is *set forth a propitiation*. He is displayed as a sun and shield, a robe of righteousness to cover our naked souls, and a garment of praise as a preservative from sorrow. That the *woman* should be *clothed with the Sun*, the church enrobed with the Lord her righteousness, was esteemed a great wonder in *heaven* ‡, and should be marvellous in *our* sight.

§ 16. 5. IN baptism is eminently exhibited the *down-pouring* of the Holy Spirit. To this John bore constant witness, Mat. iii. 11. Mark i. 8. Luke iii. 16. John i. 33. — And this our Lord confirmed, Acts i. 5. — This, moreover, Peter repeats, and further authenticates for the information and encouragement of the Gentiles, Acts ii. 38, 39. — Thus do the ancient promises and prophecies run respecting these divine influences, Prov. i. 23. Turn ye at my reproof, behold I will *pour out my Spirit* unto you. — Isa. xliv. 3. I will *pour out my Spirit* upon thy seed. — Joel ii. 28. And it shall come to pass afterward

† Paraph. *in loc.*   ‡ Rev. xii. 1.

ward, that I will *pour out my Spirit* upon all flesh, &c. that is, I presume, "Under the gos- "pel dispensation I will make an exhibition of "this invaluable privilege to Jews and Gentiles "without distinction." This prediction Peter applies to the *miraculous* effusion of the Spirit on the day of Pentecost, Acts ii. 17, 18. But that he does not exclude his *common* influences in after times from being a part of the promise, appears from *v.* 29.—To the same purpose is the language of Zec. chap. xii. 10. And I will *pour* upon the house of David, and upon the inhabitants of Jerusalem, the Spirit of grace and of supplications, &c. Such a general promise must intend an *œconomical exhibition* of the blessing; as is evident from the apostolick writings, Heb. iv. 16. James i. 5. &c. And especially from our Lord's declarations and conduct, Luke ii. 13. John vii. 37—39.—Under *former* dispensations God granted to his people his Holy Spirit; when he was comparatively but *as the dew* unto Israel, or the *small rain* on the tender herb; but now he is *poured* on the Gentiles, and *shed abundantly*, not only thro' the mediation, but also by the actual communications of Jesus Christ our Lord, Tit. iii. 6. Acts ii. 33. x. 45. John i. 33.

6. REGENERATION, or the quickening influence of the divine Spirit on a sinful soul, is another blessing exhibited in the baptismal rite. John iii. 5. Tit. iii. 5. From the evident reference baptism has to this effect of the Spirit on

the

the souls of the redeemed, the ancient Fathers termed the ordinance itself, Παλιγγενεσια, *regeneration*. And others have observed a striking analogy between the baptismal element, and the regenerating efficacy of the Spirit. " *Water* is
" the *principle* of very many *living things*, and
" in their creation the Spirit brooded on the
" *waters*, Gen. i. 3. The earth produces scarce
" any thing that has life, either of the vegetable
" or reptile kind, unless it be impregnated with
" *water*, Psalm lxv. 10. The very generation of
" the human fœtus is said to be from *water*,
" Isa. xlviii. 1. Psalm lxviii. 27. Thus in like
" manner, the blood and Spirit of Christ, as the
" mystical *water*, are the principles of our re-
" generation and new creation. John iii. 5. and
" as that is *signified* by the *water* of baptism, so bap-
" tism itself is called, Tit. iii. 5. *The washing of*
" *regeneration, and renewing of the Holy Ghost**.

7. SANCTIFICATION, or the cleansing effect of the Spirit on a polluted soul, is a mercy very significantly represented, and graciously exhibited in baptism. 1 Cor. vi. 11. Ephes. v. 26. *The washing away the filth of the flesh*, as Peter (1 Ep. chap. iii. 21.) calls baptism, is not only an apt and expressive *sign* of the Spirit's purifying influence, but also a divinely appointed *mirror*, if I may so express myself, in which God *exhibits* the blessing to all thus regularly enrolled among the subjects of his kingdom, in the most conspicuous manner. This remark is equally applicable to all the *other* particulars

---

* Witsii Oecon. Fœder. Lib. iv. Cap. xvi. § 24.

ticulars before mentioned as to this of sanctification. And it is a distinction I could wish the reader fully to enter into, being of no small moment in this debate, as will appear hereafter.

§ 17. 8. WHAT crowns all the other blessings, and in which indeed they are all virtually included, is man's chief and ALL-SUFFICIENT GOOD; and this is what baptism exhibits in a very express and glorious manner, Mat. xxviii. 29.—The ever adorable and blessed God, Father, Son, and Holy Ghost, uses and dignifies this ordinance for the purpose of *displaying* his wonderful condescension and grace to every subject, introduced thro' this avenue into the visible christian kingdom, thereby explicitly testifying, as of old to Abraham, that he is GOD ALL-SUFFICIENT. He declares himself a merciful and loving *Father*, an almighty and gracious *Redeemer*, and most holy *Sanctifier*. But it is a consideration peculiarly worthy of our regard, that herein he does not merely declare what he is in himself, but what he is in relation to guilty helpless sinners. To those who have escaped the corruption that is in the world thro' lust, or have been regularly entered as the subjects of the Redeemer's kingdom, are exhibited exceeding great and precious promises, that by these they might be partakers of a divine nature. 2 Pet. i. iv.—*Blessed is the people*, comparatively so at any rate, *whose God is the Lord*, who are authorized and encouraged to approach JEHOVAH as the object of their worship, trust and confidence;

and bleffed in a manner ftill more emphatical if their hearts, however corrupt by nature, are affimilated by grace to his moral image. Pfa. xxxiii. 12. clxiv. 15.—It is further obfervable, that the unworthinefs, yea the moral unfitnefs of the fubject, does not eclipfe this glorious truth; for as the heavenly Father maketh his fun to rife on the evil and on the good, and fendeth rain on the juft and on the unjuft, fo the *œconomical exhibition* of himfelf, under the moft illuftrious and endearing characters, is to every fubject of his gofpel kingdom without exception. Whatever reception his mercy meets with among men, *he abideth faithful; he cannot deny himfelf.* See 2 Tim. ii. 11—14. And he ftill *fhineth*, even *in darknefs*, tho' *the darknefs comprehendeth him not.* John i. 4, &c.—This hath been the common and exalted privilege of the fubjects of every difpenfation of true religion that ever was in the world, viz. That JEHOVAH gracioufly *propofed* himfelf to them as their CHIEF GOOD. But this *propofal*, or revealed exhibition, of the GREAT SUPREME made by himfelf to thofe whom his providence fingled out, tho' it feems the principal and moft diftinguifhing feature of each œconomy, from the firft to the fecond Adam, hath yet been characterized by different degrees of explicitnefs. What the wife man fays of the path of the juft, that it *fhines more and more to the perfect day*, is peculiarly applicable to the gradual openings of the difpenfations of grace. The fall of Adam brought upon his

posterity

Ch. 2.   *Design of Baptism.*   131

posterity a night of moral darkness, uncertainty, and justly apprehended danger; while additional discoveries were made of the divine will, and numerous witnesses raised to promulgate the certainty and approach of greater and better blessings; till, at length, the SUN OF RIGHTEOUSNESS appeared to illuminate the hemisphere of the gospel church, as a prelude to a state of unclouded and immortal glory. By the gospel life and immortality are brought to light, and placed in full view. What was hidden from ages and generations is now made manifest to the saints; and they are encouraged, with open face, to behold the glory of the Lord. O glorious privilege! Blessed are the eyes that see, and the ears that hear these things! The meanest christian hath no need to envy the dignity of kings, or the honour of prophets, that died without this sight. And let not the reader forget, that the very exhibition made in baptism of such blessings, is an important privilege.

§ 18. (2) THE *things signified* in baptism are either *blessings* or *obligations*; we have considered the former, and now proceed to the latter, which we shall find to be great and important. And

1. FROM christian baptism results the obligation of *repentance*. Acts xxii. 16. Every display of divine goodness obliges a sinful creature to repent, (Rom. ii. 4.) but an exhibition of mercy and forgiveness increases the obligation. And as in baptism are held forth the greatest mercies and blessings, it must proportionably oblige

to a difpofition correfponding thereto. Now tho' *remiffion of fins* be reprefented in fcripture as *generally* granted *upon* repentance, (Acts iii. 19.) it does not follow that there is no remiffion granted without it; but this is clear, that actual *impenitence* perfifted in, excludes remiffion. And thofe who are the fubjects of forgivenefs, but under a natural incapacity to repent, may be faid, notwithftanding, to be under obligation in this fenfe, viz. That the *principle* of holinefs and rectitude, from which evangelical repentance muft proceed, is what every child of Adam is *obliged* to, or *ought* to poffefs. And the natural capacity itfelf is under an abfolute obligation to fubferve the dictates of that principle.

2. From baptifm arifes the obligation to *deftroy the body of fin*. Rom. vi. 3, 4, &c. That the paffage now quoted refers to the OBLIGATION refulting from baptifm, to *renounce*, to *crucify*, to *deftroy* and *bury* fin, is evident from the connection. The apoftle had been fhewing that a finner's *juftification* was obtained freely by the righteoufnefs of Chrift imputed, and fo the privilege not founded on any deeds of the law, or any good quality whatever in the perfon juftified; no efforts or worthinefs of the guilty finner could ever deliver him from the condemnation of fin. This reprefentation of the fubject gave rife to an Antinomian objection, which the apoftle firft rejects with abhorrence, and then particularly refutes. And this he does by fhewing that *holinefs*, as well as righteoufnefs, is an

effential

essential part of the christian character; that sin must be *subdued* as well as *pardoned*; and that as our righteousness was obtained by the perfect work of Christ, so our sanctification is effected by virtue of a vital *union* with him. Now this mystical, vital, spiritual *union* is one of the great blessings exhibited in baptism; and from it result the most important obligations. Such a union requires particularly, that we should concur with the grand *design* of Christ as the Saviour of his people. In regard to *sin*, it was his *design* to resist it in every instance, to renounce it in every shape, to nail it to his cross, and so to destroy and bury it, that neither himself nor his redeemed people should be in any respect voluntary subjects of sin's power; *he* of its imputative force, *they* of its enslaving and defiling dominion. The person who is baptized into this union with Christ, (and so is every one that is baptized at all) is, from the very notion of such a union, under an obligation of universal conformity to this important design. Christ is the vine, his disciples and subjects are the branches. As divine justice dealt with sin in Christ the surety, so ought we to deal with it in ourselves. In him it was condemned, crucified, utterly destroyed and buried; our union with Christ represented by baptism obliges to a cordial concurrence in the same design. If justice spared sin in Christ, so° may we in ourselves, otherwise not. If justice avenged itself on sin in our representative and head, so should we in ourselves. Christ, in his

unparalleled.

unparalleled condescension, and by virtue of his federal engagement, became so united to our imputed sin, that he and sin must live or die together. If he had not died, sin had not died. If he had not been buried, sin could not be buried. Then the union was dissolved, when both were dead and buried. But the same glorious power that was pleased to bruise, to smite, to put him to grief, and sacrifice him to death, when united to sin; did, when he became disengaged from it, raise him up to immortal life and glory. Nor can our new man be raised, till our old man be dead and buried. Therefore, instead of cherishing and animating in ourselves the monster sin, for the eternal destruction and burial of which Christ was crucified and buried, we are under the strongest *obligation* to concur with his design, to bring it to a state of death and keep it there, putting our foot as it were on its horrid neck whenever it attempts to rise. And as Christ, the tree of life, was taken from the trees of the wood, and after his death planted in the earth, that, freed from sin, he might grow and flourish with immortal vigour; so we ought to plant ourselves with Christ, that our corrupt nature may be left with his imputed sin and weakness, and our spiritual nature may grow up with him into a similar fruitfulness, vigour and glory. Or, as a graft cannot participate of the sap, life and fruitfulness of another tree except it be first severed from its old stock, leaving it for ever behind; so we cannot partake of spiritual life and

and fruitfulness from Christ, but by being severed and entirely disengaged from our sinful selves, that we may grow up into him in all things. The apostle's similitude when treating of the resurrection is not inapplicable to the subject of this mystical union. *That which thou sowest is not quickened except it die.* All seeds, and some species of plants, never spring up into new life, but by the death and corruption of at least a part thereof. When the germen sprouts forth, the other part consumes away in the ground. Thus as baptism obliges to a concurrence with the *design of this union in general,* which is exhibited in baptism, so particularly with that of mortifying and *destroying the body of sin.*

§ 19. 3. FROM baptism results the obligation of *newness of life and heavenly-mindedness.* Rom. vi. 4, 8, 11, 13, 19, &c. And this is peculiarly enforced by the apostle from the doctrine of vital union to Christ; union of design, union of interest; a certain oneness of spirit, of life, light, and liberty. For as Christ is risen and ascended to a state of triumph over sin and hell, a state of refined pleasure, and an inexpressible, serene delight, in spiritual purity and the beauty of holiness; so every person baptized *into Christ* is baptized into *his life,* and lies under the strongest obligations of being thus conformed to him.

4. FROM our baptism arises the obligation of an inviolable *attachment to Christ* as our supreme Master and Lord. 1 Cor. i. 13. Christ is our master; he demands of us to regard him as such

136   *Of the Nature and*   Ch. 2.

such, and he alone is deserving of it: No one else deserves to be called Master on earth. And as none can serve two masters of different and opposite interests, with the same fidelity and affection; by baptism, the right of a regular entrance into his family and service, we are obliged to be faithfully attached to him and his interest intirely. Christ is a King, and his church is a kingdom (but not of this world) and every subject of this kingdom is in loyal duty bound to adhere to Christ as the lawful and infinitely worthy Sovereign.

5. An obligation is laid on the baptized person to seek and maintain *the answer of a good conscience* towards God. 1 Pet. iii. 21. God's requisitions and demands from us are very great and awful. As a holy and just God, he claims perfection of state and obedience from the creature; nothing short of perfection will God accept, or the conscience approve of. How, then, can a sinner make a *confident appeal* to God, when answering his demands as a judge, or claiming the peculiar blessings of a God in covenant? What provision is made to calm the surges of the mind? What can dissipate the gloom of adverse providences, or support the soul, conscious of much frailty and imperfection, in the apprehensions of approaching death?—A *consciousness* of being united to Christ as the risen Saviour. As united to him we are *justified* by his *resurrection*; and *saved* by his constant intercession, his heavenly and immortal *life*. In baptism

tifm, indeed, are reprefented and exhibited God's all-fufficiency, his matchlefs greatnefs and goodnefs, the boundlefs and unfathomable riches of his grace; and a cordial, confcious embracing of thefe bleffings muft fatisfy confcience and produce a ferene content in the mind. But what the confcience has to do with, in the paffage above cited, is, I prefume, more immediately, the claim of divine juftice and holinefs. The *refurrection of Chrift* is, then, the great *evidence* we have that juftice is fatisfied with his finifhed work, and fo it becomes an objective ground of confidence to the confcience (otherwife terrified with guilt and condemnation) in its reply to the divine claims. And being confcious of a *vital union* with Chrift, the confideration of his victorious refurrection and triumphant afcenfion lays the foundation of holy joy and triumph. But it is a remark not a little important, that here the remedy is *proportioned* to the difeafe; the anfwer of a *good confcience* is to the *believer*, adequate to the clamours of an *evil confcience* to the *unbeliever*.

§ 20. 6. From baptifm refults the obligation of filling up (honourably no doubt) the place of departed chriftians. Rom. xv. 29. What Solomon remarks of the generations of the world of mankind, thro' the fucceffive revolutions of time, is applicable to the church of God in the world. *One generation paffeth away, and another generation cometh* *. All alike make
their

* Ecclef. i. 4.

their exit thro' the gate of death; for it is appointed for *all men* once to die, by an irreversible decree. How, then, is the depopulated kingdom of Christ to be recruited? When persecution with its merciless attendants, and the wasting messengers of death, render the church like a desolate island, how is it to be colonized? By constant supplies from the wide world. The world is a common nursery from whence the church is planted; but the watering of baptism is not of itself sufficient to ensure the future growth, verdure, and fruitfulness of the plants; for in this plantation, the church visible, every plant which the heavenly Father planteth not (of which there have always been awful instances) shall be rooted up. Paul may plant and Apollos may water, but God giveth the increase. But notwithstanding this, ministers are commissioned to transplant and to water, leaving the event to God. But to speak without a figure, it is evident, that when any are brought into the church regularly by baptism, to fill up the room of others, they are obligated to do it honourably and usefully; even as a member that is chosen into any body corporate, or a soldier to fill a place in a rank or regiment.

7. From the ordinance of baptism arises the obligation of *waiting for the promise of the Spirit*. Acts ii. 38, 39. viii. 12—17. The gospel dispensation is eminently distinguished from all preceding it, by a rich display and communication of the influences of the Spirit, not only

in

in a miraculous way, but alfo as a *Sanctifier*, and efpecially as a *Comforter*, to the church. And as this is a bleffing of unfpeakable value, and moft explicitly exhibited in chriftian baptifm, every perfon to whom it hath been adminiftered is under the ftrongeft obligation to feek and wait for all neceffary divine influences. This is the unction from the Holy One which we all want; and, thro' the divine mercy, there is in the inftitution of baptifm a foundation laid for the moft importunate and unwearied application for all needful fupplies thereof. We can never be too ardent and importunate in our defires and prayers for the illuminating, quickening, teaching, and transforming influences of the Spirit. And this inceffant breathing of the foul after the divine influences, is not only its intereft and comfort when fo employed; but, in confequence of baptifm, where the bleffing, by virtue of the divine appointment, is clearly fet forth, it is what every fubject is abfolutely *obliged* to do. And as no one can be fo far replenifhed as not to need further fupplies, the obligation muft be conftant, thro' every ftep of our life.

§ 21. 8. ANOTHER obligation highly important refulting from chriftian baptifm, is an abfolute devotednefs to the *grace* and fovereign *will* of GOD, FATHER, SON, and HOLY GHOST. Mat. xxviii. 19.—Baptifm (εις ονομα) *into the name* of Father, Son and Spirit, implies an obligation,

(1) To

(1) To receive this God, and him *alone*, for our God, as the object of our worship, the sovereign of our heart, and our everlasting portion; to the absolute disavowal and renunciation of all competitors whatsoever.

(2) To receive him under the representation here given of himself, as Father, Son and Holy Spirit. That these three terms belong to God only, and not the first to the true God, and the other two to beings of an *inferior* class, (and if at all *inferior*, they must be *infinitely* so) seems evident from the *manner* in which they are connected; for from *this* nothing less can be observed than *equality* among them; and the importance of this remark rises still higher when we reflect, that the goodness of God, — his detestation of idolatry, — the excellency of the gospel above other religions, — and the exalted character of Jesus as the founder of it, — are necessarily *degraded* if this be not the fact. For thus to associate the terms, Father, Son, and Spirit, in a solemn ordinance of religion, the very *introductory* ordinance, on supposition that an infinite disparity subsists between the objects they refer to, appears like putting a dangerous stumbling-block at the very porch of the christian temple. But his true disciples have not so learned Christ; and wisdom is justified of her children.

(3) Every baptized person is laid under obligations of duty to Father, Son, and Spirit, *respectively*

respectively, according to the scripture representations of these divine Persons, and their several *relations* to him, whether absolute or exhibited only.

(4) ANOTHER obligation included in the form of administration is, cordially to embrace the infinite mercy, grace, and love of God, herein exhibited. Every expression of benevolence and favour from God, obliges the person to whom it is directed, to answerable gratitude;. but no one that hath been admitted, by baptism, into the number of Christ's regular subjects, can say that he hath not had represented in his baptism unspeakably great and glorious blessings, and this he may be as certain of as he can be of the *fact*—THAT HE WAS BAPTIZED. Whether he be certified of his baptism by the evidence of *sense*, or competent human *testimony*, does not alter the case; to be sure of the *fact* is to be equally sure of the exhibited blessing and the correspondent obligation.

(5) To be influenced, actuated, transformed, directed and governed by that mediatorial grace and mercy which is displayed by the medium of this ordinance. Tho' the divine mercy be like a most delightful sun-shine, in itself, yet mankind are so situated in the present state as not to be benefited by it but by reflection. (See 2 Cor. iii. 18.) The face, or person of Christ,—the inspired records,—the ordinances and institutions of the gospel,—and this initiatory rite in particular, do eminently answer this important

important end. And in proportion as this laſt does ſo, the baptized perſon is obliged by it.

(6) To be abſolutely devoted to the ſovereign *will* of God; ſo as to be at his command and diſpoſal in every reſpect. As our Creator, Redeemer, and Sanctifier, he hath an undoubted right to us; all we are, all we have, and all we do; which right being evidently repreſented, and as it were reflected, by the ordinance, to every ſubject of it, obliges to a ſuitable and adequate devotedneſs to his will.

§ 22. Having now conſidered the bleſſings exhibited by baptiſm, and the obligations reſulting from it, by an attentive regard to what the New Teſtament ſays on the ſubject, I proceed to make ſome remarks that ſeem to follow from the whole as obvious *concluſions*. And

(1) Whatever bleſſings are, according to the ſcripture account, repreſented and exhibited by baptiſm, there are *anſwerable obligations* reſulting from them, tho' not particularly ſpecified. And this appears from the very nature and ſpring of moral obligation; for one perſon is *obliged* to another in proportion as he is *indebted* to him, ſo that to be under obligation to another, with reſpect to *univerſal juſtice*, is the ſame as to be his debtor; and the nature and degree of this *debt* muſt be aſcertained by the comparative *worthineſs* of the perſon to whom we are indebted, in all thoſe reſpects in which we ſuppoſe him to have a demand or claim upon us. For inſtance, if *obedience* be the debt, then it
ſhould

Ch. 2. *Design of Baptism.* 143

should be according to the worthiness of the comparative *authority* requiring it; if the debt be *gratitude*, it should be according to the worthiness of the benefits, or expressed benevolence, of the party benefiting, compared with the worthiness or unworthiness of the party benefited; and if the debt be *love* or benevolence, it should be according to the worthiness or excellence of the person himself, which worthiness consists in the joint consideration of greatness and goodness. Let us apply these reflections to the present case. *God* is infinitely great, and infinitely good; hence every intelligent being is under infinite obligation to *love* him, because he is infinitely excellent and worthy, yea, is *worthiness itself* in every possible respect. — God's *benefits* to man are emanations from his matchless benevolence, and the greatness of those benefits exhibited in the gospel dispensation, or, which is the same thing, in its initiatory rite, are of unparalleled excellence and importance. Behold, says an inspired Apostle, what manner of love the Father hath bestowed on us! And, says another, To us are given exceeding great and precious promises. The riches of Christ are unsearchable riches; then what must be the gift of Christ himself! And what must be the mission of the Divine Comforter! What a worthiness of favour is here, and what a call to *gratitude!* Again, God's *authority* is supreme, and its worthiness is infinite; and, as every exhibition of mercy and favour designed for sinners, and *addressed* to them as
such,

such, claims from them a suitable and corresponding tribute of gratitude, and the obligation or debt rises and multiplies as the favour does, it follows, that the most free and sovereign grace of the gospel must, in this respect, have all the force, influence and authority of a law upon all to whom it is directed. All the exhibitions of gospel blessings, therefore, have an authoritative and binding power, (for this is necessarily implied in the very idea of obligation) even when they are not delivered in a commanding form; but when a disregard to gospel blessings is *declared*, in the most express terms, to be displeasing to God and destructive to ourselves; when we are positively told, that a non-compliance with the proposals of mercy is the same insult as *to charge the God of truth with impious falsehood*, (1 John v. 10.) the authority with which gospel grace appears invested is infinitely important. From these considerations it appears, that whereever we meet with a benefit or blessing exhibited in baptism, we may as safely conclude that an *answerable obligation* results therefrom, as if that obligation were mentioned in form. — Another conclusion, which is in a manner the converse of that now mentioned, is the following, viz. That whatever obligations we find specified in the New Testament as actually connected with baptism, or derived from it, we may be sure that the foundation of that obligation is laid in the exhibition of *answerable benefits*, tho' not expressly mentioned in that view.

§ 23.

§ 23. (2.) IF the above reprefentation of the nature and defign of this ordinance be juft, it may contribute to vindicate the *right ufe* of two very important terms, commonly employed in the controverfy, liable to abufe, and, may I not add, very feldom explained in a confiftent manner? I mean the terms SEAL and COVE-NANT. Hardly any thing more common in explaining the nature of baptifm than fome fuch phrafe as this — " It is a fign and *feal* of the gofpel covenant": and the authority ufually urged in favour of this application of the word *feal*, is what the Apoftle fays touching circumcifion, Rom. iv. 11. *And he received the fign of circumcifion, a* SEAL *of the righteoufnefs of the faith which he had yet being uncircumcifed.* Waving a particular difcuffion of the many ftrange things this notable paffage has been made to fpeak, and the abfurd deductions following thereupon; I would obferve, that the chief, if not the only, fource of thefe miftakes, has been owing to the want of a proper attention to the *different ufes* of SEALS among the ancients, in connection with the *different acceptations* of the term COVENANT.

THE word *covenant*, as I fhall fhew more fully afterward, frequently intends, in the holy fcriptures, a gracious *decree*, the exhibition of a free *promife*, or the like, directed for the ufe of any; and in the above text the *exhibited bleffing* is the *righteoufnefs of faith*. This is the divine proclamation, full of mercy and grace, that

H   righteoufnefs

righteousness and eternal life should be received by *faith*, as that is opposed to work and *merit*; which by no means implies, that the blessing is never communicated to any of the human race but in consequence of a certain act of the mind called believing. Prevailing *unbelief*, it is true, excludes all actual interest in the contents of the gracious charter; as it indicates a want of union with the divine Saviour, which is the grand foundation of our being accepted as righteous: and *true belief*, for a similar reason, entitles to that righteousness which faith regards. But faith, or believing, as an *act* of the mind, is not the fundamental and essential bond of union; for in *that* respect the spirit of Christ, whereby the fallen sinner is apprehended, is the bond; and which may subsist without the existence of any such act, as all must allow who admit that it appears agreeable to the divine constitution to impute righteousness to infants, who have neither works nor faith. This is sufficient to shew that the *righteousness* exhibited and reckoned to Abraham, which was the infinite merit of the divine Interposer, may have its complete effect on *some* of the human race, without any actual restipulation on their part: tho' at the same time, it lays them under *obligations* of a suitable return, whether designed for life or death. And if so, here is a *covenant*, (if we intend thereby *an application* of mercy and righteousness) without any sealing, or so much as *consenting*, on the part of the person benefited.

AMONG

AMONG the ancients, as well as the moderns, the use of SEALS was various; and by no means confined to *contracts*, or agreements between two or more parties. An act, patent, or charter, &c. of a monarch is sealed, as well as a mutual contract. Seals were affixed to *letters* and *decrees*. 1 Kings xxi. 8. Efth. iii. 12, 15. Chap. viii. 8, 10. &c. &c. In short, merchants were wont to put a seal or mark (usually on a thin piece of lead, not wax) on their commodities; different things were sealed for security against intrusion and deceit, as bags, chests, doors, &c. Thus, for instance, God says (Deut. xxxii. 34.) Is not this laid up in store with me, and *sealed* up among my *treasures*? And thus Job says, (Chap. xiv. 17.) My transgression is *sealed* up in a *bag*. When Daniel was cast into the lions' den, a stone was brought, and laid upon the mouth of the *den*, and the king *sealed* it with his own signet; (Dan. vi. 17.) and the stone on our Lord's *sepulchre* was *sealed*, (Mat. xxvii. 66.)——When, therefore, the apostle stiles circumcision a *seal of the righteousness of faith*, it seems an unwarrantable liberty to infer, that the seal here referred to must necessarily be that of a restipulator in acceding to the terms of a contract; as if the *faith* of Abraham, or of his descendants, or of any other whose faith '*should be* in uncircumcision, gave existence to circumcision *as a seal*. Why not rather consider it, as what the eternal King has thought fit to affix to an *act of grace?* What the inftrument to be fealed contained, was an *exhibition of righteoufnefs*; and, for confirmation that this righteoufnefs was recommended, as the only foundation of a finner's hope, and as an all-fufficient introduction to eternal blifs, God appointed circumcifion to ratify or *feal* it. This inftrument or *covenant* contained glad tidings of great joy, which fhould be firft to the houfe of Ifrael principally, and afterwards to all nations; it was the gofpel in miniature. And the *feal* was to continue until the feed fhould come; when exprefs order fhould be given for its abolition, to make way for another. But as long as this ordinance continued in force, it *exhibited*, not only to the fubject himfelf but to all who fhould obferve it, whether male or female — nor only while the ceremony was performed, but in every period of life — the *certainty* of thefe glad tidings. If any doubt arofe concerning either the *covenant bleffings* or *obligations* reprefented, they were to have recourfe to circumcifion, as the broad feal of heaven; whereby they might be certified, that the *former* continued in full force and virtue, by way of exhibition, for their ufe, whether male or female; and that the *latter* were unavoidably incumbent on them.

§ 24. Let us now advert to what Mr. B. has to fay on this fubject. " If Dr. Lightfoot's verfion of Rom. iv. 11. and his obfervation upon it, be juft; there can be little reafon for

for calling baptism a *seal* of the *covenant*, on account of *circumcision* being denominated a *seal* of *righteousness*. His translation of the text, and part of his remark upon it, are as follow. "*And he received the sign of circumcision, a seal of the righteousness of the faith,* which SHOULD HEREAFTER BE *in uncircumcision.* Which *should be,* not which *had been.* Not what had been to *Abraham,* as yet uncircumcised; but which should be to *his seed* uncircumcised; that is, to *Gentiles* that should hereafter imitate the faith of *Abraham.*" Which version and interpretation (adds Mr. B.) are agreeable, so far as I can perceive, both to the scope of the passage and the letter of the text. For the Apostle does not represent circumcision as a seal of righteousness to the Jews, *in common*; but to Abraham, *in particular.*—— Or, if our brethren must needs call it [baptism] a seal of the covenant, we desire to be informed, what *spiritual blessing* it ascertains, really ascertains to infants, any more than to unbelieving adults, who have at any time been baptized; or, than circumcision, to similar characters, under the former œconomy? Millions of Jews were circumcised in their infancy, and numbers of Proselytes, who lived and died in rebellion against the government and grace of God. Simon the sorcerer, professing faith in Jesus Christ, though he had it not, was baptized by Philip; and many, no doubt, in former and latter ages, have been baptized on a similar profession, whose conduct

conduct disgraced the christian character. Now, must we consider these, *all* these, as having had the *righteousness of faith*, or the *covenant of grace*, RATIFIED or SEALED to them? Far be it! Why, then, should baptism be represented at every turn, and without hesitation, as a *seal* of the covenant, when applied to infants?"† To this I will subjoin the following remarks from Dr. STENNETT. " The practice of affixing *seals* to covenants is of very early date. The use and intent of it is, to bind the parties contracting to the fulfilment of the conditions agreed on between them; and to preserve to that end, an authentic proof of the transaction.—— Now IF this be the practice alluded to, there is an impropriety in the phrase itself, of persons *having a right to the seal of the covenant:* for if sealing be a matter rather of *duty* than of *right*, to use this kind of language is much the same as to say, that persons have a right to do their duty. But what I have principally to observe is, that it follows from *this* account of the usage of sealing, that interest in a covenant does not in all instances give persons a right to the seal of it, or, in other words, make it their duty to affix their seal to it. A man may be included in a covenant or benefited by it, who is no way a party to it, and whose signature therefore is not at all requisite. Children, for instance, frequently derive advantages from covenants

† Pædob. Exam. p. 313.

nants which, with all the authentic forms of them, exifted long before they were born." † And on Rom. iv. 11. he further remarks: " Abraham believed in the promife of God refpecting the Meffiah, and by voluntarily *fubmitting* to circumcifion in obedience to the divine command, he gave clear evidence of his faith; and fo circumcifion became, in regard of *him*, a feal or authentic proof of his juftification; it was a feal affixed by Abraham himfelf to the covenant, and an atteftation, on the part of God, to his intereft in the bleffings of it. And in the fame light it might be confidered in regard of *others*, who fubmitted to it in *riper* years, and upon the conviction of their judgment. It was an expreffion of their affent and confent to the covenant, and fo a feal affixed by them to it. And it was on the part of God (to fpeak with reverence) a feal affixed by him to the covenant, that is, a gracious affurance, with refpect to thofe who thus in faith fubmitted to it, that he would pardon, accept and fave them. ‖ —— It is eafy to fee that baptifm cannot be a feal of the righteoufnefs of faith, that is, of their juftification, to infants, they not having *faith:* nor can it be in regard of them a teft of new obedience, they not *voluntarily fubmitting* to it."— And again, " Circumcifion was *a token of the covenant between God and Abraham.* A pofitive arbitrary fign, inftituted by God

H 4   to

† S's Anfwer to A. p. 105. ‖ p. 107.

to bring to remembrance that tranfaction, in the fame manner as the bow in the heavens was appointed by God, as a token of the *tranfaction between him and Noah.*" § Thus I have endeavoured to give thefe gentlemen's objections and reafons all the ftrength they admit of; nor have I defignedly evaded the force of any one circumftance; but forbear further quotations, to avoid prolixity: concluding, that if thefe pofitions are fairly and folidly refuted, as far as they tend to oppofe Pœdobaptift principles, this is fufficient for my prefent purpofe. I only obferve here previoufly, that if the reader will give himfelf the trouble to confult and weigh impartially what I have faid in the laft fection, moft, if not all that is here advanced, is in effect anfwered or precluded. However, I fhall not decline a more particular examination of what they urge.

§ 25. WHATEVER appearance of argument there is in thefe quotations, againft the propriety of calling circumcifion and baptifm *in general*, that is, confidered merely *as inflitutions*, independent of the genuine *faith* of the fubject, *feals* of the covenant, is reducible to thefe pofitions.—— " Abraham's covenant was a *contract* between God and Abraham, and as fuch required a *mutual* agreement of both parties.— Mr. B. will have it, that circumcifion was not a *feal* of righteoufnefs to the Jews *in common*; but

§ p. 109.

but to Abraham, *in particular*.. Dr. S. maintains that it was so to *all believing* Jews; but both agree, that it was not a *seal* of righteousness to Jewish infants: and the common reason is, that they were not capable of *assenting* or submitting to the contract.——And on these accounts baptism is not a seal of righteousness to any infants, or even adults who are not true believers."——— Here are several things taken for granted which ought to have been first proved. And, first, I maintain, it is not true that what is called the Abrahamic covenant was a *contract* between God and Abraham; as if it could not be properly termed God's covenant *to* or *with* Abraham, without the latter's *believing consent*. For,

1. Nothing is more clear, than that the first publication of mercy to our fallen parents (Gen. iii. 15.) was of the nature of a *free promise*. We may, perhaps, not improperly call it, The first edition of the covenant of grace that was ever published and revealed to man. Nor was it in their power to alter its nature as a covenant. Their not believing could not have made the faith of God of no effect. The revealed and exhibited blessing was God's covenant *to* man, or, if you please, *with* man, which amounts to the same thing in regard of God's transactions with sinners, independent of his assent and consent to the terms of it. For God to publish his covenant to sinners, few or many, is one thing; and for these to give it a cordial reception, is another

another. Such a tranfaction, on the part of God, may ftand on the moft abfolute foundation; and if we believe not, he abideth faithful and true to his declaration: but a *believing* concurrence, or a *difpofition* fuited to fuch an exhibited favour, is what proceeds from a very different difpenfation; that of the Spirit of grace in executing the hidden counfel of Heaven.— The covenant of grace is ONE. In its original *internal* form, which comes under the notion of a contract or mutual agreement in the ftricteft fenfe, it is perfectly *abfolute*; as founded on the fovereign pleafure and irreverfible decrees of God. It is alfo *abfolute* in its *exhibition* to fome rather than to others; for in this fenfe as well as the former it may be faid, God will have mercy on whom he will have mercy, and compaffion on whom he will have compaffion. Whatever is *conditional* of it is on account of man's *free nature* and God's *moral government*. Its publication and exhibition to man, *as a free agent*, folicits and requires his approbation — his obedient reception of what is propofed to him by his Creator and Benefactor. But mankind being univerfally finners, and *as fuch* infinitely unworthy; and what is more, totally averfe from what is required of them; no foul could be faved if the covenant in its *abfolute internal* form did not *enfure* the direction of its bleffings to the intended perfons; as alfo a difpofition fuited to their enjoyment. Thus, when God gave Adam and Eve an abftract of his covenant of redemption,

redemption, which was absolute and infallible in its internal form as settled in the divine counsel; the *exhibition* of it was also *absolute*, both to *them* and *all thofe* of their posterity who should be informed of it: importing, that there was mercy with God that he might be feared. Yes, not less absolute than his covenant of the night and of the day; which no one, surely, will maintain was sealed, certified, confirmed, or made more absolute, by the *affent* and *fubmiffion* of man, to whom it was given. It was in that very display and promulgation of it an unspeakable blessing; and, as such, absolutely *obliged* them to suitable acknowledgments; previous to, and independent on any dispositions of the persons, whether good or bad. —— And not only so, but it is highly probable the institution of *facrifices* was given to Adam, as a *feal* of the covenant, as well as a type of Christ. " For, (as WITSIUS observes) the *inftitutions* which commemorated sin, also signified and *fealed* the future expiation of it by the Messiah." * Again he says: " These *facrifices* were *feals* of God's covenant. For though there is a difference between sacrifices and sacraments formally considered; because sacraments are given by God to men, but sacrifices are offered by men to God: nevertheless, there is no reason why the consideration of a sacrament and sacrifice

* WITS, Oecon, Fœd. Lib. iii. Cap. iii. § x.

fice may not, in different refpects concur in one and the fame thing. For even facrifices are given by God to men, that is, are *inftituted* by divine authority; that by thefe ceremonies, the coming of the Son of God in the flefh, &c. might be fignified and SEALED." †

2. NOT lefs abfolute was God's covenant or *free promife* to Noah, (which Dr. S. quaintly calls a " tranfaction between Him and Noah") that he would drown the world no more by a flood. This was a feafonable *covenant* granted to Noah, to all mankind, and literally to *every creature* capable of the benefit; and particularly fo, as it was an adumbration of the covenant of grace, or connected with it. But what is very remarkable is, that God's covenant to Noah, and his feed for ever, was confirmed and fealed, by a token on the part of God *only*; independent of any confent and *fubmiffion* on the part of Noah and his defcendants. God made a covenant, and fet his *bow in the cloud* as the confirming feal of it; but where was Noah's affent and fubmiffion, on behalf of himfelf, his pofterity, &c. to render the contract valid? For if it was a COVENANT made with all flefh, fhould it not, on the principle I am oppofing, have the *confent* of the parties contained in it, as the *impreffion active*, before it could be faid to be ratified or fealed to them? Rather I would afk, is not the rainbow a fign and

† Id. Lib. iv. Cap. vii. § vii.

Ch. 2.   *Defign of Baptifm.*   157

and confirming feal of God's covenant not lefs to the atheiftical philofopher than the grave divine? Nor fhould we fuppofe that fallen finners are fo far complimented, and that God's *inftitutions* are fo liable to be degraded and nullified, as that nothing could be a *feal* of his covenant to men, but what they are pleafed to. make valid, by their *faith* and *fubmiffion*.

§ 26. 3. WHAT has been faid of the difpenfations of God's covenant to Adam and Noah,. with their refpective feals, is applicable to that publication of it made to Abraham; but with fome remarkable circumftances of *limitation* in regard of the *additional bleffings* exhibited, and the *fuperadded feal* of it, circumcifion. The *former* were principally addreffed to Abraham's defcendants in the line of Ifaac and Jacob, though. not exclufively, for a gracious provifion was made in favour of profelytes and their feed; and the. *latter* was confined to Abraham's *male* defcendants, and thofe of the profelytes. This reftriction of the feal of the covenant, to be applied. only to the males, was, we may be fure, founded on the wifeft and jufteft reafons; and may be in fome good meafure accounted for, by attending to the civil and ecclefiaftical polity of the Jews, in connection with the Saviour's incarnation. To inveftigate the particular reafons of this reftriction, my prefent argument does not require. I would only add, that as the inftitution of facrifices was a *feal* of the former difpenfations of the covenant, and a part of

family

family religion; we ought not to infer that Abraham's *female* descendants had *no seal* of God's covenant in common with the males. All that can be said of them is, that they were deprived, by an express restriction, of this *additional seal*, for reasons the most proper; while they enjoyed every thing else in common. So far then should we be from supposing, that a Jewish circumcised *male* had not in his flesh the seal of God's covenant, even from infancy; that I think it may be justly affirmed —— the *female* part was highly obliged to the divine goodness for what may be properly termed a *seal of the righteousness of faith*; — to *assure* them of blessings exhibited *to them*, and of their important obligations. If, therefore, God's COVENANT of redemption to fallen man, in its external form and manifestation, is nothing else but a DECLARATION *of sovereign grace and a divine righteousness*; which, in everlasting transcendent love and compassion, is provided for the use and service of wretched sinners, who live within the pale of such a declaration: and if to this God institute a sign, yet not a *mere* sign, but a confirming token —— a demonstrating *evidence* of the truth of what is testified, and of God's infallible, unchanging veracity ——- be that sign what it may, and directed to be applied or administered to the subjects of a dispensation indiscriminately; or else *expressly restricted*, for wise and obvious reasons, to a certain class, as in circumcision

cision to the males only: is there not the greatest propriety in calling such a token THE SEAL of God's *covenant*, perfectly unconnected with and *independent* of the *faith* of the subject, as in the case of Jewish infants?

§ 27. BUT this is not all. The principle I am opposing, is fraught with an inconvenience little short of a gross absurdity. For this implies, "that circumcision became a seal or authentic *proof* of their justification, only to those of *riper* years, who, upon conviction of their judgment, *submitted* to that ordinance; and the same rule (our opponents contend) holds as to the ordinance of baptism." *This*, it is evident, the above quotations maintain, and the following proposition is the sum. " Then *only* may circumcision and baptism be termed *seals*, when they are PROOFS of justification to persons submitting to them."— Now I ask,

1. MAY we infer that a man is certainly in a justified state, and what is more, *assured* of his justification, *because he has submitted* to an instituted ordinance, such as circumcision or baptism? If not, how can his affixing his seal to the covenant, which according to Dr. S. must be matter of duty, be any *proof* to him of his justification? Previous to this *duty* of sealing the covenant, the performer must either be *assured* of his being in a justified state, or he is *not*: if the *former*, how can the observance of such an external right be a *proof* to him of his justification? What is designed it seems, for this external

external right to perform, has been *before* effected by other means. As a *proof* then it comes too late, if the perſon was aſſured of righteouſneſs antecedently. But if he was *not* aſſured previous to his performance of the duty, and yet was conſcious of no inſincerity of heart, is the mere addition of the performance of the duty a ſeal or certain proof to him that he is juſtified? It ſhould ſeem then that no perſon who ſubmits to baptiſm upon conviction, and who is conſcious of no hypocriſy, can be at a loſs to determine upon the goodneſs of his ſtate; for baptiſm is to him a *ſeal* whereby he may be certified of his juſtification. But if this be true, how comes it to paſs that any ſincere ſouls, who have made that ſubmiſſion, are yet haraſſed with fears and doubts reſpecting their ſtate? or, muſt we pronounce them all hypocrites and unſound, who heſitate about their intereſt in Chriſt, and maintain that, in this reſpect, he who doubteth is damned?

2. If it be ſaid, that baptiſm is a ſeal to thoſe only who have *real faith*, and that ſuch perſons *only* may be *aſſured* of juſtification and the conſequent bleſſings of the covenant; I reply, that then it follows, that baptiſm can be no ſeal to any but ſuch as have the aſſurance of faith: for if they doubt of the *reality* of their faith, they muſt proportionally doubt that baptiſm is a ſeal; and the conſequence will be, that ſince, on the principle I am oppoſing, baptiſm is a ſeal of the covenant as a *duty* performed by the believer,

liever, and on the part of God, an atteſtation of his intereſt in the bleſſings of the covenant;— God's atteſtation is no atteſtation to any who doubt of the reality of their faith, and ſo is a ſeal of a certainty that certifieth nothing!

3. THERE ſeems but one method of evading this concluſion; and that is, that however doubtful a perſon may be of his ſtate before or at his baptiſm, yet, *after* he has ſubmitted to the duty upon conviction, he may be *aſſured* of his intereſt in the bleſſings of the covenant. —— Yet this evaſion is of no uſe, except we borrow for its aid another principle, which maintains, that the ordinance produces a real moral change in the ſubject, *ex opere operato*. For if it be ſaid, that the certainty is obtained from God *after* we have in faith complied with a known duty, and from the conſideration of our ſubmitting to it *as ſuch*; I would fain know how *this* rather than any *other* duty, enjoined by the ſame authority, becomes an *evidence* of our intereſt in covenant bleſſings? or, how we are *certified* of a divine atteſtation to our juſtification in any other way, than we may infer from any other chriſtian duty whatever? Is it not abſolutely inconceivable how baptiſm can be a *confirming ſeal* of our intereſt in Chriſt and his benefits, on the part of God, in any other ſenſe than all other duties may be ſo termed when performed by faith? And if ſo, it follows from our opponents' own principles, and contrary to what Dr. S. maintains, that neither baptiſm nor circumci-

sion can be any *distinguishing seals* at all, any more than any other moral duty performed in faith.

4. From the above considerations it must also follow, if Mr. B. and Dr. S. are right, that circumcision could not be a seal of the righteousness of faith, even to Abraham himself, contrary to the Apostle's express words, (Rom. iv. 11.) as an institution; without a supperadded revealed assurance given him of the *reality* of his faith and submission. And thus we are driven, at length, to this conclusion, that circumcision was no seal to Abraham or any of his descendants but in *consequence* of the sealing of the Spirit; and the purport of God's language to Abraham must be (Gen. xvii. 9—14.) "Though I enjoin upon thee, and thy seed after thee, the right of circumcision as a token of the covenant betwixt me and you; yet it shall be no token of confirmation, no seal of the covenant at all, but to such of you as have previously the infallible witness and sealing of my Spirit, to certify you of the undoubted reality of your faith and submission. And observe further, that this honour is not to be extended to thy seed who shall be circumcised in infancy; for, not having faith, it can be no seal to them: no, this honour is reserved for those who shall be bought with money of any stranger, or any proselytes not of thy seed; and these must be sealed by the Spirit, or have the certainty of their interest in the covenant, *before* they have any just grounds to conclude that circumcision is

to them the feal of my covenant." But is this a declaration worthy of God?

5. It therefore follows, on Dr. S's hypothefis, that to be of the feed of Abraham, was a privilege not worthy to be compared with that of a profelyte. To Jacob and the patriarchs for inftance, circumcifion was not a feal of the covenant, for they had *no faith* when circumcifed; but the profelyte of a day, who fubmitted to the rite upon conviction, had in his flefh a confirming feal of his juftification. Had not a native Jew here an irrefiftible temptation to envy the profelyte? A Jewifh mafter to envy the privilege of his fervant bought with his money, even fuppofing their piety to be equal? How happy thofe children above others, who, through the neglect of their parents, or any other accident, were left uncircumcifed in their minority; whereby they had an opportunity in *riper* years to *fubmit* to the important rite, and thereby of obtaining a *feal* of their juftification!

§ 28. Aware of thefe inconveniences, Mr. B. avails himfelf of Dr. Lightfoot's verfion of Rom. iv. 11. and his remark upon it —— " A feal of the righteoufnefs of the faith, which *fhould hereafter be* in uncircumcifion. Which *fhould be*, not which *had been.*" Why the Dr. fhould fupply the elliptical paffage (της εν τη ακροβυςια) *which in uncircumcifion*, with a *fhould hereafter be*, requires no fmall critical difcernment to determine.

I think it muft be allowed by any impartial competent judge, that the fupplied part of the fentence sentence is *far fetched*, and should not be preferred without manifest necessity. The Vulgate Latin renders it —— *quæ* EST *in præputio*; the Syriac Version is rendered —— *quæ* FUERAT; the Arabic —— *quæ* ERAT; and the Æthiopic thus: *Et circumcisio signaculum justitiæ ejus fuit quam ei dedit, & signum ejus, ut ei innotesceret de hoc, quod per fidem Deus justificaret Abraham quum non fuit illo tempore circumcisus.* The *scope* of the passage is evidently this: The apostle in prosecution of his grand proof, that justification and eternal life are not obtained by human worthiness, works or observances of our own, but are solely and absolutely the fruit of sovereign grace; shews that this doctrine, though more clearly revealed in the gospel, was yet the common language of preceding dispensations. That this was the import of the *Jewish* dispensation, David testifieth, ver. 6. *Even as David also describeth the blessedness of the man unto whom God imputeth righteousness without works.* And that this method of acceptance through grace and a divine righteousness, was not *peculiar* to the circumcision, but belongs to the uncircumcision also; appears from the history of Abraham, whom the Jews were so ready to boast of on every occasion. Ver. 9. *Cometh this blessedness then upon the circumcision* ONLY, *or upon the uncircumcision* ALSO? *For we say that faith* (as contradistinguished from works or any manner of worthiness of his own) *was reckoned to Abraham for righteousness.* Ver. 10. *How was it then*

Ch. 2.   *Defign of Baptifm.*   165

then reckoned? *When he was in circumcifion, or in' uncircumcifion? Not in circumcifion, but in uncircumcifion.* Ver. 11. *And* (Και) as a following confideration, many years after the righteoufnefs of faith was made known to him, *he received the fign of circumcifion, a SEAL of the righteoufnefs of the faith which* (the *relative* having a refpect either to the antecedent *faith* or *righteoufnefs* *) he had (or, poffeffed) *in uncircumcifion*; that uncircumcifed ftate juft fpoken of. That the phrafe, εν τη ακροβυσια, refers to Abraham's uncircumcifed *ftate* rather than to the *Gentiles*, in this place, may appear from what immediately follows. To the intent *that he might be the father of* ALL *believers,* — a confpicuous example to Jews and Gentiles that juftification is not the confequence of ceremonial obfervances, or any human merit, worthinefs or confideration whatever; —(δι ακροβυ-ςιας) *thro' uncircumcifion,* — by reafon of his being the favourite of God in his uncircumcifed ftate, as well as after; — to the end *that righteoufnefs might be imputed unto them* ALSO. Ver. 12. *And that he might be the father of circumcifion,* — that is, of fpiritual circumcifion ; (an inconteftible inftance that the *bleffings exhibited* in and by that rite, and of which circumcifion was the *feal*, were not intended for chriftian gentiles exclufively, but had

refpect

---

* *Quæ* (ambiguum eft, & referendum, vel 1. ad fidem: vel potius, 2. ad juftitiam fidei, h. e. quam ex fide exceperat) *eft in præputio.* Eftius.— *Fidei quæ* (vel, *quæ* fuerat; Erafmus, Pagninus, Tremellius, Flaccius Illyricus, &c. vel, *receptæ*, Beza, Pifcator; vel, *quam* habuiffe dignofcitur, Zegerius) *in præputio.* Poli Synop. in loc.

respect) *to them who are not of the circumcision ONLY, but also walk in the steps of that faith of our Father Abraham, which he had (ἐν τῇ ἀκροβυστια) being yet uncircumcised.* —— Thus the Apostle cuts off boasting on either side. The Jew had no ground to slight the Gentile, nor the Gentile to slight the Jew. The grace of the covenant was exhibited and applied to Abraham *before* circumcision; and yet circumcision was instituted as a sign and seal of the same grace, righteousness, or covenant, to the Jew. I would further remark —— as just criticism requires, that similar renderings should be given to similar phrases in the same connection, it seems an unaccountable liberty to render the same phrase, ἐν τῇ ἀκροβυστια, in ver. 11. as referring to the *Gentiles,* which in ver. 12. *must* be referred to Abraham's *state* of uncircumcision; while at the same time there is no pretended necessity for such a variation.

§ 29. Thus, I think, we may pronounce Mr. B's favourite interpretation of the passage in question — far-fetched and unnecessary. But supposing he were indulged with Lightfoot's critical weapon, I presume it would be but of little service to him; since there is another consideration that so blunts it, as to render it perfectly innoffensive.

Now supposing, without granting, that Abraham's circumcision being a seal to him, that the Gentiles should, in some after period, be justified by faith, were the meaning of the controverted

verted text; what is the confequence? Why, if ver. 11. implies that he received a feal to affure him that righteoufnefs, (or by a periphrafis, the righteoufnefs of faith) would be imputed to the future Gentiles without ceremonial obfervances, works or worthinefs of their own; ver. 12. muft in like manner, from the *connection* of the two verfes, neceffarily imply, that he had the fame confirming feal to affure him of the fame important truth in relation to the Jews. He received a feal, of what? Of righteoufnefs. What kind of righteoufnefs? That which is of faith, as oppofed to legal obfervances, works, merit, or worthinefs of the creature. Who fhould be the happy objects of this favour? The uncircumcifion; fuppofe the Gentiles. But to what end was fuch a feal given to Abraham?

1. *That he might be the father*, or the appointed and highly honoured pattern, of *all among the Gentiles* in the moft diftant periods, who fhould obtain righteoufnefs and falvation of *free and fovereign grace*, exclufive of works of righteoufnefs which they fhould do. Thus it was that he received mercy, without any works of the law; and therefore properly ftiled the *father* of all among the Gentiles who fhould have no pretenfions at all to any ceremonial and legal righteoufnefs of their own. And was this the *only* defign of his receiving circumcifion as a feal? Far from it, for,

2. ANOTHER

2. ANOTHER very important one is immediately fubjoined, ver. 12. AND that he might be *the father of circumcifion*, a SIMILAR PATTERN to the *Jews alfo*, that none of them may truft to the law, ceremonies, or any other confideration: and thofe among them who were beholden to mercy, as Abraham was, without works, were his CHILDREN in the fame fenfe as the gracious among the Gentiles are. Thus it appears, that circumcifion was to Abraham a SEAL *of the righteoufnefs of faith*, or of *free grace*, not more to the Gentiles than the Jews; and confequently, Mr. B's attempt, to confine the purport of circumcifion as a feal, with reference to *Gentiles only*, proves abortive.

§ 30. OUR laft inquiry refpected the perfons *concerning whom* Abraham received a feal; but now another queftion returns, viz. *To whom* circumcifion was a feal of righteoufnefs? Mr. B's reply is fhort and plain, " To Abraham *in particular*." * Herein, however, he differs from Dr. S. For thus the latter writes: " Though I object to the idea of circumcifion's being a *feal* of the covenant, at leaft in regard of infants, and underftand the paffage juft referred to as only faying, that it became to Abraham, and by confequence to all others who believed, a feal or atteftation to their juftification; yet I readily admit, that it was a *fign* or *token* of the covenant between God and Abraham in all who

were

* P. 313.

were circumcised †." And a little after: " Circumcision, though it became a seal of the righteousness of faith to Abraham, could not be a *seal* to his *infant* posterity, at least in the same sense it was to him." — In conformity to this principle he further adds, " It is easy to see that baptism cannot be a *seal* of the righteousness of faith, that is, of their *justification*, to infants, they not having *faith*: nor can it be in regard of them a test of new obedience, they not *voluntarily submitting* to it."

But have these assertions any foundation in scripture or reason? And,

1. Is there any truth in the supposition, That nothing can be a test of new obedience, or lay us under additional obligations of duty, without our *voluntary submission*? Is not this singular notion, so much insisted on by our adversaries, confronted with the fundamental principles of morals? For it is demonstrable, from the nature and spring of moral obligation, that if baptism be a *benefit* to infants, as we maintain, it must be to them such a test, or *obliges* them to *additional* duties. —— Again, I would ask,

2. Is there any propriety in the supposition — because infants cannot *believe*, they therefore cannot be *justified*? or what amounts to the same — because infants have not actual *faith*, therefore their *justification* cannot be *sealed*? But all this stands on another rotten pillar —— that there is no difference between a seal being *applied*

† S's Answer to A. p. 108.

plied to a person, and the *certainty* of his actual justification. On the contrary, is it not abundantly evident, that God's covenant of redemption, AS REVEALED TO FALLEN MAN, is of the nature of a gracious proclamation? If so, what necessity is there to suppose, that there can be no *sealing* of such a covenant to any person without thereby certifying his justification? May not the Eternal Sovereign institute a *memorial* of his mercy which endureth from generation to generation; to the intent, that every lost sinner to whom it is duly administered, may be certified, as far as any thing short of a miracle can do, that this gracious God does actually and incessantly exhibit *to him* the blessings of his covenant —— with the merciful design to encourage his future faith, and to engage his grateful obedience?

3. MAY we not say, that such an institution is the *seal* of God's covenant, without supposing the efficacious *grace* of the covenant experienced by the sealed? For, *who* seals? God, by his commissioned ministers. —— *What* does he seal? His own gracious proclamation, exhibited to the subject. — The voice of God's heralds is to this purpose: " Now then we are ambassadors for Christ, publishing to a lost world, the most merciful terms of reconciliation: and if any suspect the *truth* of our message, or the *faithfulness* of our divine master, behold both ratified with his own SEAL!" —— I suppose it has been proved, that circumcision *was* not designed, nor indeed *could be*

Ch. 2. *Design of Baptism.* 171

be, to Abraham or any other, as a *proof* of actual justification, without involving a great absurdity. Therefore,

4. It must be a seal, AS AN INSTITUTED RITE, which God affixed to his covenant. This *must* be its purport in reference to Abraham, as far as it *assured* him of any thing; nor can it be denied, that in *this* sense, which I think is demonstrably the true one, it *ought* to be considered, in regard of every individual subject of it. — Thus the twelve patriarchs, for instance, had in their flesh, not only a *sign*, but a *seal* also of God's covenant: purporting, that he thereby proposed himself *to be to them a God*; that they, in return, *may be to him a people*. The fact of the institution, sealing the covenant, and not their personal qualifications of any kind, was the *ground* of their obligation; and this *increased* with their years. When grown up they might thus reflect: " By this mark in our persons, we are *assured*, " in consequence of what the Lord said to our " father Abraham, that he is graciously willing "'to become, not only the object of our wor- " ship, but our all-sufficient portion. And, sure- " ly, this consideration obliges us, incontestibly, " to become his people,—to love and serve him " with all our powers." —— But will any one say, that circumcision was not *to them* a seal? or not without their devout approbation of it? That cannot be, except we maintain this absurd position, That the very essence of a divine institution depends on the precarious determination of

I 2 the

the finful creature. This, however, is in perfect confiftence with another pofition, equally abfurd, viz. That what we do not *voluntarily fubmit* to, cannot be to us a teft of new obedience.

§ 31. FROM what has been faid, we infer, that the hypothefis which maintains — infants were not *fealed* by circumcifion, becaufe of their not having *faith*, or not *fubmitting* to it upon conviction, — is untenable. Yet, as our opponents have treated this fubject with undeferved contempt, we fhall, *ex abundanti*, take another turn with them.

Now, if circumcifion was a feal of righteoufnefs to Abraham, and not to the infant fubjects of it in the *fame fenfe*, it muft be owing—either, to their being *incapable* — or, to fome *difference* in the original *inftitution*, fpecified or implied — or, to fome fcripture evidence whereby this diftinction is made neceffary. I affirm, then, in general,

THAT none of thefe cofiderations, nor any other fufficient reafon whatever, can fhew the *neceffity* of the pretended *diftinction*. Now, the queftion is not, Whether or no circumcifion, as a ftanding rite, had *other ufes* of an ecclefiaftical or political nature; but, Whether it was a *feal*, on God's part, to circumcifed infants? The former is not difputed; and therein it agrees with the inftitution of facrifices, which were not only a type of the Meffiah's atonement, but, in a fecondary view, anfwered the end of a tribute, to fupport the priefthood. Nobody, I prefume,
will

will deny, but one inflitution may, by divine appointment, fubferve *various* purpofes — moral, typical, ecclefiaftical, and political; as numerous inflances in the Jewifh œconomy fupport the fact. Therefore, to enumerate feveral purpofes, for which we may fuppofe circumcifion was inftituted, *befides* that of a feal of righteoufnefs, is impertinent; when intended to conclude againft the idea of its being a feal to infants. Yet Dr. S. expatiates largely upon the different ufes of circumcifion, as a reafon why it was not a feal of the covenant to infants. But how fhall we reconcile the following paffages with truth, or with each other? " As to circumcifion, it was a *token* of the covenant between God and Abraham. — But what was the *purport* of that tranfaction? I readily agree, that the *grand* object of it was the coming of the Meffiah, and our redemption by him; on which account the gofpel is faid to have been preached unto Abraham. But this furely was not the *only* object of it [*]." And again: " Thofe matters in the covenant between God and Abraham, which feem to be the *chief*, if not the *only* ground or reafon of circumcifion, and which that rite was peculiarly adapted to exprefs, are matters to which *baptifm* hath no reference at all [†]." Has baptifm, then, *no reference at all* to our redemption by Chrift? Or, is it conclufive to infer, that becaufe the coming of the Meffiah, and our redemption by him, was the *grand object* of circumcifion

[*] Dr. STENNETT's Anfwer to Dr. ADDINGTON, p. 112.
[†] Ibid. p. 118.

circumcifion, but not the *only* one; therefore, it was not a feal of righteoufnefs to infants?

§ 32. CONSIDERING circumcifion as an inftituted rite, defigned to afford the ftrongeft evidence, that righteoufnefs was attainable *only* as a free favour —— that it was God's *feal*, as the impreffion active of his authority, adminiftered by his fervants; attefting, not that the fubject is actually poffeffed of the fpiritual bleffings reprefented by it, (for *this* no external rite whatever is capable of, as before fhewn, § 27.) but, that it is the divine pleafure to *exhibit* therein to him the bleffings of his covenant — that the fact of an exhibited *benefit*, lays earlieft infancy under obligations of future returns (§ 22.) — confidering, I fay, thefe things, it is evident,

1. THAT infants were CAPABLE of circumcifion as a feal; if not, we muft fay, that the incapacity lay either in their apparent *ftate*, or in their want of a profeffed *fubjection*. But *neither* of thefe is *effential* to being the fubjects of the feal of God's covenant; and therefore are required qualifications in certain circumftances only, viz. in perfons who are capable of diffenting and rejecting, as well as affenting and fubmitting. If any again infift, that the concurrence of the fubject is abfolutely neceffary to conftitute the fealing, as this muft be on the part of God and the creature; this would be only objecting to the fenfe, in which I have explicitly declared I underftand the term and notion of fealing; and which I think is demonftrably the only confiftent

tent fenfe in which it can be taken in reference to the inftitution either of circumcifion or baptifm. For the *general* thefis under confideration, requires me only to fhew — That there is a proper and confiftent fenfe in which *any* divine ordinance intended to *exhibit* the bleffings of the covenant, and to *oblige* the fubject to a cordial reception of them, and other anfwerable returns, *may* be termed a SEAL *of the covenant:* and that baptifm, being proved an ordinance of that nature, is properly denominated *fuch a feal.* And the argument under prefent confideration is — That *fuch* an ordinance, is *equally applicable* to infants and adults; and, therefore, that no pretended incapacity in the Jewifh infants could be a fufficient reafon why circumcifion was not to *them* as well as *Abraham* a feal of righteoufnefs. Let any one, therefore, reflect in what fenfe I underftand the word *feal,* and he may immediately perceive the validity of this branch of the argument, that infants are *not incapable* fubjects of it.

§ 33. 2. BUT tho' circumcifed infants were thus *capable* of having the *feal* of God's covenant in their flefh, is there not fomething in the INSTITUTION ITSELF, whereby it appears, that circumcifion was a *feal* to Abraham, while it was only a *token* to his infant feed? I think not. The words are very exprefs and particular. Gen. xvii: 7. " And I will *eftablifh* my covenant between me and thee, AND THY SEED AFTER THEE, in their generations, for an everlafting lasting covenant; TO BE A GOD UNTO THEE, AND TO THY SEED AFTER THEE. ver. 8. — AND I WILL BE THEIR GOD. ver. 9. And God said unto Abraham, Thou shalt keep my covenant therefore, THOU AND THY SEED AFTER THEE, in their generations. ver. 10. This is my covenant, which YE shall keep between me and YOU, AND THY SEED AFTER THEE; EVERY MAN CHILD AMONG YOU shall be circumcised. ver. 11. — And it shall be a token of the covenant betwixt me and YOU. ver. 13. — And my covenant shall be in YOUR flesh for an everlasting covenant." On these words I observe,

(1.) THAT Abraham and his seed are here considered as one aggregate body, as well as in strict conjunction. God not only addresses Abraham in these terms, respecting the covenant and its token, " thee AND thy seed," which abundantly shews a *similarity* of design in their direction to Abraham's *seed* as well as to himself; but they are also addressed in these collective terms, YE, YOU, YOUR, without any discriminating clause. There is, therefore, in the institution itself no ground of distinction, why circumcision should be a *seal* to Abraham and not to his seed, of which the latter were equally capable.

(2.) THE grand covenant *blessing exhibited* to Abraham, extends *equally* to his seed. I will establish my covenant —— to be A GOD unto thee

thee AND to thy feed after thee. And I will be THEIR GOD.

(3.) THE *obligations refulting* from the inftitution are the *fame* to Abraham and his feed. For God faid unto Abraham, "Thou fhalt KEEP my covenant therefore, THOU, AND THY SEED. This is my covenant, which YE SHALL KEEP between me and you." There was not indeed an *application* of grace to all the circumcifed alike, but there was an *exhibition*, and the *obligation* was general.

§ 34. IT has been confidently afferted by our opponents, as before obferved, "That there were *other* ends, ufes, and fignifications of circumcifion to Abraham's own perfon, than thofe for which it was difpenfed to his feed; fuch as — that he fhould be the father of all believers — that his feed fhould inherit Canaan — that Chrift fhould come out of his loins." From whence they infer, "That the covenant of circumcifion, *in every* of thofe refpects in which circumcifion was given Abraham as a *feal* of it, was not given to all the Jews and their children: nay, which his feed (indefinitely) had no promife of at all *." But is there any thing in thefe dogmatical affertions better than magifterial trifling? For,

1. To fay that circumcifion was a *feal* of Abraham's *fatherhood* of all believers, or of his feed inheriting Canaan, is directly contrary to the apoftle's affertion, that it was a feal of the *righteoufnefs of faith*. That thefe particulars were

included

* FISHER's Chriftianifmus Redivivus, p. 18, 19.

included as *inferior* parts of the Abrahamic charter, is granted; but it is abfurd to make them fynonymous with the righteoufnefs of faith; which our opponents muft do to be confiftent. Nor is it *true*, that the promife of Canaan was *peculiar* to Abraham, in any other fenfe than that he was *foremoſt* upon the lift. See Gen. xvii. 19. chap. xxviii. 13—15. Was not Jehovah a God to Ifaac and his feed, and to Jacob and his feed, as well as to Abraham and his feed; and in the *very fame* refpect? And, fays the Lord to Jacob, in the paffage laft cited, " The land whereon thou lieft, TO THEE WILL I GIVE IT, AND TO THY SEED." Seeing, then, that this divine charter includes Abraham and millions of his defcendants *in common*; and, as before fhewn, without any ground of difference; and feeing the fame charter has been confirmed, to Ifaac and Jacob, and their feed — to make the circumftance of Abraham's *priority* on the lift of perfons benefited by the grant, the foundation of the pretended diftinction, is to the laft, nugatory and impertinent.

2. To urge that the claufe " of Chrift's coming out of his loins," was a privilege *peculiar* to Abraham, in fuch a fenfe as that circumcifion was to *him* a *feal* of it, but not to his feed; is equally futile. For tho' it was granted him, that he fhould be the progenitor of Chrift; yet it was faid to Jacob as well, " IN THEE, AND IN THY SEED SHALL ALL THE FAMILIES OF THE EARTH BE BLESSED." Nor muft

must we confound Abraham's *carnal privilege* with the *righteousness of faith*. Circumcision is said to be a seal of the *latter* expressly, but not of the *former*; nor does there appear any reason or propriety in saying that the carnal privilege was sealed to Abraham, but so far as it was subservient to the Saviour's infinite and everlasting righteousness. Thus it appears, that as infants were *capable* of circumcision as a *seal*, so there is abundant evidence from the *institution itself*, that it was equally applicable to them as to Abraham.

§ 35. However unfavourable to the purpose of Antipædobaptists might be the institution itself of circumcision, were there notwithstanding any *other* producible evidence from a subsequent divine statute in their favour, it would alter the case proportionably. But this, I believe, is what none of those whose interest it is to produce it, attempt to do; except Rom. iv. 11. which has been already considered; and I think fairly shewn from the scope and design of the apostle, to be inconsistent with their confined view of it. The apostle's argument is, that both Jews and Gentiles are justified by the same divine righteousness, and not by the observance of any law whatever, or any worthiness of their own: now, is it any thing else but ridiculous trifling to contend, and still worse to make the apostle maintain, that the inestimable privilege of *righteousness imputed without works* is COMMON to Jews and

and Gentiles, BECAUSE circumcifion was to Abraham ALONE a feal of righteoufnefs?

THERE is, indeed, another paffage that has been occafionally fubpœnaed to ferve this tottering caufe; and that is, John vi. 27. *Him hath God the Father fealed.* " In the fame fenfe," fays the author laft quoted, " in which the Father is faid to *feal* the Son, to be the giver of meat that endures to eternal life, i. e. authorifed to that bufinefs, honoured with that office, is God faid to give circumcifion to Abraham, whereby to feal him up, and fettle him for ever in that glorious title, viz. *The father of all that believe*; in which fenfe circumcifion was never given to any one of Abraham's pofterity at all*." To this I reply,

THAT there were in ufe among the ancients fealings for *different* purpofes, as before obferved; and a *perfon* may be faid to be fealed when he receives a *commiffion*, is invefted with *authority*, or bears well authenticated *credentials*, &c. And thus was Chrift fealed of the Father. His miracles were inconteftible proofs of his divine miffion. But how does this help the notion, that neither Ifaac, Jacob, or any other befide Abraham, received circumcifion as a feal? For where is it faid or implied, that God *fealed Abraham?* It is faid, indeed, that he *received* the fign of circumcifion, a feal of rightcoufnefs. But who would infer, that becaufe a promife, a law, or a facred rite, was *received* by an individual for the ufe and fervice of himfelf and

* Ibid.

and his posterity; it must signify one thing to the first receiver, and another thing to all the rest; when no such distinction is intimated, and when the case does not require it? Is it reasonable to conclude, that, when a person *receives* a certain privilege for himself and his heirs, collectively and indefinitely, it has one meaning when it regards himself, and another when it refers to his heirs; where there is no manner of necessity for such an interpretation? Would any one conclude, that because Moses *received* the law for himself and the Israelites, it spoke to *him* one thing, to *them* another? —— Finally; I conclude it must appear to the impartial reader of the preceding pages, that the rite of circumcision, CONSIDERED AS A DIVINE INSTITUTION, was appointed to all the subjects of it, indiscriminately, a SEAL of the *righteousness of faith*; viz. a declarative and *certifying* token that a man, whether Jew or Gentile, is justified by faith, as opposed to merit or worthiness of his own; or *saved by grace*. And I presume, it must further appear highly proper, to term circumcision a *seal* from the very NATURE of the institution; as it most assuredly *exhibited* the grand blessings of the everlasting covenant, and was attended with suitable *obligations**. And moreover,

---

* As to what some have urged from Acts xv. 10. where circumcision is called *a yoke*, and Gal. v. 3. where the circumcised are represented as *debtors to do the whole law*; it is manifest that nothing can be fairly concluded against what has been here advanced; since these passages refer, not to the NATURE and

over, since the ordinance of christian baptism, *exhibits* the same spiritual and principal blessings, with the same infallible certainty, and *obliges* to similar corresponding duties; it follows, that baptism is properly and strictly a *seal* of the christian covenant, or the exceeding great and precious promises of the gospel, to every person, indiscriminately, to whom it is duly administered, and may be so denominated *from its very* NATURE.

§ 36. FROM what has been said respecting the *nature* of baptism and of circumcision, and the propriety of calling them *seals of the covenant of grace*; it follows, that there is an equal propriety in calling the *Lord's supper* a SEAL; as it is a divine institution in the church, most assuredly *exhibiting* the great blessings of the covenant, and *obliging* the subjects to answerable returns of gratitude and obedience.

§ 37. (3.) ANOTHER general conclusion from the nature and design of baptism is, That the actual unworthiness of minister or subject has no invalidating influence on the blessings and obligations represented in the ordinance. For if baptism be a *seal*, and does really represent the aforementioned particulars, *as a divinely instituted ordinance*, neither the holiness nor the sinfulness

and genuine design of circumcision, but to the ABUSE and perversion of it by legalists. Paul himself circumcised Timothy; but did this champion for sovereign grace, and gospel liberty, put on his neck a yoke, which, in its proper nature, use and tendency, subjected him to legal bondage? Surely not.

Ch. 2. *Defign of Baptifm.* 183

nefs of the *minifter* can alter its nature and defign; for to fuppofe it a feal to a proper fubject when adminiftered by a *good* man, but not fo if by a *bad* man; is to reft the validity of a divine ordinance on a bafis totally unworthy of God. It would alfo render the *baptized* liable to conftant doubt and fufpenfe, nay, abfolute uncertainty, whether he has received the feal of God's covenant or not, in proportion as the moral ftate of the adminiftrator was not certainly known; which inconvenience would be a fource of perpetual confufion in the church; and therefore the fuppofition is inadmiffible for the cleareft and ftrongeft reafons. Again: to fuppofe that baptifm, duly adminiftered, is a feal only to the *true believer* and not to *other* baptized perfons as well, is attended with the fame inconvenience. For if baptifm be valid and a feal to none but *true believers*, none but fuch can infer, that any benefits are exhibited to *them* in particular *as baptized*, or that any confequent and anfwerable *obligations* are thereby incurred; and it alfo follows, that altho' the fubject be a *true believer*, yet if he do not *know* it, or have not a *certainty* that he is fo; he muft be proportionably at a lofs whether the ordinance be or be not to him a mere nullity. For, on the fuppofition, it is not the *truth* but the *affurance* of faith, can enable him to draw the inference, that he is in confequence of his baptifm under any additional obligations of duty. But how abfurd to fay, that none are thus *obliged* except
they

they are *aſſured* of the truth and reality of their faith !

§ 38. (4.) From what has been ſaid we may draw another corrollary, viz. That for any perſon to deſire *rebaptization* (I mean, on ſuppoſition of agreement about the mode) from a pretence that he was not properly qualified for his former baptiſm, or cannot recollect it, or was not active and voluntary in it ; is virtually to deny that goſpel bleſſings are at all exhibited therein *to him*, and that his baptiſm did lay him under any obligations of duty reſulting from this inſtitution, *becauſe* he was not *then* duly qualified. But I think it has been demonſtrated, that conſent is no neceſſary prerequiſite of future obligation — that an adminiſtrator of baptiſm has a diſcretionary power of determining who is a qualified ſubject and who not — that no unworthineſs in miniſter or ſubject renders the baptiſmal act a nullity ; — for a perſon, therefore, who has been baptized before properly, as to the *manner*, by a goſpel miniſter, under the aforeſaid pretence of non-conſent, &c. to be *rebaptized*, or to *deſire* it, is wrong, unreaſonable and unſcriptural. This being the caſe, is not a deſire in any to *make void* the firſt, that they may *ſubmit* upon *conviction* to another baptiſm, which they apprehend requires them to make an open teſtimony of their allegiance to Chriſt ; too much like the ſubject of a ſtate, who deſires to *rebel* againſt his

his sovereign, by a temporary withdrawing of his allegiance, tho' introduced into his kingdom when an infant — that he might have the pleasure of *submitting upon conviction* to the legal and rightful authority of his sovereign? For, if baptism *does* lay every person, however unworthy, that has been baptized by a christian teacher, under the obligation appertaining to that ordinance; to renounce, *that* baptism, is to renounce *its* obligation; and consequently to rebel: and this *rebellion* is for the specious, but spurious, reason of personally, openly and fully acknowledging *future allegiance!* Again: Is not this desire of *rebaptization* too much like that of a person who enjoys the privileges, and even *seals* of friendship, on another's part; but who has a mind to introduce a *quarrel*, by declaring that he has been hitherto under no *obligation* to his friend on account of any *former* seal of his friendly disposition and conduct, to the intent — that he may, after the quarrel was made up, take occasion to *profess* his friendship to his benefactor!

I WOULD here remark, that it is pretty evident from the natural dictates of conscience, that one who rejects christianity after he has been baptized *in due form* in his infant state, and brought up in a christian family, is in a more *wretched condition* than an infidel who has not been *so devoted* to God. Nor is this a begging of the question, but an appeal to the common notices and impartial practical conclusions of
mankind

mankind. Let but an intelligent apostate reflect, that IF what is represented in baptism be *true*, however unfit he was to comprehend and receive it; whether or not his *guilt*, in renouncing christianity, would be the *greater* on account of his having been recognized by baptism a subject of Christ's kingdom? I verily believe there is no sensible person of that description, but must conclude, from an attentive regard to the nature and design of the ordinance, that he incurs *additional* blame, (supposing christianity to be *true*), in consequence of his infant baptism. This then argues, on the supposition, a *benefit* received, and *obligation* incurred; for otherwise there could be no ground of blame. If a gospel minister, who has a *discretionary* commission relative to the fitness and qualification of an admissible subject, *judge* (supposing, for argument sake, he were under some mistake as to his determination of fitness) that an *infant*, in some cases, may be baptized according to the nature and design of the ordinance, and the institutor's intention; must this *act* of a discretionary commission, and, I will boldly assert, an act consistent with the strictest sincerity of determination, regarding the glory of God, the will of the Redeemer, and the good of the subject, — must this act be deemed a mere nullity? When the baptized afterwards reflects upon the fact, must he conclude, that because it was done without his consent, therefore he is not *obliged* by it as true baptism? For an answer to this question, I appeal, not

to

to the paſſions, but to the rational powers, and deliberate impartial judgment, of thouſands who love their Lord and his authority more than their own lives; and doubt not that their reply is, WE ARE UNDER OBLIGATIONS, even all thoſe which reſult from the ordinance, as a divine inſtitution. When I expreſs my own ſentiments on this head, thoſe of my brethren will be echoed; and they are theſe,— I look upon my baptiſm as exhibiting to me inceſſantly the forementioned bleſſings, and find my conſcience conſtrained to anſwerable obligations of love, gratitude and obedience, and all the particulars abovementioned. I have a rational certainty of the fact, and I am *certain* (pardon the expreſſion) that the action of a profeſſional miniſter pouring water upon me, when an infant, in the name of the Father, &c. does really and *truly* oblige my conſcience according to our Lord's intention in chriſtian baptiſm. Nor can I conceive of baptiſm anſwering the ends of exhibiting and obliging *more truly and powerfully* if adminiſtered this very day, than in earlieſt infancy; of its having any better moral tendency, or being better calculated to ſtrengthen faith or adminiſter comfort *. For if I cordially

* " Sacraments were never intended by God to exert their virtue only *in*, or *during* the adminiſtration For then it would follow, that the baptiſm once received, at whatever age, is no further to be improved by the party receiving it; and ſo, either baptiſm muſt be altogether a barren ſacrament all our lives, but only during the little time of its adminiſtration: or elſe to *renew the* BENEFIT thereof, we muſt often *renew the adminiſtration* itſelf." Dr. FORD's Practical uſe of Infant Baptiſm. Dial. ii. p. 10.

dially and morally approve of this tranfaction, of which I was confeffedly a *capable* fubject, performed thirty or forty years ago, and on fuppofition that it is to be done but once in my life time, I am at a lofs to conceive, why it may not anfwer every valuable purpofe in reflecting upon and approving the fact, as if done this day. If it be a *fact* that I was *baptized into Chrift*, in the fenfe before explained, as I am perfwaded it is, the obligation to *put on Chrift* is inceffant and perpetual, and not at all weakened but rather *ftrengthened* by the diftance of time.

§ 39. (5.) THOSE, whether ancients or moderns, who fuppofe a *real communication* of fpiritual bleffings *conftantly attendant* on the ordinance of baptifm, are under a miftake, if a juft account of its nature and defign has been given in the preceding pages. For there we find, that what the inftitution does *infallibly*, is to *exhibit* bleffings, and *oblige* to duties; but as to any moral and fpiritual favour *communicated* by it, this we fhould refer, not to any virtue in the duty, or any *certain connection* between this and any fuppofed favour, but to the *fovereign pleafure* of the God of means. Much lefs have we ground to infer that baptifm is the true chriftian *regeneration*, or that a certain *immortalizing fpirit* is imparted with it, as fome have whimfically affirmed.

§ 40. (6.) FROM an attentive and impartial furvey of the nature and defign of baptifm, deduced from all the paffages of the New Teftament

ment relating to it, we may again infer, That to make the death, burial, and refurrection of Chrift the *only* or even the *principal* FACTS reprefented in the ordinance, is partial and unjuft. Mr. B's third chapter is entitled, " The DESIGN of Baptifm; Or the Facts and Bleffings reprefented by it, both in regard to our Lord, and his Difciples." And under this title he mufters together no lefs than *fifty fix* pœdobaptift writers; who, having made fome *conceffions* refpecting the propriety and expreffivenefs of immerfion to reprefent the facts of Chrift's *death, burial* and *refurrection*, he imagines greatly affift his caufe. It appears that the chief reafon of thefe conceffions was their fuppofing the apoftle, Rom. vi. 3 — 6, and Col. ii. 11 — 13. alluded to the mode of *dipping* the fubject when baptized. But is there any *neceffity* for fuch a fuppofed allufion? or is that the moft *natural* and *fignificant* import of thefe texts? I think not; but am of opinion with Mr. HENRY's Continuator (and more than *fifty fix* others that might be collected, were the controverfy to be decided by *numbers*, as certainly it is not) that the allufion is not to any *mode* of baptifm whatever, but to a *fpiritual difpofition* to which baptifm as a divine inftitution, *obliges* the fubject. " Why this burying in baptifm fhould *fo much as allude* to any cuftom of dipping under water in bap*t*ifm, any more than our *baptifmal crucifixion* and death fhould have any fuch reference, I confefs, I cannot fee. It is plain, that it is not the *fign*, but the *thing fig-*
nified

nified in baptism, that the apostle here calls being buried with Christ; and the expression of *burying* alludes to *Christ's* burial."—— And again, " We are both buried, and risen with him; and both are signified by our baptism; not that there is any thing in the *sign* or ceremony of baptism, which represents this burying and rising, any more than the crucifixion of Christ is represented by any *visible resemblance* in the Lord's supper ‖." In addition to this, and what was said before on these passages (§ 18, 19, of this chapter) I would propose it to any impartial person, acquainted with the nature of the mystical union between Christ and his church, of which Paul often speaks, whether it is not a strict and weighty truth, — that every christian, tho' UNBAPTIZED, is *dead, buried* and *risen* with Christ? and, as baptism is an *initiatory* ordinance, representing these things *in common* with various *other* momentous facts of a *quite different* nature, whether it is not *most natural* to conclude, that the Apostle in these places urges a *particular branch* of duty, of being *conformed to Christ's death* &c. from the GENERAL NATURE of the exhibitory rite, however administered, and not that he should press them to the same duty from the supposed *manner* of administration? And is not the *former* a topic far more noble and powerful than the *latter*, to answer the apostle's grand design?

§ 41. BUT, it may be objected, " Supposing the

‖ HENRY's Commentary on the Rom. vi. 4 and Col. ii. 12.

any *correspondency* between the sign and the things that are signified by it; immersion *must* be the mode of administration†." Here is a bold conclusion drawn from premises couched under three hypothetical propositions; the *second*, I presume, is sufficiently enervated already; to the *first* and the *third* I shall make the following replies. And,

1. I AFFIRM there does not appear, from any thing said in the New Testament or any thing urged by Mr. B. that the *death, burial,* and *resurrection* of Christ are the PRINCIPAL facts designed to be represented in baptism. For, if no passages of scripture are adduced, nor any consideration urged by our author to support his conclusion, except the two places above mentioned;—and if the direct meaning of these passages amount to no more than this, viz. That as baptism exhibits the blessing of the church's union to Christ and communion with him *indefinitely*; so it lays the baptized under obligations of *conformity* to him as the surety; and hence his *incarnation,* his *obedience,* his *sufferings*—when he was devoted to the curse as the sacred victim, and (dreadful *baptism!* Luke xii. 50. Mark x. 38.) when the cup of divine justice was *poured out* § on him without mixture ⸺ his *crucifixion*,

† p. 71.

§ The almost constant scriptural mode of expressing God's infliction of punishment when the metaphor is taken from water. See Psa. lxix. 24. lxxix. 6. Jer. vi. 11. x. 25. xiv. 16. Ezek. vii. 8. xiv. 19. xx. 8, 13, 21. xxi. 31. xxx. 15. Hos. v. 10. Zeph. iii. 8. 2 Chron. xii. 7. xxxiv. 21, 25. Jer. vii. 20. xlii. 18. xl v. 6. Ez. xxii. 22, 31. xxxi. 18. Rev. xiv. 10. and xvi. throughout, &c. &c.

the apostle does urge the *special* duty of the mortification of sin, from the consideration of the *general nature* of baptism as *binding* the subject to *universal* duty, and consequently *that* very important one; and supposing that the apostle PRINCIPALLY alludes to this *general obligation* of duty resulting from the *nature* of the ordinance; does it not follow that the motive would be yet *stronger* if the mode was immersion?

I ANSWER, with Mr. B. that "we have no more authority to *invent* a signification for any rite of holy worship, than we have to *appoint* the rite itself‖." And if the texts in question do not *require* this additional allusion, it must be either *invented* to serve an hypothesis, or it must be sought in some *other* part of holy writ. There is no alternative, and therefore let our opponents take which they please, their fond conclusion is not *proved* from these premises. That the sacred passages referred to, do not *require* an allusion to the *mode* of baptizing, has been shewn, and whether or not immersion appears to be the most proper mode from *other* considerations, is not to the present argument, therefore to *suppose* an additional force and propriety in them on that account, is no better than begging the question.

§ 42. LET us hear Mr. B. "Now, if such [to represent the death, burial and resurrection of Christ,] be the *chief design* of the ordinance; if *these passages* of holy writ [Rom. vi. 4. Col. ii. 12.] be pertinently applied; and if there be any

‖ p. 70.

crucifixion, when his body was bathed in its own blood, the circumstance which above all others St. Paul preached and gloried in — his dying for sin — his burial for three days and three nights — his victorious resurrection and triumphant ascension to heaven, —— are ALL illustrious FACTS, by which the christian, in virtue of the said union, is bound to all suitable conformity; —— if this, I say, be the apostle's meaning, as before shewn; it is plain Mr. B's conclusion is ill founded. For, maturely reflect, reader, do not christians *suffer* with Christ? are they not *crucified* with Christ? do not they *live*, and *sit* and *reign* with him in heavenly places? and are not these privileges in virtue of *union*? does not baptism represent that union *in general*? If so, why *confined* to these *three particulars* to the exclusion of others? " Know ye not, as if the apostle had said, that so many of us as were baptized *into Jesus Christ*, were baptized into him *at large*, (see Gal. iii. 27.) and *of course* into his death, that as he died *for* sin, so should we die *to* sin; as he buried our sin with his mortality, we should concur with his design by unremitted efforts to keep under subjection the body of sin; and as he rose to triumph over sin, we should not continue its deluded captives, but act as becomes a *royal priesthood, an holy nation, a peculiar people* ||." Was not *Christ crucified* the *most impor-*

K *tant*

1 Pet. ii. 9.

tant theme of Paul's apostolic teaching? (1 Cor. ii. 2.) And, God forbid, says he, that I should glory save in the *cross* of our Lord Jesus Christ. I am *crucified with* Christ; nevertheless I live.— Now this union being *general*, when any one branch of it is selected, it is according to the moral purpose in view. For it is evident, from the consideration of the *general and universal nature* of union and communion between the church and the divine Sponsor, represented in baptism, that had the circumstance of *crucifixion* answered the apostle's *moral design* better, he might have properly said, " being *crucified* with him in baptism."

Now who sees not, that the restrictive notion of baptism *principally* representing the death, burial and resurrection of Christ, is inadmissible, being repugnant to an equitable axiom of interpretation, (§ 9. ax. 3.) That no meaning of a text, which is contrary to another passage *more evident than itself*, can be the true one. Nothing can be plainer than this, that the apostle Paul, repeatedly, considers baptism as representative of union and communion with Christ and his people *indefinitely*; (1 Cor. xii. 13. Gal. iii. 27. &c.) but this Mr. B's limiting hypothesis virtually denies. For it is the same as to say, *that a part is greater than the whole:* that a few particulars, (however important) are *more principal* than the whole aggregate of the Redeemer's vicarious substitution.

Upon the whole, then, it appears, that to

confine

confine the fignification of baptifm to this part of the furety's meritorious work, is contrary to the fcriptural idea of baptifm reprefenting union to Chrift at large in *all thofe refpects* in which he is the finner's fubftitute. Nor is it eafy to fay, how *any mode* of miniftration whatever is adapted to exprefs this more than another. From whence I infer, that neither the death, burial, refurrection of Chrift, nor any other *corporal ftate* thro' which he paffed, were to be *at all* reprefented by the ordinance. For the church has union and communion with him in *all the ftates* of his furetyfhip, which were fo various as not to be *capable* of an external reprefentation in one *fingle act* as baptifm is. Which leads to another conclufion, that may ferve as a fufficient reply to Mr. B's remaining argument, which implies, that " if there be any *correfpondency* between the fign and the things fignified, *immerfion muft* be the mode of adminiftration," and that is,

2. From the cleareft teftimonies of fcripture, and from Mr. B's own maxim, it follows, That *if any facts at all*, of an *external* denomination, are reprefented in the mode of adminiftration, we are referred, above all others, to the VISIBLE DESCENT of the Holy Spirit. Now this, as it is exprefsly called, without controverfy, a BAPTISM, is a more certain clue to find out and afcertain the mode, moftly ufed, than any other. I fay *moftly ufed*; for I own it does not appear to me likely that one uniform

mode prevailed even in the apoſtolic age. When, therefore, I object to the baptiſt ſenſe of Rom. vi. 4. &c. what I would be underſtood to mean is — theſe paſſages do not amount to a *proof*, either that our Lord's death, burial and reſurrection are the *principal facts*, ſignified by baptiſm, or, that the ordinance was *deſigned* viſibly to repreſent thoſe facts — that, ſo far from countenancing the *eſſentiallity* of dipping, they are *no evidence at all* of any alluſion to ſuch a mode. For further confirmation of which poſition, I refer the reader to that part of our ſubject which treats profeſſedly of the *mode*.

But why ſhould Mr. B. exert himſelf ſo much in an attempt to eſtabliſh, from *two* controverted paſſages, that the death, burial and reſurrection of Chriſt are the principal facts alluded to and repreſented, while there are *many more* texts, and thoſe *uncontroverted*, which repreſent the *deſcent and influences* of the Holy Ghoſt to be the things ſignified? Nay, I ſcruple not to aſſert it, there is *no object whatever* in all the New Teſtament, *ſo frequently* and *ſo explicitly* ſignified by baptiſm, as theſe divine influences, ſee Mat. iii. 11. Mark i. 8—10. Luke iii. 16, 21, 22. John i. 33. Acts i. 5. ii. 38, 39. viii. 12—17. v. 47. xi. 15, 16. &c. &c. Yet theſe things he *prudently* overlooks. The reaſon is at hand; *plunging* is practiſed by himſelf and his conſtituents, and there is a greater reſemblance between that practice and a burial, than between the
ſaid

Ch. 2.   Design of Baptism.   197

said plunging and the active communication and application of divine influences to the soul.

BESIDES, Mr. B.'s maxim may be thus retorted; if in baptism there is an *expressive emblem* of the descending influences of the Spirit, *pouring must* be the mode of administration, for *that* is the scriptural term most commonly and properly used for the communication of divine influences.

To conclude, when we impartially consider these things, and withal, that the Gospel dispensation is in the strictest sense THE MINISTRATION OF THE SPIRIT ||, it appears *most probable*, that the *various influences* of that divine Agent are *principally* represented in baptism. I own there appears to me great beauty in this scriptural view of the ordinance, especially when considered in connection with the other standing institution of the gospel. The *initiatory* rite, which is not to be reiterated, represents the *promised influences* of the spirit of grace; and by *exhibiting* these blessings as about to be imparted repeatedly and successively, *obliges* the subject to unremitted and earnest applications for them. While the *confirming* ordinance, which is to be repeated, represents the *death of the Lord* §, and by *exhibiting* this important transaction as a past event, *obliges* the subject to celebrate it eucharistically, or in thankful remembrance of the great sacrifice. The *former* teaches what the subject may *expect*, the *latter* to what he is *beholden*.

K 3   CHAP.

|| 2 Cor. iii. 8, &c.   § 1 Cor. xi. 26.

C H A P. III.

Of the proper Subjects of baptism; particularly, whether it is the WILL OF CHRIST that the infants of believing parents should be baptized?

§ 1. *Of the proper point in debate.* § 2. *How we may know what is the will of Christ in this matter.* § 3. *Pretended scriptural evidence against Pœdobaptism, and the supposed silence of the New Testament about it.* § 4. *All these Antipædobaptist objections confronted with two propositions.* § 5. (I.) *Baptism is* APPLICABLE *to infants; as appears* (1) *From the nature and design of the ordinance.* § 6 — 9. (2) *From the scriptural account of necessary qualifications.* § 10. (3.) *From the concessions and principles of our opponents.* § 11. (II.) *It is the* WILL OF CHRIST *our children should be baptized, as appears,* § 12 — 17. (1.) *From the dictates of the law of nature, which are his will, when not contravened by positive authority, to* BENEFIT *our children.* § 18 —— 28. (2.) *From God's constant approbation of this principle, in all preceding dispensations.* § 29 — 35. (3.) *From the language of prophecy respecting children in gospel times.* § 36 —— 54. (4.) *From New Testament passages, which corroborate the preceding arguments.* § 55. *Corrolaries.*

§ 1.

§ 1. HAVING, in the former chapters, investigated the nature of positive institutions in general, together with the nature and design of baptism in particular; we proceed next to consider, who are the proper subjects of that ordinance? And here it would be impertinent to enlarge on the evidence we have in scripture, that Jews and Heathens upon renouncing their *false* and embracing the *true* religion were baptized; for about this we have no dispute. We do not inquire, whether it be right or not to baptize qualified *adults* who had not been baptized *before*; nor, whether a profession of faith and repentance and a consistent moral character be necessary for *such*; but whether *any infants* are to be baptized? or, to bring the question to a still narrower compass, "Whe-
" ther it is the WILL OF CHRIST that *believing*
" *parents*, should endeavour to have their children
" *baptized*; and, virtually, being the other's
" correlate, whether it is the WILL OF CHRIST
" that *his ministers* should comply with their
" request in baptizing them?" The Antipædobaptists adopt the *negative*; it is my business to make good the *affirmative*. Nor am I apprehensive that our opponents themselves will object to this statement of the controversy, but will allow, that if what is proposed be *fairly demonstrated*, our cause as Pædobaptists is good, and our practice commendable.

§ 2. THIS being the matter in debate, our

next inquiry muſt be reſpecting the *allowable medium* of determining the queſtion. I doubt not but it will be allowed, to ſave proving what is ſo evident, that whatever ſhall appear to be the will of GOD, is equally the will of CHRIST, and *vice verſa*. When I ſpeak of Chriſt's WILL, I mean that will, *upon the whole*, as diſcoverable by us. This *will* being to us the *Supreme Law*, it is evident that wherever it appears, upon the whole, to preponderate, we are under proportionable obligation of concurring with that preponderation. —— Again, no one, who deſerves to be reaſoned with, will deny, that it is *perfectly indifferent* by *what means* this is aſcertained, provided *it be* but aſcertained; for if all *poſſible mediums* of proof be not allowed, then Chriſt's will, *upon the whole*, or all things conſidered, is not the deciding ſtandard, which is abſurd. Beſide, this rule is conſiſtent with our opponents' own principles; for, when they appeal on every turn to baptiſm as a poſitive inſtitution, they can mean nothing elſe than that it is Chriſt's will, *all things conſidered*, we ſhall *not* baptize our infant children.

THE *poſitive evidence* of ſcripture, in reference to baptiſm, or any other doctrine, privilege, or duty, holds the ſame rank in theology, as *experimented evidence* does in reference to any hypotheſis in philoſophy. As, in the latter caſe, there is no diſputing in favour of a ſyſtem *againſt facts*, phenomena and experiments; ſo, in the former caſe, no reaſoning can be valid in oppoſition

sition to *positive evidence*, or exprefs difcernible authority. This authority muft be *difcernible*, elfe it is no authority at all, for then *nothing* would remain to influence our determination. Nor can it be *positive*, but in proportion as it is exprefs and unequivocal. For, in the prefent cafe, *positive authority* is that, the reafon of which we do not, and cannot *otherwife* find out. Therefore, that pofitive evidence, for or againft, which, if afcertained, muft needs preclude all further inveftigation, fhould *firft* be attended to. And if on examination no fuch evidence appear, the inquiry muft be transferred to another *medium*, the neareft, in the fcale of importance, to which it is applicable. Let any one propofe a more juft and fatisfactory mode of inveftigating the fubject, *(et erit mihi magnus Apollo)* I fhall venerate his abilities, and will fincerely thank him for the difcovery.

§ 3. The firft inquiry to be made being concerning the *pofitive evidence* of fcripture, I fhould produce all thofe paffages out of the New Teftament which relate to the fubject, were not this done already; but as it is done, the reader is referred to the beginning of the laft chapter, to prevent needlefs repetition. Now fince it would be endlefs, as well as unneceffary, for me to examine every facred text produced againft us, or which may be fo produced, — and fince that would be impofing on myfelf to prove a negative, — it only remains that I fhould bring to the teft thofe which our opponents lay the greateft greateſt ſtreſs upon; and this ſtep is the more reaſonable, inaſmuch as it is to be preſumed their own intereſt in the debate would prompt them to produce the ſtrongeſt. And here I muſt beg of my reader he will give me credit when I ſay, that I ſhall endeavour all along to place the Antipœdobaptiſt objections in what appear to me the ſtrongeſt light, and dwell chiefly on thoſe points which are of the moſt radical importance in the controverſy.

WHEN we conſider the dictates of nature in parental feelings; the verdict of reaſon in favour of privileges; the relation children bore to the inſtitutions of ALL preceding diſpenſations; and eſpecially the language of prophecy in reference to the children of the goſpel church; — it may reaſonably be preſumed, from their inflexible oppoſition, our opponents have ſomething very expreſs to urge out of the *New Teſtament* to counteract ſo ſtrong a *probability* in our favour. And, ſurely, *expreſs* they muſt be, to reſiſt the united forces of ſuch conſiderations. And yet, ſtrange to think! I do not find that any of the Antipœdobaptiſts pretend to adduce ONE SINGLE TEXT as an expreſs and poſitive teſtimony for this purpoſe. Therefore, the mercenary forces they place in front muſt be ſuch as theſe. "There is no *expreſs precept*, or *prece-*
" *dent*, in the New Teſtament for pœdobaptiſm.
" —That ſuch paſſages are our *only* rule of doctrine
" and worſhip. — That the ſcripture *forbids* what
" it does *not mention*.—That in religious matters
" it

" it is not only finful to go *contra flatutum*, but
" to go *fupra flatutum.*" — To thefe they add,
" that to imagine the firft pofitive rite of religious
" worfhip in the chriftian church, is left in fo vague
" a ftate as Pœdobaptifm fuppofes, is not only
" contrary to the *analogy* of divine proceedings
" in fimilar cafes, but renders it morally im-
" poffible for the *bulk* of chriftians to difcern
" the *real* grounds on which the ordinance is
" adminiftered. — We have both exprefs *com-*
" *mands* and exprefs *examples* for baptizing fuch
" as *profefs faith* in Jefus Chrift; but for *none*
" *elfe.* — That the *qualifications* required of thofe
" for whom our Lord intended the ordinance,
" do *not agree* to an infantile ftate. — That *faith*
" and *repentance* are pre-required in baptifm. —
" Hence Philip faid, *If thou believeft with all*
" *thy heart, thou mayeft*, Acts viii. 37. The com-
" mand of Peter was, *Repent and be baptized,*
" Acts ii. 38. — That the facraments are not
" *converting* but *confirming* ordinances.—The fol-
" lowing fcriptures are alfo urged. Mark xvi. 16.
" *He that believeth and is baptized.* Acts ii. 41.
" *Then they that gladly received his word were*
" *baptized.* 1 Pet. iii. 21. *The like figure whereunto,*
" *even baptifm, doth alfo now fave us (not the put-*
" *ting away the filth of the flefh, but the anfwer of*
" *a good confcience towards God) by the refurrec-*
" *tion of Jefus Chrift.* Again, That the fcrip-
" tures *confine* its adminiftration to fuch as *pro-*
" *fefs faith* in the Son of God. — That our
" practice reftrains it almoft *intirely* to fuch as lie
" under

"under a natural incapacity of profeſſing repen-
"tance and faith. — That poſitive laws imply
"their negative; — that our Lord having given
"a commiſſion to baptize thoſe that are *taught*,
"without ſaying any thing elſewhere, by way
"of precept or of example, concerning ſuch as
"are *not* inſtructed being included in that com-
"miſſion; there was no neceſſity for him to
"*prohibit* the baptizing of thoſe who are *not*
"taught: much leſs the baptizing of infants,
"that *cannot* be taught, in order to render the
"baptiſm of them unlawful. — That ſince office,
"or duty, means an action conformable to
"*law*, it is plain that duty cannot be conceived
"without a law; that he does not perform
"a duty, when the *law*, or the *reaſon* of the
"law ceaſes †." —— Theſe, I believe, are Mr.
B.'s *moſt capital* objections, which are *excerpta*
taken out of his eighth chapter, entitled, *No
expreſs precept, or precedent, in the New Teſtament, for Pædobaptiſm.* But numerous as they
are, their whole collective force from van to
rear, conſiſts in theſe two things,

1. That ſuch are the *qualifications* for baptiſm, required in ſcripture, that children are
incapable of it.

2. That, ſuppoſing they were qualified, ſince
infants are not *expreſsly* and uncontrovertibly
mentioned in connection with baptiſm, it is *not
the*

† Pædob. Exam. p. 168, 174, 176, 179, 181, 183, 184, 185, 187, 188, 190.

the *will of Chrift* they fhould be baptized; becaufe in a pofitive inftitution, nothing fhort of an *exprefs precept* or *plain example* can indicate his will.

§ 4. ON the contrary; to confront, to break, and to rout this boafted fophiftical phalanx, I fhall fhew,

I. THAT the ordinance of baptifm *is applicable* to infants, not lefs than to adults : or, in other words, that infants are poffeffed, according to fcripture, of all *neceffary qualifications* for baptifm, and therefore *are capable* of it.

II. THAT there is fufficient *pofitive evidence* it is the WILL OF CHRIST baptized believing parents fhould endeavour to get their children baptized. Let us begin with the former.

§ 5. (I.) THAT the ordinance of baptifm is applicable to infants, as well as adults, appears hence,

(1.) THAT there is nothing in the *nature* and *defign* of it, but is equally applicable to an infant as to its parent. For,

1. WHAT is its *nature?* It is a *feal*. This, I flatter myfelf, has been demonftrated in the foregoing chapter; and am bold to fay, is capable of manifold demonftration. But *what* does it feal? Not that the fubject, *rightly baptized*, as fome have affirmed, is affured thereby that he is juftified and faved : which muft imply, if any thing, that he who is *notfo affured* was *not rightly* baptized; than which nothing need be

be more abfurd. For, then, numbers baptized by the apoftles themfelves were not *rightly* baptized. And yet, being a feal, it muft affure the rightly baptized fubject of fomething. But what is this fomething? Is it that the fubject is *fincere*, that he HAS *a good confcience*, is *actually poffeffed* of certain perfonal endowments, or *certainly entitled* to new covenant bleffings? This is impoffible, on any other hypothefis than the Popifh figment of facraments being effectual to the fubject, *ex opere operato*. What it *affures*, therefore, is not any thing *fubjectively* to the baptized, whereby he is diftinguifhed from others; but as the only alternative, the *fealing* muft imply an *objective certainty* afforded him by the Inftitutor. Now,

2. WHAT is the *defign* of this objective fealing? and what are the *truths* thus certified? (I fay *truths*, for nothing which is not *true* does the God of truth certify.) The anfwer is plain — *That he will be* A GOD *to all the fealed*. Or, more fully, this is the record, " That God gives i. e. *exhibits* to fuch eternal life, thro' the mediation of his Son, and the influences of his fpirit." But when I fay, that God affures the baptized in and by the *fact* of the ordinance, he will be *a God* to him, I do not intend the erroneous, but too common notion, that a declaration or promife of his being A GOD to any, in the œconomical revelation of mercy, implies a *certain connection* between the *promifee* and his future (much lefs his prefent) *poffeffion* of the

Chief

Chief Good. For such declarations and promises cannot, I think, be conceived of, when addressed to man, under any other notion than that of a *proposal* from a first mover of covenant terms; for the *free nature* of man requires that he should be addressed in this way. But how man *answers* the divine requisitions, or how he *comes by* a nature and disposition which, as an echo, makes a suitable reply to such a proposal, belongs intirely to *another dispensation*, namely, that of SOVEREIGN EFFICACIOUS GRACE; the Holy Spirit therein executing the decree of election. It is evident, therefore, that the Lord may be properly said to be *the God* (or the *chief good*) of a person or people, in divine ordinances, independent of any adstipulation from the creature. For he was, in this sense, *the God* of the infant Jews, and uncircumcised in heart, no less than Abraham himself. But,

3. WHO sees not that if it be a *truth* he may be *a God* to any, infants or adults, independent on their gracious disposition, the same truth may be consistently *sealed* and certified to them. This I insist *was* done to all, adults or infants, rightly circumcised; and this *is* done to all, adults or infants, rightly baptized. However some have made an improper use of the topick of circumcision in the baptismal controversy, one would think there is *one thing* at least that may be inferred from it —that the seal of God's covenant to man, be that seal and that covenant what they may, is APPLICABLE to an infant as well as to its parent. If, indeed, God's requisitions *could not*
be

be anfwered in *any other way*, than by the *believing confent* of the finner, there would be fome force in the objection of infants' incapacity and incapability of being the fubjects of God's covenant feal. But this is not the cafe. For tho' infants are finners, and have no believing confent; yet fome infants, our opponents being judges, anfwer God's requifitions, or, in other words, are juftified. The truth is, the infant of a day, and the convert of three-fcore years, are accepted on the *fame account*, tho' attended with different circumftances. Union with the Saviour, formed by a fovereign act of grace, anfwers all demands. All other confiderations are merely circumftantial. If, then, infants are capable of anfwering the *grand condition* of acceptance, nay *equally* fo with adults, it is evident that they are capable of being under obligations, and ftill *more capable* of baptifm, the feal of the objective certainty of exhibited bleffings.

§ 6. (2.) THAT infants are *capable fubjects* appears, alfo, from the fcriptural account of *neceffary qualifications* for baptifm. Infants are capable. not only of what is *equivalent* to faith, repentance, the anfwer of a good confcience, a profeffion of Chrift, &c. and a *fubjective fuitablenefs* for the inftitution; but alfo of *that very thing*, from which thefe *qualities* derive all their value.

1. INFANTS are capable of what is *equivalent* to faith, &c. in the moft important concerns, fuch as acceptance with God, juftification to life,

life, &c. and where these very things are pronounced *as necessary* as in the case of baptism. For instance, He that *believeth* shall be *saved*; but he that *believeth not* shall be *damned*. Without *faith* it is impossible to *please God*. Except ye *repent*, ye shall all likewise *perish*. He that *believeth not* God, hath made him a *liar*. With the heart man *believeth* unto *righteousness*, and with the mouth *confession* is made unto *salvation*. Now, what can be more evident than that these, and innumerable similar passages, are *not intended* to exclude from the benefits of redemption, all *infants*, but UNBELIEVERS, IMPENITENT sinners, DISPLEASERS of God, and DISOWNERS of Christ. This conclusion does not, indeed, appear from the passages themselves, for they are as express and peremptory as can be, in *restricting* the qualifications for SALVATION, to FAITH, REPENTANCE, &c. yet, when we consider infants' capacity for the *former*, as moral and immortal beings, and their incapacity for the *latter*, (however peremptorily the conditions and qualifications are specified;) and when we consider the favourable regard shewn them, in every dispensation, by the Great Father of all; we are fairly led to conclude, that such passages of holy writ do not affect infants, as *non*-believers, *non*-penitents, *non*-pleasers, or *non*-professors. For the positive virtues and graces which divines call conditions of salvation, *sine qua non*, are opposed, not to the *mere absence* of those qualities in their activity and exercise, but to their *active opposites*, unbelief,

unbelief, impenitence, &c. which can take place only in adults.

From the premises, then, it is clear, that if infants are *capable* of those things which are *equivalent* to faith and repentance, as qualifications for the *most important* privilege of salvation, they are also capable of what are equivalent to them as qualifications for the *less important* privilege of baptism. For, if the one be denied, so *may* the other; and if the one be granted, so *ought* the other. Infants are capable of a divinely constituted *union* with the infinitely worthy Saviour, not less than adults; and are they incapable of the *symbol* of that union? Infants are capable of the *influences* of the holy Spirit, not less than adults; and are they incapable of the *symbol* of those influences? He that CAN believe it, let him believe it.

§ 7. 2. INFANTS are capable of a *subjective suitableness* for the institution. The nature and design of baptism require, as is plain to common sense, that *ostensible foes*, such as unbelievers, impenitents, and the like, ought not to be treated as *apparent friends*; that those who *evidently* love darkness rather than light, because their deeds are evil, should not be ranked with the *visible* children of light; but does it follow that infants must be classed with the former, and not with the latter? There is a *suitableness* in excluding *open enemies* from an external token of a *supposed fitness* to be subjects of the gospel kingdom. But does it follow that infants ought

to

Ch. 3.   *Subjects of Baptism.*   211

to be alfo excluded? Again, there is a *fuit-ableneſs* in this, that none but believers, penitents and profeſſors ſhould be baptized, *among adults*, becauſe if they are not ſuch, they muſt be poſitively the reverſe; for in *them* there is no alternative; there is no medium between faith and unbelief, between repentance and impenitence. Of *them*, he that is not *for* Chriſt, is *againſt* him. But can the ſame be ſaid of infants? Becauſe they are not *intelligent* and *voluntary* ſubjects, muſt they be treated as foreigners? nay, as rebels? Is there no *medium* between loyal active obedience, and rebellion? And becauſe the infants of any community do not make an active part of the ſtate, does it follow that there is no *ſuitableneſs* in their being ſubjects at all? But if there be a ſuitableneſs in infants being admitted proper ſubjects of a civil kingdom, *much more* is there a ſuitableneſs in their being admitted ſubjects of the goſpel kingdom; the requiſitions of the *latter* having a reſpect to *grace*, which is applicable to both alike, but thoſe of the *former* having a reſpect to *reaſon*, of which infants are incapable.

MOREOVER: it is apparent, that faith and repentance are no diſtinguiſhing characteriſticks of a chriſtian *as ſuch*, but of a chriſtian *as adult*; theſe qualifications are not *eſſential* to chriſtianity, (if we intend thereby ſalvation thro' Chriſt) for this may exiſt without them. Now if the initiating ordinance of chriſtianity has relation to the *eſſence, nature* and *deſign* of chriſtianity, and

not

not merely to a *particular mode* of it, it follows that the ordinance is applicable to infants. To fay, that this initial rite refers not to chriftianity itfelf, but only to a certain mode or circumftance of it, is flatly to contradict its nature and defign. For baptifm exhibits *the whole* of chriftianity, and not merely *a part*; its *effence* and not a mere *circumftance*; as appears from the preceding chapter. It *exhibits* regeneration, fanctification, myftical union, falvation, &c. which are common to infants and adults. Nor does it appear, I believe, that *any thing* is therein exhibited, which is not *equally applicable* to both. Nay, were we, for argument' fake, to allow Mr. B. 's account of what it reprefents, viz. The death, burial, and refurrection of Chrift, and communion with him therein, it ftill follows, that infants are not lefs *capable* of thefe bleffings than believers, penitents and profeffors. They are alfo *capable* of being put under *obligation*, except we adopt one of the moft abfurd pofitions — That we ought not to be grateful, when grown up to manhood, for a benefit received in infancy. Thus we fee, that *fuitablenefs* to the nature and defign of baptifm, belongs to the infant no lefs than his parent.

§ 8. 3. AGAIN: they are capable of *that very thing* from which faith, repentance and profeffion derive all their value. That there is in fcripture a connection formed between *believing* and *baptifm* in *adults*, is clear from particular paffages, as well as the nature and defign of the

the ordinance; but it is not lefs clear that this connection depends on thefe qualities, not as they are *in themfelves*, but only as they are *indicative* of fomething more effential †. Thefe qualities are no further valuable than they are *expreffive* of the perfon's moral and relative *ftate*. For, on our opponents' own principles, a preponderation of evidence *againft* the latter, would abolifh the pretenfions of the former. They will allow, that the moft plaufible *profeffion* of knowledge or faith, is *of itfelf* no fufficient ground for baptizing adults; for if fuch a defect in a candidate's moral character, as demonftrates to the minifter at the time of baptization, the infincerity of his profeffion, and the badnefs of his ftate, be proved againft him, it would certainly difqualify him for the ordinance. It is clear from the nature of the cafe, that the beforementioned qualities, rather than any *other* chriftian virtues, are connected with baptifm, becaufe they are the moft ftriking and decifive *indications* of a real change of ftate, or at leaft fuitablenefs of ftate and difpofition to commence a fubject of the gofpel kingdom. Does an infidel become a *believer*? Does a criminal become a *penitent*? Is the ignorant become *knowing*? Then they give a minifter the beft evidence the cafe can afford, that they are proper fubjects; that is, in a ftate fuited to the nature and defign of the inftitution. Could we fuppofe a perfon poffeffed of the cleareft underftanding

of

† See Mr. BOOTH's Apology for the Baptifts. p. 2.

of chriftian doctrines; making the moft devout and abundant profeffions of fincerity, of the foundnefs of his faith and the genuinenefs of his repentance; the integrity and circumfpection of his conduct for a length of time paft;—but, while the candidate is ftanding ready for the ordinance, and the minifter is going to execute the command of Chrift, inconteftible evidence is produced of his being that very day guilty of a notorious deliberate crime, which he had ftudioufly concealed; what can the minifter do? Muft he forbid water? On what ground? His knowledge, profeffion of faith, repentance, &c. are now fuperfeded on a *moral* account. On the fuppofition, his baptifm was to have taken place *becaufe* of thofe qualifications, but now he is excluded *becaufe he wants* THAT VERY THING of which children are *capable*, viz. a ftate of grace and acceptance. But, if it be faid, that the reafon of his rejection was becaufe his profeffion was not *fincere*, it amounts to the fame thing; for what is the difference between a ftate of *fincerity* and a ftate of *grace*?

§ 9. SHOULD it be ftill urged, that " what is deemed by the Antipædobaptifts as the grand qualification, is a *credible profeffion*; not grace apart, nor profeffion apart, but the *union* of both; of which infants are incapable:" I anfwer,

THIS diftinction, however fpecious, is a mere evafion. For if there be any force in it, it militates alike againft their *falvability*. For we are

Ch. 3.   *Subjects of Baptism.*   215

are *saved* by grace, *thro' faith.* We are *saved* by *hope.* With the mouth *confession* is made to *salvation.* If any man *love not* the Lord Jesus Christ, let him be anathema maranatha. *Repent*—that your sins may be blotted out. Now if this *union* be requisite in *one* case, it must be so in the *other*, since it is required with *equal* explicitness in both. And salvation is connected, not with grace apart, nor profession apart, but with the *union* of grace and the expressions thereof in faith, hope, confession, love to Christ, and repentance. But whatever shews this latter instance to be fallacious is proportionably conclusive against the objection. Suffice it to observe, as before—that in *each* case, the scriptures require these expressions and signs of a gracious state, of those *only* who are capable of their active opposites, or the contrary vices. And they derive their value intirely from the *circumstances* in which they are placed †, and not from any supposed excellency resulting from their union as such.

Besides, that there is no such *union* as the objection supposes, no such indispensible connection between these qualities and baptism, as founded on divine *positive authority*, is apparent hence; that in the New Testament *different qualities* are required of *different persons*, according to the circumstances in which these persons are found. If any are charged with some notorious sins, the exhortation is, *Repent* and be bap-

† See Pædobaptismus Vindicatus, p. 15, &c.

baptized; if any are in a ſtate of inquiry after ſalvation, the qualification is, *believing on the Lord Jeſus Chriſt*; if any heſitate in giving their aſſent to his meſſiahſhip, *believing with the whole heart* is required. In like manner the *confeſſion of ſins, receiving the word with joy, the anſwer of a good conſcience, &c.* are required in different circumſtances. But what renders this argument irrefragable is, that our Lord was a *ſuitable ſubject of the baptiſm of repentance*, tho' *incapable of repentance*. He poſſeſſed, indeed, what was *equivalent* to it, but not the *thing itſelf*. The ſame may be ſaid of *regeneration, &c.* The baptiſm of John required repentance and the confeſſion of their ſins of thoſe only who were in circumſtances *capable* of theſe things, but they were not *eſſential* qualifications; for what was eſſential to the nature and deſign of the inſtitution, Chriſt muſt have poſſeſſed, elſe there was no propriety and ſuitableneſs in his being the ſubject of it.*

As to what is called a *credible profeſſion*, it is plain the epithet *credible* is predicated of profeſſion to ſhew, on the one hand, the inſufficiency

---

* " Neque obſtare debet, quod non *omnia* quæ itidem per
" baptiſmum ſignificari ſolent, in iſtam ætatem [ſcil. infantiam]
" proprie congruant. Nam et *pœnitentia,* quam ſcimus baptiſmo de-
" ſignari, *majorem* certe in iis qui, cum vitam diu impuram
" egiſſent, vitæ totius mutandæ propoſitum teſtabantur, quam
" in aliis, locum habebat; in CHRISTO vero, quem Johannes
" baptizavit, NULLUM; qui, ut TERTULLIANUS loquitur, *nul-*
" *lius pœnitentiæ debitor vinctus eſt.*" POLI Synopſ. in Matth.
xix. 14.

ciency of *mere* profeſſion, and on the other, that the *ſuppoſed poſſeſſion* of the thing profeſſed, gives to profeſſion *the whole* of its value. Thus in reſpect of promiſes and oaths, they are no further valuable, in a moral and religious ſenſe, than they are exact delineations of the reſpective principles from which they are ſuppoſed to proceed. A promiſor or a juror, known to be *falſe* in the matter promiſed or ſworn, is detected. The value of theſe things ariſes from their *credibility*, that is, from the *ſuppoſed connection* between the ſign and the thing thereby ſignified. So far, then, it is clear, that if there be any profeſſion *at all*, that profeſſion ought to be *credible*. But from the conſideration, that no profeſſion is available but what is credible, it does not follow, that *profeſſion* of this or any other kind is *neceſſary*. For the nature of the goſpel kingdom, and of this inſtitution, do not require, any more than the nature of civil government, that infants, becauſe not capable of *profeſſing* allegiance to their reſpective kings, ſhould be conſidered as *no ſubjects*; tho' the nature and deſign of the one and the other require, that where it is ſuitable there ſhould be a profeſſion at all, it ſhould be a *credible* one.

§ 10. (3.) It may be made to appear, from the principles and conceſſions of our opponents, that infants are not *naturally incapable* of baptiſm; but the incapacity they object to is deduced, from the ſuppoſed eſſentiality of faith and profeſſion, as qualifications for the ordinance. For thus Dr. S. writes in reply to Dr. Ad-

DINGTON's enumeration of benefits refulting from infant baptifm: " Now, Sir, IF thefe advantages, which no doubt are very great and important, were the natural and proper effects of the application of baptifm to infants; or IF the ceremony were *appointed* by God to thefe ends; or IF the omiffion of it did at all leffen the obligations of parents to take care of the education of their children, or of children to make all fuitable returns to their parents and to demean themfelves well in life, or of minifters to inftruct and exhort them both to their feveral duties: IF this were the cafe, *I acknowledge it would be both cruel and impious to deny them to children* ||."

HERE it is plain, from the *avowed connection* fubfifting between the confequence and the hypothetical antecedents, that nothing is neceffary to render infants equally CAPABLE of baptifm with adults, but a *divine appointment* of its application to them, or its *ufeful tendency* when applied. And, therefore, no *incapacity* in infants, Dr. S. being judge, can be fairly objected, but what arifes from a begging of the queftion in debate. For, if it fhall appear, that it is the *will of Chrift* believers fhould get their infant offspring baptized; or, if it fhall appear, that there is a preponderation of *folid advantages* in its favour, the pretended incapability urged is totally annihilated.

§ 11. (II.) I AM now to fhew, that it is the WILL OF CHRIST baptized believing parents fhould endeavour to get their children baptized. When I exprefs myfelf thus, I would not be underftood

|| p. 291.

Ch. 3.   *Subjects of Baptism.*   219

stood to mean, that those parents who are *not baptized*, and do *not believe*, are under *no obligation* with respect to their own baptism and that of their children; but our controversy with the Antipædobaptists does not require a greater universality than is expressed in the proposition. It must be left to the candid reader to determine, whether the preceding pages evince the *capability* of infants to answer the nature and design of the institution. But our opponents contend, " That, supposing they were capable and qua-
" lified, since infants are not *expresly* and incon-
" trovertibly mentioned in connection with baptism,
" it is not the *will of Christ* they should be bap-
" tized; because, in a positive institution, no-
" thing short of an *express precept* or *plain ex-
" ample* can indicate his will." The fallacious impropriety of connecting the abstract notion of a positive institution with the ordinance of baptism in its complex form, and especially in extending its *positiveness* to the moral *qualifications* of the subjects, has been shewn in the first chapter; to which the reader is referred. Now, against the remaining part of the objection I maintain, that *on supposition* infants are not expresly and incontrovertibly mentioned in connection with baptism, there is sufficient *positive evidence* in favour of Pœdobaptism. For,

§ 12. (1) THE *law and light of nature* require, and consequently the *will of Christ*, that parents should introduce their children to all the *benefits* and privileges of which they are capable.

That infants are subjects capable of baptism (*capable*, I mean, in the properest sense) has been demonstrated. For, *baptism* being the SEAL of God, to be ministerially applied to all the subjects of the visible gospel kingdom; and *circumcision* being a SEAL of the righteousness of faith; the latter therein eminently agreeing with the former; it follows, that if an infant be *capable* of the one, it is *equally* so of the other.—It remains therefore that we attend to the remaining parts of the complex proposition. I say, then,

1. Baptism is a *benefit* and privilege when applied to capable subjects, possessing all the qualifications necessary to answer the scriptural design of the ordinance. That it is a *benefit* to such is apparent, when we consider what baptism when applied necessarily includes. It includes a relative change of state; thereby the subject is translated, ministerially, from a state of distance to a state of nearness; is separated from the world and joined to the universal church; is thereby legally entitled to all the other external privileges of the gospel dispensation, of which the subject is capable, this being the right of *initiation* into them. Again, it includes, a dedication of the subject to Father, Son, and Spirit; is a *seal* of God's covenant to the subject, assuring him to his dying day, that therein are *exhibited* to him exceeding great and precious promises; and, of course, lays a foundation for the most rational and interesting obligations of duty. And, indeed, the single

single consideration of baptism laying all suitable subjects to whom it is ministerially applied under such obligations, is alone decisive in support of the point under consideration. And here we may ask, If infants are capable and suitable subjects, as we have proved they are, and if the above important particulars belong to all these when baptized, *as such*; what greater *benefit* can we conceive to appertain to a divine institution? Could Paul himself regard his baptism in a more *beneficial* light? For, if it be said, that an adult has an opportunity at his baptism to *testify* his faith and repentance, to *profess* his subjection and allegiance to Christ, it is plain this is only confounding what are in themselves distinct, divine *benefits* and human *duties*. To call the discharge of duty a divine benefit, in strictness of speech, is to say that the *grounds* of moral obligation, and the *discharge* thereof, are one and the same thing, which is absurd. The grounds, motives and encouragements of duty are divine benefits, together with the ability, inclination and the effective cause of compliance with duty; but, properly speaking, *duties themselves* are not so. And this must necessarily be the case while man is free in his actions and accountable for them.

§ 13. IF the above reasoning be just, and if I do not greatly misunderstand our opposers, *their* notion of baptism is *no benefit at all*. We consider the baptismal ordinance as a *seal* of God's covenant to *fœderati*, and of consequence the right

right to it a *benefit*. To this Dr. S. replies, "If sealing be, as you have seen, a matter of *duty* rather than of right, to use this kind of language is much the same as to say, that persons have a right *to do their duty*†." But be it known, that this worthy author does not say, as indeed he could not with any colour of plausibility, that infants are *incapable* of being *benefited* by free grants and covenants, for thus he subjoins: "A man may be included in a covenant or BENEFITED by it, who is *no way a party* to it, and whose signature therefore is not at all requisite. CHILDREN, for instance, frequently derive *advantages* from covenants which, with all the authentic forms of them, existed long before they were born ‖." The Reason, therefore, why infants, according to him, are not proper subjects of baptism, is not because of any incapacity in them of being *benefited*, but because they are incapable of *duty*. And so essential is the subject's *duty*, on these principles, to the ordinance of baptism, that separate from this obsequious concurrence, the institution itself is not a benefit or a privilege, but a mere non-entity. Consequently, for any to disregard baptism, is not to disregard a *benefit* mercifully held forth to them, but the neglect of a *duty*, in the same sense as prayer, or any other moral duty is neglected. On these principles, therefore, which represent baptism as *no benefit* in any sense but that in which the *performance of any duty* is so,

it

† Ans. to Dr. ADDINGTON's Reasons, p. 106. ‖ Ibid.

it is no wonder that our antagonists should pronounce the baptizing of infants an abfurd practice, for it is the same as to put an infant on performing duty! But if it be so, it equally follows, that baptism is *no benefit*, properly speaking, to believers. And if no benefit, it can lay them under no obligations of gratitude, for gratitude necessarily supposes a benefit. What they must lay for a foundation of gratitude on these principles is their *own performance* of duty, and that properly being no divine benefit, their gratitude must terminate on *themselves*. But what are our opponents' *avowed grounds* of obligations of duty in this matter? Dr. S. replies: " There can be no doubt that we are to consider it [baptism] as a solemn test, whereby we VOLUNTARILY BIND OURSELVES to new obedience.——Nor can it be in regard of them [infants] a test of new obedience, they not VOLUNTARILY SUBMITTING TO IT*." Is this the language of a protestant orthodox divine? Is our NEW OBEDIENCE founded on our OWN SUBMISSION? Is our OBEDIENCE obligatory in proportion as we BIND OURSELVES to it? Be it so; there is one consequence inevitably follows, viz. That no person in the world is under any *obligation* to perform what he does not voluntarily submit to, or to regard any thing as a *duty* until he *binds himself* to the performance of it. A doctrine this, that will be always grateful to the human mind, in proportion as it is

* *Ut supra*, p. 109.

is disaffected to the requisitions of its Creator! How much more rational and scriptural the supposition, That baptism, as a divine institution, is a *benefit* conferred on all who are the capable and actual subjects of it; and, as such, exhibiting blessings and obliging to answerable duties? To conclude this paragraph, I will subjoin the words of a Prelate on this subject, in whom the power of godliness, sound learning, and judicious moderation, seemed to unite their splendors: " Either baptism is a *benefit* to
" fants, or it is not. If none, why then admi-
" nistered at all; but if it be [which was his
" real sentiment] then why should the poor
" innocents be prejudged of it for the parent's
" cause, if he profess but so much of a chris-
" tian as to offer his child to that ordi-
" nance†." We now come to shew,

§ 14. 2. THAT as baptism is a *benefit* applicable to infants, the *dictates of nature* require our applying it to them; and, provided these dictates are the *will of Christ*, and if they are not contravened by positive authority, the conclusion is clear as the day, That it is the WILL OF CHRIST professing parents should solicit baptism for their children, and gospel ministers should baptize them.

LET us not mistake the state of the question, and the force of the argument. I do not say that BAPTISM is discoverable by the light of nature; but that the *revealed* account of it considers it as a BENEFIT

† Archbishop LEIGHTON's Select Works. Let. No. 1.

FIT; and that the law and light of nature require we fhould confer on our children all the benefits of which they are fuitable fubjects, and which lie within our power. This is of importance to be obferved; for there is a very obvious difference between the *difcovering* of a benefit and the *application* of it, when difcovered, to one rather than another. This diftinction Dr. S. overlooks, when he thus interrogates and replies: " Is *infant baptifm* a duty the *light of* " *nature and reafon* teaches? This furely will " not be pretended*." But this is artfully blending what are in themfelves perfectly diftinct. We do not fay that BAPTISM, viz. The chriftian purification in the name of the Father, and fo on, is taught by the light of nature and reafon; but is, on the contrary, a *pofitive appointment*. And what then? Does it follow that the light of nature and reafon is not concerned in the *application* of baptifm to one fubject in preference to another? The minifterial commiffion to *baptize* (as well as to *preach*) is a *difcretionary truft*; the gofpel revelation is the RULE and pofitive directory; but can any one, who properly confiders the nature of divine laws, their feparate and refpective influence, the nature of pofitive authority in particular, hefitate a moment about the neceffity of the *light of nature and reafon* to affift in the *application* of that rule? To fuppofe that, by infifting on the neceffary aids of the dictates of nature in the *application* of the fcripture rule in many cafes,

* Anf. to Dr. A. p. 291.

we derogate from the *true perfection* of the sacred volume, is a surmise demonstrably weak and impertinent. Suffice it to observe with St. Austin: " To reject the conduct of the *light of* " *nature* is not only foolish but also impious*." With Tertullian: " Those *notions* and " persuasions of the human mind that are *com-* " *mon*, are capable of making us wiser, even " in *divine matters*, provided we employ them " in defence of truth, not for the support " of error †." With Hooker: " The will of " God, which we are to judge our actions by, " no sound divine in the world ever denied to " be in part made manifest even by *light of na-* " *ture* and not by scripture alone ‡." With Chillingworth: " It is very meet and rea- " sonable and necessary that men, as in all " their actions, so especially in that which is of " greatest importance, the choice of their way " to happiness, should be left unto — *right* " *reason*, grounded on *divine revelation* and *com-* " *mon notions*, written by God in the hearts of " all men ; — deducing, according to the ne- " ver-failing rules of logic, consequent deduc- " tions from them. And he that follows this " in all his opinions and actions, and does not " *only seem* to do so, follows always God∥."

The

---

* Augustinus de Trin. cap. vi. *Luminis naturalis* ducatum repellere, non modo stultum est, sed et impium.

† Tertullianus de Resur. carnis. cap. iii. Est quidem et de *communibus sensibus* sapere in *Dei rebus*, sed in testimonium veri, non in adjutorium falsi.

‡ Hooker's Eccles. Polity, B. III. § 8.

∥ Chillingworth's Religion of Protestants, Pref. § 12.

The influence, therefore, here afcribed to the light of nature, is not the *difcovery* of baptifm as a *pofitive* appointment, (which would imply a contradiction) but the *application* of baptifm to fome perfons rather than others, with the affiftance of the fcripture rule. If the fcripture rule *clearly counteract* what *feemed* before a natural dictate, this latter, it is evident, fhould fubmit to the former; if not, and fuppofing revealed pofitive evidence out of the queftion, the natural dictate continues in full force, being, on the fuppofition, the *only* evidence remaining in the cafe. But if to this laft mentioned evidence be *fuperadded* any given degree of fcriptural authority, the force of obligation is *increafed* in that proportion.

§ 15. WHEN I fpeak of the *Law of nature*, in this connection, I would be underftood to mean nearly with GROTIUS: " That [regular] " DICTATE OF RIGHT REASON WHICH SHEWS " that there is in any [human] act, from its " AGREEMENT OR DISAGREEMENT WITH " [OUR] RATIONAL [AND SOCIAL] NATURE a " moral turpitude, or a moral neceffity; and, " of courfe, that fuch an act is either FORBID-" DEN OR ENJOINED BY GOD THE AUTHOR " OF NATURE*." And, with CALDERWOOD, I would term any human act INDIFFERENT " which has no *moral* goodnefs or pravity; " that is, which is neither enjoined nor for-" bidden, by any law natural or divine.†"

All

* GROTIUS De Jure Belli ac Pacis. Lib. I. Cap. I. § x. 1.
† CALDERWOOD Altare Damafcenum. Cap. ix. De rebus adiaphoris et ceremoniis. p. 366.

All human acts, therefore, *morally* confidered, in their general and univerfal nature, are either GOOD, BAD, or, *fecundum fpeciem*, INDIFFERENT; tho' no human act, in its particular and fingular nature, *fecundum individuum*, terminating in actual exiftence and attended with all its circumftances, can be morally *indifferent*. By the *light of nature* I underftand with DODDRIDGE: "That part of the law of nature which man "by the exercife of his reafon *has actually dif-* "*covered* ‖," and not merely what he *may difcover*, by that means.

HERE let it be obferved, that as the reports of *fenfe* may be taken for true, when there is no reafon againft them; becaufe when there is *no* reafon *not* to believe, that alone is a reafon for believing them: fo, the reports of the *law of our nature* may be taken for true, when there is *no revelation againft* them; for to do otherwife would be to deny our affent to what, on the fuppofition, is the *beft evidence*. And where *certainty* is not to be had, probability muft be fubftituted in the place of it: that is, it muft be confidered, which fide of the queftion is the *more probable*. With whatever contempt fome may affect to treat this rule, they fhould be reminded that the object of fuch contempt is *truth itfelf*. Befides, unlefs it be reafonable to put out our *candle*, becaufe we have not the light of the *fun*, it muft be reafonable to direct our fteps by probability when we have nothing
clearer

‖ DODDRIDGE's Lect. Definit. LXII.

clearer to walk by. The only alternative is to wander and fluctuate in *abfolute* uncertainty †.

Nor can it be denied, " that every man," as Puffendorf obferves, " of mature age, and a " found mind, poffeffes fo much of this natu- " ral light, that ufing proper means and due " attention, he may very well difcover at leaft " the general precepts and principles of the law " of nature; and, at the fame time, judge, " that thefe are perfectly fuitable to his nature " and ftate *. But if any thing be determined, by " rational inveftigation, to be a part of the law of " nature, this muft not, on that account, be pro- " nounced *oppofite* to what the facred fcriptures " deliver *more clearly* on the fame fubject; but " fhould be diftinguifhed as it were by *abftraction*§."

§ 16. Having premifed thefe things re- fpecting *natural dictates*, as being of divine ori- gin, and of univerfal and perpetual obligation, when not contravened by the exprefs will of the fupreme Lawgiver, who alone has a right to controul them; we proceed to inquire what are fome of the moft important and *univerfally ac- knowledged parts and principles thereof*, that relate to our prefent purpofe.

The following things feem to be of that defcription: " That man is a focial creature: " and

† See Wollaston's Religion of Nature, § III. 14, 15, 16.
* Vid. Puffendorfium De Officio, Lib. I. Cap. I. § 4.
§ Id. Pref. § 4.

" and the subject of moral obligation. That
" all injustice is wrong and evil, and *vice versa*.
" That to render all their due, is justice: and
" to detain any thing that is another's, is injus-
" tice. That infant children are to be regard-
" ed as parts of their parents. That parents
" have a just right of putting their children,
" even in earliest infancy, under future obliga-
" tions: or, in other words, that they *ought to*
" *benefit* their children, when it is in their
" power to do so. That parents ought to take
" the *best care* of their children they can, en-
" deavour to provide for them, and to be al-
" ways ready to assist them. That in order to
" the good of children, there must be some
" authority over them lodged by nature in the
" parents: that is, the nature of the case is
" such, as *necessarily requires* there should be
" in the parents an authority over their chil-
" dren *in order to their good*. That parents
" ought *to dispose* of their children according to
" the *best* of their judgment. That as the
" child *grows up*, the case is still the same in
" *some degree* or other, till he arrives at the age
" reckoned mature; and very often longer.
" That parents, in consulting the *good* of their
" children, ought to adopt those means, which,
" according to the best of their skill, abilities,
" and opportunities, they find most conducive
" to *that end*. That children are laid under
" *obligations* to their *parents* in proportion as
" they are *benefited* by them; and to GOD su-
                               " premely

"premely, as the ultimate source and first cause
"of all. That the *natural affection* which re-
"gularly and mutually subsists in parents and
"children, ought to be observed and followed,
"when there is no reason to the contrary. For
"when there is no reason why we should not
"comply with it, its own very solicitation, and
"the agreeableness we apprehend to be in com-
"plying, are *preponderating* arguments. This
"must be true, if *something* is more than *no-
"thing*. Nay, if this ϛοϛγὴ be only a kind
"of *attraction* in the mere matter of parents
"and children; yet still this physical mo-
"tion or *sympathy* ought not to be over-ruled
"if there be not a *good* reason for it. On the
"contrary, it ought to be taken as a *suggestion*
"of nature, which should always be regarded,
"when it is not superseded by something *su-
"perior*; that is, by *reason*, &c. — Therefore
"not to act *according to* it, is not to act ac-
"cording to reason, and to *deny* that to be which
"is ‖. Consequently, That when parents do
"not act according to these *dictates*, without a
"divine warrant to act otherwise, they lie a-
"gainst the truth, and *deny* themselves and their
"children to be *what they are*; and the *relation*
"that subsists between them. That when any
"do not *benefit* their *offspring*, and those in their
"*house*, who are not of age to *reject* the pro-
"posed favour, act an *unnatural* part."

§ 17. FROM what is said, the conclusion is
inevitable

‖ See WOLLASTON's Relig. of Nat. § VIII. *passim*.

inevitable — That it is the WILL OF CHRIST, his difciples fhould devote their infant children to him in baptifm. ——For,

THE dictates of nature, uncontrouled by revelation, are the *will of Chrift*, and our rule of duty. (§ 15.) — The WILL OF CHRIST, exprefled in thefe *dictates*, requires us to *benefit* our children as they are capable. (§ 16) — *Baptifm*, as the initiatory *feal* of God's cove‑ nant, is a *benefit* of which infants are *capable*. (See chap. II. § 23—25. and ch. III. § 5—10.) — This evidence is not *eclipfed*, but *brightened*, by fcripture authority, as we fhall fee in the fequel of this chapter.

LET the reader carefully notice, that we do not fuppofe, by infifting on this argument, the infufficiency of *direct fcripture* evidence: for *this* has been frequently urged with advantage, to fatisfy perfons of the beft difpofitions and abi‑ lities. That is, reader, " fome of the moft eminent Pœdobaptifts that ever filled the Profeffor's chair, or that ever yet adorned the Proteftant pulpit." But fince our opponents infift, that what has been fo often urged, is not conclufive ; and *modeftly* affirm, it is only calculated to catch " the eye of a *fuperficial* obferver ;" they are defired once more impartially to weigh this rea‑ foning, and then, if they are able, to refute it. Let them know, however, that hackneyed phrafes without meaning — principles taken upon truft — and empty declamation — muft not be palm‑ ed on us inftead of folid arguments.

WERE it neceffary, it would be eafy to fhew, that

that the principles above urged are no *novelty*; but are perfectly agreeable to experience, — and to the practical judgment of the moſt ſerious Pœdobaptiſts, both illiterate and learned. But waving this, proceed we next to another corroborating proof of the main propoſition.

§ 18. (2) WHAT we contend for is, That it is the WILL of CHRIST we ſhould *baptize* our infant children. In proof of this we have ſhewn, firſt, that the *dictates of right reaſon* require us to *benefit* them, and conſequently to *baptize* them; as baptiſm is always a benefit when adminiſtered to *capable* ſubjects. We come, ſecondly, to ſhew —— That God has conſtantly *approved* of *this principle*, in all *preceding* diſpenſations. In other words —— That the *principle* of the laſt argument is ſo far from being *weakened* by ſcripture evidence, that the Lord's *approbation* of IT, in his conduct towards the offspring of his profeſſing people, in all the diſpenſations of true religion, is abundantly *illuſtrated* and *confirmed*.

Mr. B's miſapplied but favourite maxim — " Poſitive laws imply their negative," has no force in the baptiſmal controverſy, until he demonſtrates, in oppoſition to what is advanced, that the dictates of right reaſon muſt be *ſmothered*, or elſe, that revelation *countermands* their influence. But to *demonſtrate* the former, in matters about which, on the ſuppoſition, ſcripture is ſilent, is no eaſy taſk. And the difficulty will be *increaſed* in proportion as the ſacred oracles corroborate

corroborate reason's verdict. Let us now appeal to these oracles.

§ 19. 1. WE appeal to that period of the church, and dispensation of grace, which extended from Adam to Noah. The inspired narrative of this long space of time is very short: on which we make the following remarks. We then assert,

(1) WHATEVER exhibition of grace was made to antediluvian *parents*, was constantly made to their *offspring*; and consequently whatever *seals* of grace were granted to the former, must equally appertain to the latter, if not voluntary *rejectors* of them. Therefore, all such parents had a *revealed* warrant to regard their offspring as entitled to the *seals* of the covenant, in *like manner* as themselves, according to their capacity. For,

(2) ALL allow that Gen. iii. 15. contains the promulgation of gospel grace; nor are we authorised to question the interest of *children* therein with their parents, without an express contravention. For, it were *unnatural* for a parent to *confine* such a *benefit* to his own person to the exclusion of his children, who are not only parts of his family but of *himself*. To which we may add, that the phrase THY SEED, tho' principally referring to the Messiah, respected Eve's *natural seed* as sharers in common with herself in the exhibition of mercy; and we suppose not less so than her HUSBAND. For this application of the phrase *thy seed*, compare Gen. xvii. 7. and Gal. iii. 16. Again,

(3) IT

(3) It is generally agreed, that not only the inftitution of *facrifices*, but alfo the *coats* of fkin (Gen. iii. 21.) were *emblematic* of covenant bleffings; and not only fo, in common with mere types, but *feals* of the covenant, as earnefts and pledges of exhibited favour. "Who will deny," fays WITSIUS, "that God's cloathing our firft parents was a *fymbolical* act? Do not Chrift's own words (Rev. iii. 18.) very clearly allude to this*?" As for *facrifices*, they were flain at God's command after the promulgation of the covenant. For, if Abel *offered by* FAITH, (Heb. xi. 4.) it prefuppofes the divine *inftitution* of them. And this inftitution, moft probably, took place when God — taking occafion from the infufficiency of the aprons of fig-leaves, which the fallen pair fewed together, to cover the fhame of their nakednefs — himfelf cloathed them with coats of fkins. And moft divines agree, that it is very probable, thefe were the fkins of thofe beafts which were flain for *facrifices*. However, God gave teftimony to thefe oblations of the antient patriarchs, that they were *acceptable* to him; but this cannot be fuppofed without admitting them to be *divinely inftituted*. Befides, a diftinction of *clean* and *unclean* animals was obferved before the deluge; which was not from *nature*, but the mere divine pleafure; and may we not add, with a particular refpect to *facrifices?* Now

(4) IF

* WITS. Oecon. Fœd. Lib. iv. cap. vii. § 4 — 7.

(4) IF, according to WITSIUS and others, these *skins of beasts*, and *sacrifices*, were appointed SEALS *of the righteousness of faith*; I would ask —— Was the *covenant* (using the term in the sense before explained, chap. ii. §. 23, &c.) directed for the use of their SEED *in common* with the parents, and not the *seal* in like manner? For, if the seals be affixed to the covenant for *confirmation* of its contents, as well as, in another view, for signification; I would fain know, by what rule of construction we can infer, that the covenant *itself* belongs to the parents and their seed *in common*, while the *confirmation* of it belongs *exclusively* to the former? Is it not contrary to *custom* and *unreasonable* to conclude, that a charter of privileges, or a testamentary instrument, (which by the way express the nature of the covenant) belongs to a man and his heirs ALIKE, but the confirming seal respects the former ONLY; while on the supposition, the sovereign, or the testator, has given *no ground* for such partiality? Besides,

(5) IF the covenant itself be a *benefit* to the persons to whom it is directed, as it certainly is in *every* dispensation of it, it follows that the *confirmation* of it is so; for parents, therefore, to *deny* their offspring all the share in such common benefits they are capable of, without a divine warrant, is *unnatural*, and an act of *injustice*. We may therefore conclude —— that from Adam to Noah, the *covenant* and its *seals* appertained

appertained to *infants* in common with their parents.

§ 20. 2. WE appeal next to that period of the church which extended from Noah to Abraham: On which we observe,

(1.) WHATEVER benefits and privileges belonged to the former dispensation, continue to flow on to the present, if not *expressly* repealed; for the change of a dispensation, *of itself*, is no adequate cause of their abrogation. That would be as unreasonable as to suppose that the bare change from night to day was, *of itself*, an adequate cause of a man's being disinherited. Or we may as well say, that the abstract notion of an epoch in chronology has a real influence on the sequence of events. Whatever covenant privileges, therefore, belonged to Noah and his family *before* the deluge, if not expressly repealed, must belong to them *after* the deluge. But,

(2.) So far were these privileges from being abridged at this period, that they were greatly enlarged and confirmed, by additional discoveries. For thus we read, Gen. vi. 18. *But with thee will I* ESTABLISH MY COVENANT; *and thou shalt come into the ark, thou, and thy sons, and thy wife, and thy sons' wives with thee.* Again, chap. vii. 1. *And the Lord said unto Noah, Come thou,* AND ALL THY HOUSE *into the ark; for* THEE *have I seen righteous before me in this generation.* And again, chap. viii. 20. *And Noah builded an altar unto the Lord; and took of every clean beast, and of every clean fowl, and* OFFERED BURNT OFFERINGS

INGS *on the altar.* Once more, chap. ix. 8, 9, 12, 13. *And God spake unto Noah, and to his* SONS *with him, saying, And I, behold, I* ESTABLISH *my covenant with* YOU, *and with* YOUR SEED *after you. And God said, This is the* TOKEN OF THE COVENANT —— *I do set my bow in the cloud.* Hence we further learn,

(3.) THAT the covenant or divine charter, first given to Noah, *included* the preceding; it was the SAME *covenant* with *additional grants:* for the Lord says, " I will ESTABLISH my covenant." Lest Noah should infer that the drowning of the world in wrath disannulled the well known covenant, God dissipates his fears, by saying, " I will *establish* my covenant."

(4) ON Noah's *account,* or *as belonging* to him, ALL HIS HOUSE or family was privileged. The privilege is, — " Come thou, and *all thy house* into the ark." The ground and reason of that privilege —— " *for THEE have I seen righteous.*" It is true, the natural dictates of reason and affection, whereby a *father pitieth his children**, and whereby an infidel *careth for his own, especially those of his own house* ‖, would have prompted this righteous person to bring *all his family,* (except any adults *refused* compliance) into the ark, *(the like figure whereunto is* BAPTISM, as an inspired teacher assures us, 1 Pet. iii. 21.) yet the Lord was pleased to brighten his evidence and strengthen his obligations of duty by express revelation.

(5) AFTER

---

* Psalm ciii. 13.   ‖ 1 Tim. v. 8.

(5) AFTER the flood the inftitution of *facrifices* continued as the feal of the *firft* part of the covenant; and the *rainbow* was inftituted as the feal of the *additional* part, or, as PAREUS calls it, " *appendix* of the covenant of grace †." And here it is worthy of notice, that as the firft exhibition of the covenant and its feals refpected the offspring of *fœderati*, and the *renewal* or *eftablifhment* of it to Noah retained that privilege in full force: fo alfo the *appendix* of the covenant comprehended his SEED.

(6) RESPECTING this appendix of the covenant of which the rainbow was the feal, tho' we fuppofe, with WITSIUS, it was not formally and precifely the covenant of grace; yet we obferve, with the fame excellent author, " it " does not feem confiftent with the divine per- " fections, to make fuch a covenant with every " living creature, but on *fuppofition* of a cove- " nant of grace, and having a *refpect* to it. ‖" And as this covenant, in its univerfality, implied the covenant of grace, we are not to deny, but the promifes of it were alfo *fealed* to Noah and his feed by the rainbow. (See Rev. iv. 3. x. 8.)

(7) IT is obfervable, finally, that NOAH, his SONS, and THEIR SEED were *fœderati*, in this ratification of the covenant; confeqently whatever *feals* of the covenant belonged to Noah, belonged to *his fons*, and *their feed*, while nondiffentients. § 21. 3.

† Ap. WITS. Oecon. Fœd. Lib. iv. cap. vii. § 19. ‖ Ibid.

§ 21. 3. APPEAL we next to a very important period of sacred hiſtory, viz. From Abraham to Moſes. On this alſo we make the following remarks.

(1) THE Abrahamic covenant *included* the preceding diſpenſations, on the general principle — that grants and privileges continue in force until *repealed*. Which repealing, if it be not either *expreſs*, or ariſe from the nature of the caſe, in itſelf *plain*, can have no binding influence, that is to ſay, no exiſtence at all: except we maintain, that we are *bound* to reſign an important good without an aſſignable cauſe; which is in fact to maintain that we ought to *deny* that to be, which is.

(2) I SUPPOSE it will be granted, that the *principal bleſſing* exhibited in the foregoing diſpenſations was THE RIGHTEOUSNESS OF FAITH; the great importance of which to the human race, in every age of the world, no one will deny who confiders things *as they are*. This covenant, therefore, was in force to Abraham *prior* to what is called the Abrahamic diſpenſation; and in this connection we might mention Lot and his family. But, behold,

(3) A MOST explicit ratification of it, with *ſuperadded* favours, Gen. xii. 3. —— IN THEE SHALL ALL FAMILIES OF THE EARTH BE BLESSED. Chap. xvii. 7. *And I will* ESTABLISH MY COVENANT *between me and thee, and thy* SEED *after thee, in their generations, for an everlaſting covenant;* TO BE A GOD UNTO THEE AND

AND TO THY SEED AFTER THEE. *v.* 10. *This is my covenant which ye shall keep between me and you,* AND THY SEED *after thee:* every MAN-child *among you shall be* CIRCUMCISED. *v.* 12. *He that is* EIGHT DAYS OLD *shall be circumcised among you, every* MAN-*child in your generations; he that is born in the house,* OR BOUGHT WITH MONEY OF ANY STRANGER, *which is not of thy seed. v.* 24—27. *And Abraham was* NINETY YEARS OLD AND NINE, *when he was circumcised in the flesh of his foreskin. And Ishmael his son was* THIRTEEN YEARS OLD, *when he was circumcised in the flesh of his foreskin. In the* SELF SAME DAY *was Abraham circumcised, and Ishmael his son. And* ALL THE MEN OF HIS HOUSE, *born in the house, and* BOUGHT WITH MONEY OF THE STRANGER, *were circumcised with him.* Hence we learn,

(4) THE *nature* and *extent* of the ABRAHAMIC COVENANT or PROMISE. Whatever *blessings* are *promised* to ruined man, must be *in virtue* of the covenant of grace. All promised blessings, therefore, must *imply* an EXHIBITION of *gospel grace.* And the glad tidings of salvation thro' Christ preached to the GENTILE WORLD, is expresly called — THE BLESSING OF ABRAHAM (Gal. iii. 14.) Not that this *link* is the FIRST in the chain of exhibited mercy to the fallen race *in general,* or with an universal and unlimited aspect, if the reasoning in the last sections be just: but for its *explicitness,* and *precious* (because expresly diffusive) intend-

ment, it may be juftly termed a GOLDEN LINK. In this refpect Abraham may well be ftiled — *The* FATHER *of us all*; not to the difavowal of Noah, with whom the covenant was before ratified, or Eve, who received the *firft* intimation of it, and who in *this* refpect eminently may be called —— *The* MOTHER *of all living.* The *covenant* of grace, in its external manifeftation, containing *an* EXHIBITION of *exceeding great and precious* PROMISES to every human being on the face of the globe, to whom providence directs the joyful news, may be compared to a flowing ftream: it proceeds ultimately from the immenfe ocean of fovereign grace in Chrift; its *firft* vifible fource we trace to paradife, where it rifes in a fmall fpring, and glides on to Noah. During this part of its progrefs, there were but few comparatively who participated of its cleanfing and healing virtues, tho' none were debarred from it. This continuing to glide along, without interruption, (notwithftanding God's awful vifitation of a corrupt world by the deluge) we difcern thro' the perfon of Noah *another* fource, whence is poured forth a fecond ftream which empties itfelf into the former channel. The ftreams thus *united* become a river, which flows on to Abraham —— a river to which *all* are invited, but *few* come, and thefe made willing by the omnipotent energy of *divine influence* which obferves the laws of another —— a HIDDEN difpenfation, running parallel as it were

were with the former; which was also the case in the preceding period. Then, thro' the highly honoured person of Abraham we behold another mighty spring copiously pouring forth the waters of salvation, and again uniting itself to the former river; and from him to Christ, with a wide majestic flow, it proceeds along the consecrated channel of the Jewish nation; gradually increasing by the accession of other streams, till it arrives at the Saviour's finished work; where, impatient of confinement, it breaks over its banks on every side, and the healing waters flow to the most distant regions—THAT THE BLESSING OF ABRAHAM MIGHT COME UPON THE GENTILES. (Gal. iii. 14, 8. compared with Gen. xii. 3. xviii. 18. xxii. 18.) Paul expressly says, that " the GOSPEL (even the very same as the New Testament contains —*salvation by* GRACE) " was preached to Abraham:" And (Heb. iv. 2.) it was preached to his unbelieving descendants in the wilderness.

(5) As it is *natural* to expect, that whatever exhibition of privileges the parents enjoyed should be extended to their children, in common with themselves; so we find that *in fact* they are *expresly included* in *this* dispensation as well as the preceding. The covenant is established between God and Abraham's SEED, *in the* VERY SAME *sense* as with Abraham HIMSELF; the essence of which is— TO BE A GOD TO HIM AND HIS SEED. And lest it should be objected that the term *seed* refers to his *adult posterity*

posterity who should tread in his steps, to the exclusion of infants, all doubt is dissipated by the appointment of applying the *seal* of the covenant in early infancy.

(6) *Sacrifices* continuing in full force to SEAL the covenant, till the divine oblation should be made; and the *bow* of the covenant continuing as a token and SEAL of it, until the Messiah's *second* coming; at the commencement of this period is given an *additional* seal—CIRCUMCISION. The very *nature* of the rite shews that all *females* are excluded from being the subjects of it; as well as the discriminating specification—*every MAN-child*. Here observe in general, that children, in this rite, have the same privileges as their parents. The males are treated as Abraham, and the females as Sarah: *These*, therefore, had the covenant sealed in the same manner as their honoured mother. Again: tho' Sarah and her sex were not the *subjects* of this rite, they were constant *witnesses* to the institution; and therefore there was an important sense in which circumcision was a seal to Sarah and her daughters: a sense analogous to that in which sacrifices were.

(7) EVERY domestic head being, in truth, a prophet, priest, and king, in his own family; a question must arise, Whether the covenant and its seals are restricted to the parent head of the family, and his children, or else extended to the *other domestics?* Nor would the question be unimportant; for his *instructions*, his *prayers*, and *commands*, answerable to his three-fold

fold office, muft be directed accordingly. To this queftion right reafon replies : If the covenant and its feals are *beneficial* to all capable fubjects, benevolence requires that they fhould be extended to the other *non-diffenting* members — except forbidden by indifputable authority. This is the voice of reafon; and we find that this is the voice of God. The privilege is common to the feed, and to *him that is born in the houfe, or bought with money of any ftranger*, WHICH IS NOT OF THE SEED, Gen. xvii. 12.

§ 22. IT has been objected, " that the covenant with Abraham was a covenant of *peculiarity* only, and that circumcifion was no more than a token of *that* covenant;" but if fo, as Mr. HENRY obferves, " how came it that all PRO-" SELYTES, of what nation foever, even *the* " *ftrangers*, were to be circumcifed ; tho' not " being of any of the tribes, they had no part " or lot in the land of Canaan ? The extending " the feal of circumcifion to *profelyted ftrangers*, " and to THEIR SEED, was a plain indication, " that the New Teftament adminiftration of the " covenant of grace would reach, not to the cove-" nanters only, but their *feed**." But it has been proved that circumcifion *fealed* to Abraham and his feed *the righteoufnefs of faith* ; and therefore it does not affect the point in debate to contend that temporal promifes were fealed *alfo*. The reader is referred to Chap. ii. § 23, &c. where the fubject has been confidered at large.

§ 23.

* Treatife on Bapt. p. 89.

§ 23. 4. WE next appeal to the long and interesting period from Moses to Christ. On which let the following observations be considered.

(1) WHATEVER appertained to the Abrahamic covenant was not disannulled by the Mosaic dispensation. This St. Paul asserts in plain terms, Gal. iii. 17.

(2) IT may not be amiss to take notice, before we proceed, of Job's family; who, being as is generally supposed, cotemporary with Moses, and unconnected with his history, deserves a previous regard. Of him it is said, that " he " *sanctified* his children, and rose up early in " the morning, and *offered burnt offerings*, ac-" cording to the *number of them all* — Thus did " Job *continually*," or, all the days. (Job i. 5.) On this I would only observe, let the *sanctifying* be what it may, the *sacrifices* must have been of divine institution, and used by Job, being an eminently righteous man, as the *seals* of the covenant of grace ;—with respect to his children *separately*.

(3) SUPERADDED to the foregoing seals of the covenant, is the PASSOVER; a divine rite of the nature of a sacrifice, instituted in memory of Israel's deliverance out of Egypt, representing and sealing spiritual blessings. " As to the *guests*, " says WITSIUS, they were, first, all native " *Israelites*, who were not excluded by legal un-" cleanness. For *all the congregation of Israel* is " commanded to solemnize the passover. (Exod. " xii. 6. 47.) And, next, the *Proselytes* circum-
" cised

"cifed and become Jews; (Efth. viii. 17.)
"whether bondmen born in the houfe or bought
"with money, &c. Exod. xii. 48. *When a*
"STRANGER *will fojourn with thee, and keep the*
"*paffover to the Lord, let* ALL HIS MALES *be cir-*
"*cumcifed, and then let him come near and keep it,*
"*and he fhall be as one that is born in the land*‡."
On this paffage in Exodus, Dr. JENNINGS obferves thefe two things: "*Firft,* That when a
"man thus became a Profelyte, *all his males*
"were to be circumcifed *as well as himfelf,* where-
"by his *children* were admitted into the vifible
"church of God, *in his right,* as their father.
"*Secondly,* That upon this, he fhould be *entitled*
"*to all the privileges* and immunities of the
"Jewifh church and nation, as well as be fub-
"ject to the whole law: He fhould be as "one
"born in the land§." In fhort; not only men
and women, but alfo young children partook of
this ordinance, *as foon as they were capable* of
anfwering the revealed defign of it, for — no
POSITIVE rule was given them on this head,
like that of circumcifion. It is manifeft that
fince the injunction refpected not only individuals of fuch a defcription, but alfo families *as
fuch,* every member without exception had a *legal
right* to the ordinance; and nothing prevented
infants from a participation, but what lay in the
natural incapacity to anfwer the defign of it.

(4) " BESIDES

‡ WITS. Oecon. Fœd. Lib. iv. cap. xii. § 11.
§ Jewifh Antiq. vol. 1. p. 132.

(4) "Besides the *ordinary* and *univerſal*
"ſacraments of *circumciſion* and the *paſſover*,
"ſome *extraordinary* ſymbols of divine grace
"were granted to the Iſraelites in the wildernefs,
"which in the New Teſtament are applied to
"Chriſt and his benefits, and ſaid to have the ſame
"ſignification with our ſacraments. And they are
"in order theſe — The PASSAGE in the cloud
"THRO' THE RED SEA— the MANNA which was
"rained from heaven — The WATER iſſuing out
"of the ROCK — and the BRAZEN SERPENT
"erected by Moſes for the cure of the Iſ-
"raelites*." To this we may add, among other
things, with the author now referred to — the
clear and familiar diſplay of the DIVINE MAJES-
TY — and the adumbration of divine myſte-
ries daily *ſcaled* by religious CEREMONIES.
Our ſubject does not call for an inveſtigation of
theſe particulars, but I would remark in general,
that the principle for which we contend, is ſo far
from being weakened, that it is abundantly cor-
roborated by the inſpired teſtimony of every
diſpenſation, and the Moſaic in particular—
That it is a common dictate of right reaſon,
children ſhould from their earlieſt infancy ſhare
in their parents' privileges, as far as they are capable, when no poſitive authority contravenes it.

§ 24. FROM the preceding induction of ſacred evidence in favour of children being ſharers
of the ſeals of grace in common with their
parents, we conclude, that for the ſpace of four
thouſand

* WITSIUS *ut ſupra*, cap. x. § 1.

thousand years, that is to say, FROM THE CRE-
ATION TO CHRIST, it was a rule *universally* incumbent on parents to treat their children as
entitled to religious privileges *equally* with themselves, according to their capacity. — And as a
counterpart of what was observed of privileges,
we may remark that, in virtue of the same uniform principle, often when the parents were
punished with excommunication or death, their
infant children were included with them. As
might be instanced in — the deluge—the destruction of Sodom, and Gomorrah — the case of
Achan the Son of Zerah (Josh. vii. 24.) — the
matter of Korah, Dathan, and Abiram — the
case of the conquered nations (Deut. xx. 16,
17.)—and many more instances, down to the
destruction of Jerusalem. Far be it from us to
suppose, that the parents' crimes and impenitence
made their suffering children incapable of *mercy*
—that mercy which proceeds on an invisible plan,
and belongs to a purely spiritual dispensation.
Yet, that children, during their *dependence* on their
parents, should share equally with them in judgments and mercies externally, is the effect of an
all-wise constitution coeval with mankind.

§ 25. Mr. B. when treating of *external covenant relation*, objects: " All reasoning from *data*
of a moral kind and the supposed fitness of
things, or from the natural relation of children
to parents, is wide of the mark. As baptism is
not a duty *naturally* resulting from our relation
to God, as *reasonable* creatures; for then it
would

would be incumbent on *every man* to be baptized: as our obligation to regard it does not arise from any moral, or civil relation, in which we necessarily stand to our fellow creatures; for then the same consequence would inevitably follow: and as this duty does not originate in the natural relation between parents and children; for then *all* parents, *whoever they be*, would lie under an obligation to have their infants baptized: so it is altogether vain to search any where for the proper subjects of baptism, except in the appointment of Christ and apostolic practice; these being the only rule and law of its administration†." But this objection, however plausible, does by no means affect the above reasoning. For, *data* of a moral kind are very good ones, when no positive evidence lies against them. Besides, there appears to me a manifest impropriety (not to say impertinence) in making the *kind* of argumentation an objectionable matter. For it is demonstrable, that positive laws, tho' they conclude *affirmatively*, do not conclude *negatively*, except in matters that are absolutely indefensible on all *data* whatever. Nothing can possibly be established by sound reasoning, but what is *reasonable and right*; and when this is done, it is plain that nothing but *affirmative* positive evidence can invalidate the conclusion. The conduct of our opponents in this instance is not unlike that of Arminians when disputing with Calvinists. It is objected to

† Pædob, Exam. p. 286.

Ch. 3.   *Subjects of Baptism.*   251

to the latter that their reasoning is *metaphysical*, or may be reduced to the science of *metaphysicks*, and to the Pœdobaptists that their reasoning is of the *moral* kind. But the cavil is well refuted by a masterly pen; part of which refutation, *mutatis mutandis*, we here apply: " If the reasoning be
" good, 'tis as frivolous to inquire what science
" it is properly reduced to, as what language it
" is delivered in: and for a man to go about to
" confute the arguments of his opponent, by
" telling him, his arguments are *metaphysical* [or
" of a *moral* kind] would be as weak as to tell
" him, his arguments could not be substantial,
" because they were not written in *French* or
" *Latin*. The question is not, Whether what
" is said be Metaphysicks, Physicks, Logick, or
" Mathematicks [*morality*, divinity or criticism]
" *Latin, French, English*, or *Mohawk?* But,
" whether the reasoning be GOOD, and the ar-
" guments truly CONCLUSIVE? The foregoing
" arguments are no more metaphysical [or
" *moral*] than those which we use against the
" Papists, to disprove their doctrine of *transub-*
" *stantiation*; alledging, it is inconsistent with
" the notion of corporeal identity, that it should
" be in ten thousand places at the same time.—I
" am willing my arguments should be brought to
" the test of the justest and strictest reason, and
" that a clear, distinct and determinate meaning
" of the terms I use should be insisted on; but
" let not the whole be rejected, as if all were
" confuted

" confuted, by fixing on it the epithet‖"—*moral,*
confequential, or analogical.—"As to the arguments
" I have made ufe of, if they are *quibbles* [adapted
" to dazzle " the eye of a fuperficial obferver"
" only] they may be fhewn to be fo: fuch
" knots are capable of being untied, and the trick
" and cheat may be detected and plainly laid
" open. If this be *fairly* done, with refpect to
" the grounds and reafons I have relied upon,
" I fhall have juft occafion for the future to be
" filent, if not to be afhamed of my argumenta-
" tions. I am willing my proof fhould be tho-
" roughly examined; and if there be nothing
" but *Begging of the queftion,* or mere *Logomachy,*
" or difpute of words, let it be made manifeft,
" and fhewn how the feeming ftrength of the
" argument depends on my *ufing words without*
" *a meaning,* or arifes from the ambiguity of
" terms, or my making ufe of words in an
" indeterminate and unfteady manner; and that
" the weight of my reafons refts mainly on fuch
" a foundation: and then I fhall either be ready
" to retract what I have urged, and thank the
" man that has done the kind part, or fhall be
" juftly expofed for my obftinacy †."

§ 26. But what has Mr. B. to urge in fupport of his affertion, that " reafoning from *data* of a *moral* kind, and the fuppofed *fitnefs* of things, or from the *natural relation* of children to parents

is

‡ Edwards's Inquiry into the freedom of the will, p. 390.
† *Ut fupra,* p. 393.

is wide of the mark?" *His* reasoning is, " If *baptism* were a duty, naturally resulting from our relation to God, as reasonable creatures, then it would be incumbent on *every man* to be baptized." And what a dreadful consequence! But will our author favour us with the curious intelligence of *any man* unbaptized, in a christian country, on whom it is *not* incumbent to be baptized? The objection confounds two things which in reality are quite distinct. It makes no difference between an obligation to perform a duty *before* it is revealed, and *after* it is revealed. Neither the righteousness of faith, nor any part of the gospel mystery, demand the belief and cordial reception of mankind, *before* they are promulged; such a revealed exhibition of mercy depending on the divine pleasure, with which only a small part of the human race is actually favoured; but does it follow, either—that the African Hottentots, who are without such a revelation, 'are under obligation to believe what they have not heard, or—that any in a christian land *are not* laid under obligation to believe and practise what is revealed to them? And does not this obligation " naturally result from our relation to God as reasonable creatures?" For can any thing be more reasonable than that we should thankfully receive what revelation testifies is a proffered mercy? Methinks it requires no great labour to shew—that if the exhibition of grace be a *benefit* to man, it is his DUTY to receive it; and that the denial of this tends directly

to

to sap the foundation of religion and morals. In like manner *baptism*, as a seal appended to the gospel covenant, is as much a matter of *revelation* as the covenant itself; but *this* is no sufficient reason why the seal should not be obligatory in as extensive a manner as the instrument sealed. On new discoveries being made to the creature, or benefits bestowed on him, new relations commence; and hence duties *naturally* result, answerable to these relations, with all that certainty and universality which belong to duties resulting from *unrevealed* relations.

AGAIN: our Author draws another consequence equally formidable: " If the duty of parents to baptize their children originate in the *natural relation* between parents and children, then [sad alternative!] *all* parents, *whoever they be*, would lie under an obligation to have their infants baptized." We are still at a loss to find out wherein lies the inconvenience of the intended conclusion. For we have no objection at all to the idea, that *all* parents, *whoever they be*, IN A CHRISTIAN COUNTRY, lie under an obligation to have their infants baptized; but if my opponent objects to the clause *in a christian country*, as acknowledging *others not* being under the obligation, and therefore not originating in a *natural relation* between parents and children, it will do him no service; until he demonstrate either — that this *natural relation does* NOT *oblige all* parents without exception to BENEFIT their children, in every part of the globe and every period of time, as

Ch. 3.   *Subjects of Baptism.*   255

as we maintain; or—that baptism is NO BENEFIT to infants, in oppofition to thofe arguments that fhew it IS a benefit. But the *nature* of the benefit, or the *manner* whereby it appears to be fo, make no part of the *criteria* whereby we fhould judge, that the duty originates in the natural relation between parents and children. Whether the *benefit* relate to the body or the mind, to property or liberty, to politicks or morals, to time or eternity, to the chief or an inferior good,—is out of the queftion: and, Whether it *appear to be a benefit* by the medium of fenfe or teftimony, of right reafon or revealed facts, by direct affertion in fcripture or juft confequence, by pofitive or moral evidence, or by any other mode whatever of collecting the *fact*, —is equally immaterial. For it ftill follows, that the parent's *duty* originates in a *natural relation* between him and his child, be the *nature* of the benefit, and the *mode* of afcertaining it, what they may.

§ 27. OUR author ftill objects: " Were it allowable to reafon from *covenant intereft*, to the enjoyment of a *pofitive rite*, Abraham and his pofterity might —— have circumcifed their FEMALES! in fome way or other*." His reafons are,—" circumcifion is a *fign* of the covenant —that covenant extends its benign influences to *both* fexes — God has made us *reafonable* creatures; and he requires that we fhould ufe our intellectual powers, on the nature, the application, and the defign of all his inftitutions. Hence it appears

* Pædob. Exam. p. 287.

appears, (says he) that a little *reasoning* on the covenant made with Abraham, and a few deductions from the nature and fitness of things, would have inferred the right of Jewish *females* to circumcision, in a manner similar to that by which our brethren endeavour to authenticate the baptism of infants *." On this singular argument *ad hominem* I make these two remarks.

1. Our author seems to make no manner of difference between the solid deductions of right reason, and the specious pretences of sophistry. For, according to him, nothing more is necessary to establish the propriety of female circumcision, but to admit this *datum* of arguing from *covenant interest*. But we deny that any such consequence would follow, for two plain reasons. First, the *most evident* revealed account of the *nature* and *design* of the institution forbid it; in confirmation of which, we appeal to impartiality itself, and the *universal* suffrage of Jews and Christians. *Secondly,* The phrase —*every MAN-child*—is so decisive in itself, and so often repeated in the institution, as to put it out of all doubt; in favour of which we might again refer to the whole body of Jews and Christians, who *(nem. con.)* understand the males *exclusively*.

2. Tho' we contend for the *proper use* of moral and analogical arguments, we do not suppose that they conclude *in opposition* to positive evidence, but only *in subordination* to it. Common-sense, like common law, ought to influence our proceedings

* Pædob. Exam. p. 287.

proceedings when not controuled by *superior* authority; but in proportion as decisive statute evidence appears, the operation of the *inferior* principle is suspended.

§ 28. ONCE more: " It is worthy of consideration, says Mr. B. whether this doctrine concerning the *federal interest* of infants, be not calculated *to harden their consciences* in an unconverted state, and to flush them with *false hopes*, when grown to years of reflection." This objection has been frequently urged by the Antipœdobaptists, but with how little justice and force, may appear from the following observations.

1. IF this federal interest consist, as the current of Pœdobaptist writers hold, in the children's being entitled to the *external privileges* of the covenant *in common* with their parents; how can this *tend* " to harden their consciences," or " to flush them with false hopes," *more* than their *parents?* Or when these latter *abuse* their privileges, are we to infer, that such privileges are *calculated* " to harden their consciences," or " to flush them with false hopes?" But if such arguing be fallacious in the *one* case, it must be equally so in the *other*.

2. IT seems absolutely unaccountable, nay demonstrably absurd, to suppose that this federal interest, including divine grants, blessings, benefits and privileges, should, in its *native tendency*, " flush any with *false hopes*." The effects it is cal-
" culated" to produce are such as these—repentance
— cau-

—caution—thankfulnefs,—gratitude—obedience, &c. With equal propriety may we pronounce, on the principle of the objection, that the *federal intereſt* of Jewiſh infants, their church memberſhip, their right to the ſeals and ſhadows of grace in common with their parents;—that the poſſeſſion of Canaan, the worſhip of the temple, the ſpirit of prophecy, and the promiſe of the Meſſiah;—that our Lord's preaching and mighty works among the Jews—were all "calculated" to *harden* the conſciences of that people, and to fluſh them with *falſe hopes!*

3. It is the united language of thoſe who maintain the children's *federal intereſt* in their parents' privileges, that an *abuſe* and *miſimprovement* thereof heighten their guilt and danger; which neceſſarily implies, that the thing itſelf is a real good. Thus Mr. STRONG: " That it is a ſpe-
" cial privilege for *parents* and *children*, that they
" [the children] are taken into their parents'
" covenant, will appear by theſe arguments and
" demonſtrations.——It will *aggravate their ſin*
" if they *abuſe* it; therefore it's a mercy and a pri-
" vilege *in itſelf:* for what is not a mercy and
" privilege in itſelf, that *cannot* add to a man's
" ſin and judgment. Now as it is in riches and
" honours, and all the bleſſings in this life, they
" will be unto a man *judgments* if they are
" *abuſed*; therefore they are bleſſings in them-
" ſelves; bleſſings in the *thing*, tho' a ſnare to
" the *man.* So this very argument, that is
" brought to prove that they are no bleſſings, and
" give

" give no benefit, doth clearly prove, that the
" *thing itself* is a privilege and a *bleſſing.*——For
" a child to be diſinherited, and caſt out of his
" father's covenant, is a very great *judgment*, and
" the foreſt of all outward afflictions that can
" befal a man; as we ſee in Cain—*Thou haſt*
" *caſt me out from the face of the earth, and from*
" *thy face I ſhall be hid.* It is the ſentence of
" excommunication that the Lord paſſeth upon
" Cain: and ſo upon Iſhmael—*Caſt out the*
" *bond woman and her ſon:*——Now if it be a
" great judgment to be *caſt out*, ſurely it is a *great*
" *privilege* to be *taken into* their parent's cove-
" nant.—— It is promiſed as a ſpecial *bleſſing* for
" the viſible church of God to continue in any
" man's poſterity. So it was in Seth, Gen. iv.
" 25. in Shem, Gen. ix. 27. In the family of
" Aaron, and afterwards of Phineas, and David.
" —And it is looked upon as a great *judgment*
" for a family and a poſterity to be diſinherited:
" as in Eſau, Saul, and Cham.——It is the
" greateſt wrath that God doth pour out upon
" men in this life, to caſt them out of external
" church privileges. The Apoſtle ſaith [of the
" Jews] *Wrath is come upon them to the uttermoſt:*
" therefore if the wrath be ſo great in a caſting
" out, ſurely there is a great deal of mercy
" ſhewed in the taking in.—The Apoſtle ſpeaks
" even of an intereſt in the external privileges
" of the covenant as a very great matter, Rom.
" iii. 1, 2.—To be caſt out from being a viſible
" member is the greateſt judgment that can be-
" fal

"fal a perfon or people in this life. 1 Cor.
"v. 5.——Hof. 1. 1—9. There is a pedigree
"of judgments fet down, but yet the higheft
"is *Lo-ammi* ∥."

§ 29. (3.) We come next to confider the language of prophecy refpecting gofpel times. On which obferve in general,

1. That the *evidence* of prophecy, in its own nature, is direct and pertinent; and when its meaning is afcertained, its verdict *(cæteris paribus)* is indifputable.

2. There are fome *fubjects* of prophecy which, in their own nature, are more plain, while others are intricate. It is often difficult to afcertain with exactnefs points of chronology, the duration of empires, the identity of fovereigns, and the like; but the nature of the cafe is fuch, that —— while we are inveftigating this queftion, Whether the offspring of parent fubjects of the gofpel difpenfation are or are not to be confidered as parts of their parents, to fhare with them in all the church privileges of which they are capable—— we may with comparative eafe learn the infpired meaning. Befides,

3. Whatever affirmative pofitive evidence our fubject derives from prophetic language is *ex abundanti*; for fince infants did actually make a part of God's church at the time of delivering thefe prophecies, and ever had been held in that relation from the beginning of the world, it is evident that we ought to be influenced by nothing
short

∥ D. fcourfe on the two Covenants. p. 208, 209, 212.

short of a decisive contravention from the Supreme Head of the church, to alter our conduct towards our offspring: and whatever the spirit of prophecy pronounces in their favour, is the addition of light to light.

4. AND, relative to the *national* aspect of prophecies, tho' addressed to *individuals*, Bp. NEWTON, (when speaking of the curse of Canaan, the blessing of Shem, and the enlargement of Japhet) says: " It is thinking meanly of the an-
" cient prophecies of scripture, and having very
" imperfect, very unworthy conceptions of them,
" to limit their intention to particular persons.
" In this view the ancient prophets would be
" really what the Deists think them, little better
" than common fortune-tellers; and their pro-
" phecies would hardly be worth remembering
" or recording, especially in so concise and com-
" pendious a history as that of Moses. We
" must affix a larger meaning to them, and un-
" derstand them not of single persons, but of
" *whole nations*; and thereby a nobler scene of
" things, and a more extensive prospect will be
" opened to us of the divine dispensations∥."

§ 30. IF any prophecies represent decidedly christian conversions in a *national* view, I think it must be allowed, that the *infant* part, on a fair construction, must be included in such an idea. Out of many passages that might be adduced to this purpose, I shall insist but on the few following.

GENESIS

§ Dissert. on Proph. vol. i. p. 14.

GENESIS xii. 3. *In thee shall* ALL FAMILIES OF THE EARTH *be blessed.* - And chap. xxvi. 4. *In thy seed shall* ALL THE NATIONS OF THE EARTH *be blessed.* These passages are not only precious *promises*, but also important *prophecies*; the former delivered to Abraham, the latter, being a repetition and confirmation of it, to Isaac. And the same was expressly made to Jacob afterwards (chap. xxviii. 14.) It is evident, the terms *families* and *nations* are here used synonymously; nor does there appear any necessity, or sufficient ground, for understanding them otherwise than *indefinite*, comprehending the *general body*, great and small, of people inhabiting certain territories and provinces. Whether our Lord intended such *national conversions* in his commission to—*disciple all* NATIONS, Matt. xxviii. 19. shall be further considered.——Again, when Isaac unwittingly blessed his son Jacob he said, chap. xxvii. 29. *Let* PEOPLE *serve thee and* NATIONS *bow down to thee*, &c. " When the gentiles were converted " to christianity, the prophecy was fulfilled li-" terally, and will more amply be fulfilled, when " *the fulness of the gentiles shall come in, and all* " *Israel shall be saved*†."

PSALM lxxii. 11. *Yea all kings shall fall down before him* [the Messiah]; *all* NATIONS *shall serve him.* ver. 17. *ult. all* NATIONS *shall call him blessed.* I believe it is generally agreed, that divers passages in this Psalm are quite inapplicable to Solomon, tho' entitled, " *A Psalm for Solomon,*" and

† NEWTON's Dissert. *ut supra.* p. 83.

Ch. 3.   *Subjects of Baptism.*   263

and equally fo to any other King but the *Messiah*. It should therefore be confidered as referring to Solomon but imperfectly, while it has its clear and full accomplishment in Chrift and the gofpel difpenfation. And from thefe paffages of this prophetick fublime Pfalm it appears,

1. THAT the Meffiah's kingdom, in its *external* afpect, fhould have kings and their fubjects, or *whole nations*, as fuch, included in it.

2. THAT in fome future period this fhould be *univerfally* the defirable cafe. *All* kings fhall fubmit and worfhip; *all* nations fhall become his fubjects, to ferve him and call him bleffed. To the like purpofe is Pf. lxxxii. 8. *ult.*

ISAIAH xix. 23—25. *In that day, fhall there be a hight-way,* &c. On which paffage Bp. NEWTON thus remarks: " By the means of the Jews and profelytes dwelling in Egypt and Syria, Ifrael, Egypt and Syria were in fome meafure united in the fame worfhip. But this was *more fully* accomplifhed, when thefe countries became chriftian, and fo were made members of the fame body in Chrift Jefus. And we pioufly hope and believe, that it will receive its moft perfect completion in the latter days, when *Mohammedifm* fhall be rooted out, and *Chriftianity* fhall again flourifh in thefe countries, when *the fulnefs of the gentiles fhall come in, and all Ifrael fhall be faved*§." On the whole it appears, That *Egypt* and *Affyria*, whether they ftand for the converted Gentile nations indefinitely, or thofe countries literally, fhould be on the *fame footing* with Ifrael in this particular, viz. Their converfion would be

§ Ib. p. 378.

be *national*, and *not* confined to adults *only*. On Antipœdobaptift principles, none fhould be deemed fubjects of the gofpel kingdom externally, but thofe adults who make a credible profeffion; but how well this agrees with the prophetick reprefentations of *national* converfions, let the impartial judge.

VERY remarkable to the fame purpofe is another text in the fame prophet, chap. lii. 15. *So* *fhall* HE SPRINKLE MANY NATIONS. On which obferve,

1. THAT the term HE refers to Chrift, is very evident from the context; and many of the Jewifh doctors, as well as the Chaldee paraphraft, apply it directly to the Meffiah; and fo ftriking is the reference to *Chrift*, that it is faid, " divers Jews have been convinced and converted to the Chriftian faith, by the evidence of this prophecy."

2. IT is as clear, that the ACTION here afcribed to him relates to the *New Teftament*. Difpenfation.

3. THE obvious and natural acceptation of the term SPRINKLE, in this connection, is that of *purifying*; and it undoubtedly *alludes* to thofe Jewifh ceremonial purifications which were performed by fprinkling perfons and things.

4. THO' thefe ceremonial fprinklings under the law reprefented and typified the atoning blood of Chrift, and the cleanfing efficacy of his grace, yet it would be forced and unnatural to afcribe this internal, fpiritual, and faving influence, to MANY NATIONS. Therefore,

5. THE prediction properly and directly intends that *external holinefs* whereby *Chriftian nations* are

pro-

Ch. 3.   *Subjects of Baptism.*   265

profeffionally *diftinguifhed* from others. And how great the privilege, how fignal the honour, conferred on fuch nations! They are *fet apart* by a gracious diftinguifhing Providence, and by the profelyting ordinance, to be to the Lord *a people*, while he exhibits himfelf to be to them *a God!* Bleffed is the people that is in fuch a cafe, yea bleffed is the *nation* that has *the* LORD for its God! But

6. MUST we *exclude* infants from being parts of thefe *nations*, and from the privileges of their parents? The law of nature, that is, the *law of God*, and the analogy of all divine difpenfations that were ever made known to man, forbid the contracted thought, while unfupported by any fo much as pretended divine warrant.

7. IT appears from the New Teftament records that the appointed ordinance of initiation into this ftate of relative holinefs, individually and *explicitly*, is, the Chriftian purification — BAPTISM. Confequently,

8. FROM the premifes it unavoidably follows — That the fpirit of prophecy, in this paffage, affords a venerable and facred fanction to Pœdobaptift principles.

WHETHER the interpretation now given, or Dr. S's, who fays of this text, " The plain meaning is, that his doctrine fhould defcend like rain upon many nations and people †," be moft agreeable to truth, let the impartial reader judge.

§ 31. THIS *national* (and confequently *Pædo-*
N   *baptift*)

† Remarks on the *Chriftian Minifter's Reafons*, &c. p. 3.

baptift) view of the gospel dispensation, is implied in many more prophetick passages, Isa. lv. 5. *Behold thou shalt call a* NATION *that thou knowest not, and* NATIONS *that knew not thee shall run unto thee, because of the Lord thy God,* &c. Jer. iv. 2. ult. *The* NATIONS *shall bless themselves in him, and in him shall they glory.* Dan. vii. 14. *And there was given him dominion and glory and a kingdom, that all* PEOPLE, NATIONS, *and languages should serve him.* Ver. 27. ult. *And all* DOMINIONS *shall serve him.* Mic. iv. 2. *And* MANY NATIONS *shall come, and say, Come, and let us go up to the mountain of the Lord,* &c. Zech. ii. 11. *And* MANY NATIONS *shall be* JOINED TO THE LORD *in that day, and shall be* MY PEOPLE. To which we may add, Matt. xxi. 43. *Therefore say I unto you,* THE KINGDOM OF GOD *shall be taken from you, and* GIVEN TO A NATION *bringing forth the fruits thereof.* Rev. xi. 15. ult. THE KINGDOMS OF THIS WORLD ARE BECOME THE KINGDOMS OF OUR LORD AND OF HIS CHRIST. Here I observe,

1. THAT the phrase, " the kingdoms of this world," in the last text, must be understood in its plain literal import, from the obvious opposition intended between it and the other, " the kingdoms of our Lord;" and for a like reason, the *latter* must intend KINGDOMS PROFESSEDLY CHRISTIAN. For the words are a prophetick representation of what *should* take place in some future period of the Christian church. Now in what sense can the KINGDOMS OF THE WORLD

BECOME

become the kingdoms of the Lord, and of his Chrift, if not in that we contend for? They were *his* in every other fenfe *prior* to the date of this prophecy. They were *always* the Lord's as the God of *providence*. By him kings have ever reigned, and princes decreed juftice. Nor was there ever a time when the whole earth was not his, and the fulnefs thereof, with all its nations and kingdoms; to enlarge or contract them; to raife or to fink them; to caufe and regulate their revolutions and fucceffions in every age. It remains, therefore, that Chriftian kingdoms are the *Lord's* in a fenfe fimilar to that in which Ifrael was *his*; with this difference, that the yoke of Mofaic ceremonies fhould be removed, and a fpiritual evangelical worfhip introduced.

2. Our Lord (Matt. xxi. 43.) fpeaks of the kingdom of God being transferred from one *nation to* another *nation*. Now what lefs can we infer hence, than — that the kingdom of God was not *abolifhed* but *transferred* from one people to another — and that the *national* afpect of the former (at leaft fo far as to *include* the children with their parents) fhould be the fubject matter of the transfer. If it be faid that what was *taken away* from the one, and *given* to the other, did not imply, notwithftanding, the *church-memberfhip* of infants: I reply, if the church-memberfhip of infants, in the kingdom of God *to be* transferred, be an *effential* part of that kingdom, this effential part muft be included in what *was given* to the other nation, or the gentile part

of the world. But the former is true, as might be easily shewn; and therefore so is the latter. And that by the *kingdom of God* we are not to understand merely the *preaching of the gospel*, is decisively clear hence, viz. That *this* was not what they once *possessed* and *gloried* in, but their *national adoption*, their church state and privileges; and therefore this latter (from the scope of the text) must be what was *taken away*, and not merely a preached gospel. It is true the rejection of the Messiah, as the most signal instance of unfruitfulness, was the *cause* of their vineyard being laid waste, their branches cut off, and their kingdom transferred; but the apostolick resolution — *lo! we turn to the gentiles*, was by no means the full accomplishment of the prediction. It intended, as what resulted from their rejecting the counsel of God against themselves, a *disinheriting* of the Jewish nation, which differs from their *not receiving the gospel*, as the effect differs from the cause. Besides, the phrase, " shall be given to another nation," is to be considered as a *judgment* on those from whom it is taken; but this could not have been the case if it meant no more than — henceforth the gospel, which is preached to you, shall be preached to the gentiles *also* — for that could be no judgment to any, but a blessing to all. Nor is it true *in fact*, that the gospel was *taken from* the Jews otherwise than from any unbelieving gentiles. The commission was, *Go, preach the gospel to every creature,* BEGINNING AT JERUSALEM. And Peter assures his brethren, that

that the *gospel* promise, or the exhibition of mercy, is *to them and their children*, as well as to *those that were afar off*. Nor do we find any *repeal* of this grant, this *universal* aspect of the gospel promise, and therefore what was *taken from* them was their CHURCH STATE, whereby *wrath* — this predicted wrath — *came on them to the uttermost*. *From this* they were *broken off*, (and not from the gospel call) and *to this* the gentiles were *adopted*. The *fall* of the one, became the *riches* of the other. What the one *fell from*, the other was *promoted to*; and what can this be, but their *church state* as a body of people?

3. THAT remarkable text in *Zechariah* (chap. ii. 11.) speaks of *many nations* that should, under the gospel dispensation, be *joined to the Lord*, and accounted *his people*. On Antipœdobaptist principles, which deny the church-membership of infants and the validity of their baptism, this prophecy neither has been, nor is ever likely to be, fulfilled in whole or in part. Nay, according to them, it is absolutely *incapable* of being fulfilled. For infants and children ever have made, and ever will make, a very considerable part of a *nation*. But if none, on our opponents' hypothesis, are to be deemed as *joined to the Lord*, but such as make a profession of faith and repentance, not only all infants and young children are struck off from visible church-membership, but, for aught we have *yet* seen, the *bulk* of a nation, or the *far greater* part. Nor will it avail them to say, that this prediction refers to the latter day glory

glory; for be the day ever so glorious, and the success of the gospel ever so great; let it be that all the adults in a nation shall be born to God in one day, still the *younger part* of the nation, which is very considerable in number, must not be joined to the Lord; and therefore, if our opponents be right, no NATION, properly speaking, is *capable* of being *joined to the Lord*, and of being *his people*, in any period of the gospel church however glorious.

§ 32. To this view of *national conversions* it may perhaps be objected, " That the term *nation* in the above places is taken *improperly* and *figuratively*, not for *the whole* of a people small and great, but for a considerable *part*, i. e. for those in a nation that would make a profession of their faith and repentance. As in Isa. xvii. 12, 13, &c. I answer,

1. IN all equity the term should be taken according to the nature of the subject; which has no reference to the incursion of *armies*, but the accession of *proselytes*; which latter ever included the children with their parents.

2. IN the passages first produced (§ 30.) the words *nations* and *families* are used synonymously; which latter cannot be understood in that connection to the *exclusion* of children. Therefore, to *limit* the term nation, to signify those in a nation who profess faith and repentance, is taking an unwarrantable liberty; a liberty for which no tolerable reason, I think, can be assigned.

As

As to the objection, "That religion is a *personal* thing ‖; either it has no force at all againſt Pœdobaptiſt principles, or it muſt condemn all preceding diſpenſations. But loth to impeach infinite wiſdom for giving ſanction to infant church-memberſhip in every age of the world, we conclude, that whatever truth is contained in the propoſition—" religion is a perſonal thing"—ſtands in perfect conſiſtency with our principles.—But if by religion's being a *perſonal* thing, be implied—that a perſon's *own conſent* is neceſſary to make him the ſubject of religious obligations; I dare affirm that the propoſition in that ſenſe is of moſt pernicious tendency. Not leſs ſo, than the modern notion of the —"innocence of mental errors!"

WILL it be objected, "That God requires to be worſhipped *now* in ſpirit and in truth?" And pray, *when* was it that he did *not* require to be ſo worſhipped? Was Abraham's worſhip, for inſtance, of a *carnal* complexion? Was his family religion *leſs ſpiritual* than that of thoſe who reject infants, as far as in them lies, from the boſom of the chriſtian church? We cannot help thinking, that thoſe objections which are urged againſt the church-memberſhip and baptiſm of infants, drawn from the great *ſpirituality* of the goſpel diſpenſation, favours not a little of the *Socinian* leaven †, which degrades the Old Teſtament as much as poſſible, to keep its votaries in countenance when explaining the New. On the contrary

‖ Dr. STENNETT's Anſwer to Dr. A. p.
† Vid. MARKII Medul. Cap. xii. § 4, 8, 12, 15, &c.

trary, we think it reasonable to conclude, that the more spiritual and excellent the dispensation is, the *stronger* the argument in favour of Pœdobaptist principles and practice.

OR will any say, " Supposing *all former* dispensations admitted infants to a participation of the same religious rites with their parents, it does not follow that they *now* must." We say it *does* follow, by the most just and certain consequence, if we have no scriptural affirmative evidence to the contrary. For whatever source it proceeds from, it is a privilege in itself. Whether this *universal fact* of infant children having been included with their parents in church privileges, arises from its natural reasonableness, and the apparent incongruity, unreasonableness and unnatural severity of the contrary; in other words, from the original *constitution of human nature*, whereby its divine Author has not only characterized it as *social* and communicative of benefits, but also formed the strongest *connection* between the parents and their offspring, as to all the benefits and privileges of the former: Whether the fact arises from this, I say, or from a *covenant grant*,—it should not be renounced but by the highest authority. And this authority must be, if at all existing, either an explicit repeal, or an implicit and virtual abrogation. We maintain that *neither* exists; and therefore we cannot renounce the church-membership and baptism of our infant children, without denying these things to be a *privilege*, that is to say, without DENYING a plain FACT.

§ 33. BUT

§ 33. But an objection still more formidable yet remains, viz. "If the above prophecies refer to *national converſions*, does not that lead to *national churches?* And what then becomes of the diſſenting and congregational plan?" I reply,

That a national eſtabliſhment, if well ordered, appears more agreeable to the prophetick paſſages we have been confidering than the Antipœdobaptiſt plan; nay more agreeable to the geral tenor of revelation. I ſay, "well ordered;" for, in the preſent caſe, the queſtion is not how they *are*, but how they *may be* eſtabliſhed. Nor does there appear any irreconcileable difference between a national eſtabliſhment and congregational difcipline.

It is neceſſary that infants make a part of nations, but it does not at all follow, that the civil magiſtrate ſhould — be the vifible *head* of the church — prefcribe to all the nation, to the greateſt nicety, the terms of chriſtian communion — publiſh acts which impoſe *uniformity*, rigid uniformity, in religious matters, under heavy penalties — require obedience in things which no one pretends to be vindicable on fcriptural or rational grounds — and efpecially ſhould require of miniſters the fubfcribing of *plain contradictions*.

On the whole it appears, that the language of prophecy, refpecting *nations* becoming vifibly *chriſtian*, is quite inimical to the Antipœdobaptiſt hypotheſis. — We now proceed to inveſtigate a few prophetick teſtimonies of another kind.

§ 34. Out

§ 34. OUT of many that might be urged in favour of infants, let the following be confidered. Pfalm cii. 28. *The* CHILDREN *of thy* SERVANTS *fhall continue, and* THEIR SEED *fhall be eftablifhed before thee.* On which I obferve,

1. THAT thefe words moft undoubtedly belong to the Chriftian difpenfation, as appears from St. Paul's quotation (Heb. i. 11, 12.) of the foregoing verfes; for *thofe* he exprefsly applies to Chrift, and *this* ftands in ftrict connection with them. It therefore follows, that thefe *fervants* are the fervants of Chrift, and who can thefe be, but either his *real* or *profeffing* people? And whether the one or the other be intended, it follows,

2. THAT their *children* fhall *continue.* But in what refpect fhall the children of chriftians CONTINUE? Does it refer to the *continuation* of the *human race* thro' their inftrumentality? Is *this* the full import of the facred text, that chriftians fhould not be furpaffed by *infidels*, but fhould be fruitful and multiply, and replenifh the earth, *as well as they?* We cannot fuppofe that fo low and jejune a meaning is worthy of the pen of infpiration. It therefore remains, that the prophetick promife refers to the religious privileges of the children of chriftians, and imports — that they fhould *continue* (*Jifhconu*) dwell, abide, or tarry in the vifible church of God, as they were wont to do, along with their parents in every other œconomy of grace that ever was. To this is added,

3. THAT *their feed* fhall be *eftablifhed.* It is hardly

hardly neceſſary to obſerve here, that by *ſeed* is meant *offspring* as ſuch, without excluding the youngeſt infant. And whether the pronoun *their*, relates to the antecedents *ſervants* or *children*, is immaterial, (tho' the connection ſeems to refer it to the latter,) it ſtill follows that the offspring — yes, the *infant* offspring — of chriſtians are to be *eſtabliſhed before* the Meſſiah. In what ſenſe *eſtabliſhed?* and how *before* the Lord Chriſt? It cannot mean that the ſeed of believers ſhould be eſtabliſhed in the *grace* of the covenant. We conclude then that the purport of the words is, —that the offspring of chriſtians were intended by the ſpirit of prophecy to be *eſtabliſhed*, confirmed, unmoved from and ſettled in their former ſtanding *before the Lord* in his church.

SHOULD any contend for this general meaning, that the chriſtian church ſhould be a kingdom in perpetuity, to continue for ever as what cannot be moved, it will not alter the caſe; for the words clearly point out the *manner* and *means* whereby this is effected, viz. by the children of profeſſors, and their ſeed being continued and eſtabliſhed in the church.

§ 35. THE next paſſage I ſhall advert to is Iſaiah lxv. 23. *They ſhall not labour in vain, nor bring forth for trouble: for they are* THE SEED *of the bleſſed of the Lord, and* THEIR OFFSPRING WITH THEM. Hence obſerve,

1. THAT the prediction refers evidently to *goſpel* times, and the accompliſhment muſt be ſought among *Chriſtians*. For tho' it were maintained, that the ſpirit of prophecy here eyed the Jews

Jews in their glorious reſtoration to church privileges after the fulneſs of the Gentiles was brought in, *that* can make no manner of difference; for the Jews when *called* will be CHRISTIANS as well as the called Gentiles. The *middle wall of partition*, which cauſed the celebrated diſtribution of the human race into Jews and Gentiles, has been taken down. And it is obvious that what the Gentiles now *do enjoy* by right of evangelical privileges, is the *very ſame* as what the Jews *would have enjoyed*, if wrath had not come upon them to the uttermoſt, to their un-churching and diſperſion. The removal of the ſeparating wall evidently implies an intended incorporation, and a community of privileges. And it is equally plain, that what they *would have enjoyed* if they had then received the Meſſiah, was the ſame as what they *ſhall enjoy* on their future reception of him. Therefore, whether the converted Gentiles or Jews be intended in the words, they are CHRISTIANS, or ſubjects of the *laſt* and unalterable œconomy of mercy.

2. WHATEVER honours and privileges belong to THE SEED *of the bleſſed of the Lord* (and whoever be intended thereby) their OFFSPRING are pronounced *bleſſed* WITH THEM, co-participants of the ſame benefits. But all religious benefits being either *internal* and real, or *external* and relative; and the *former* bleſſings do not devolve on the children, as *their* children, (which needs not to be formally proved to Antipœdobaptiſts;) it follows — that theſe privileges, of which

which the *offspring* of chriftians are co-participants *with their parents*, are the external and œconomical benefits of the chriftian church. And if *baptifm* be a *benefit*, as it demonftrably is to all capable fubjects, and it is equally demonftrable that infants are fuch, it irrefragably follows that, according to the language and defign of prophecy, the infant children of chriftians are entitled to baptifm with their parents. On the whole, the *connection* between parents and children, relative to church privileges and facred ordinances, fo reafonable and conformable to the law of nature in itfelf, and fo countenanced by the fanction of Heaven, is here ratified and confirmed.

§ 36. (4.) THAT it is the WILL OF CHRIST we fhould introduce our infant children into the chriftian church, by the initiatory ordinance of baptifm, will further appear from the corroborating evidence afforded in the NEW TESTAMENT.

BUT, previous to our inveftigation of particular paffages, it is neceffary to repeat a remark before made—that the TRANSITION from one difpenfation to another, is *of itfelf* no adequate reafon for abrogating any benefit or cuftom appertaining to the former, which would be really a benefit under the latter. Hence we find, (conformably to that wife and benevolent apophthegm, Mark ii. 21, 22.) that the change from the Jewifh to the Chriftian œconomy, was *gradual* and moft tender. Nothing was altered without a manifeft neceffity, and that always for the *better*. Our Lord and his apoftles, being native Jews, not only were obfervant servant of the *religious* worship and ceremonies of the Jewish church, but also complied with their innocent *civil customs*. It is beyond all reasonable doubt, that *baptism*, as a purifying rite, and the holy *supper*, as a solemn Jewish festival, were in use before their appointment as standing ordinances in the church*. The Apostle Paul assures us (Heb. ix. 10.) there were *before* Christ *divers baptisms*. Therefore the baptism of the New Testament has nothing new but its appointment to the *particular purpose* of proselyting into the Messiah's visible and universal church. And this is perfectly conformable to the divine proceedings in former periods; as might be instanced in the appointment of the *rainbow* as a token and seal of the covenant, the Mosaic institution of *sacrifices*, &c.

THESE things duly considered, it must be a weak prejudice, a false notion taken upon trust, unsupported by one solid principle, That there is any thing in the *mere change* of a dispensation, which implies an abolition of former *privileges*, and a promiscuous annihilation of *every part* of church relations and connections. The *substance* of true religion is the same in all periods; and to suppose otherwise, would be as ridiculous as to suppose that whenever a man changes his *clothes*, his *body too* is metamorphosed! The spiritual and moral parts of religion are the same now as ever; and tho' the gospel presents to us new *objects*,

or

---

* See, among others, the following authors on this head: WITSIUS's Oecon. B. iv. chap. xvi. § 2. also § 3—10. GODWYN's Moses and Aaron, Lib. iii. chap. ii. HAMMOND's Letter, Q. iv. § 5. GROTIUS in Matth. iii. 6. xxvi. 26—30. xxviii. 18.

or rather the same objects in a clearer light, yet the *principles* of true piety, *faith, love*, &c. continue invariably the same in every age. Again: duties of *natural obligation* are no more superseded by any change of dispensation in the church, than the principles of common sense are superseded by true philosophy. Whatever, therefore, appears of natural obligation, and meets with no revealed *positive* interruption, flows on uniformly and quite unaffected by a mere change of œconomy.

Of this *invariable* nature, we insist, is the obligation of parents to *benefit* their children by introducing them to a participation of their *own* privileges, even *all* those of which they are suitable subjects, be these privileges what they may: for, properly speaking, their *nature* does not constitute the *criterion* whereby we judge of the obligation, but the *capacity* and *suitableness* of the subject. It has been, I think, demonstrated, that baptism is an ordinance of which infants are not less capable than their parents, that they possess all necessary suitableness and qualifications to answer its nature and design; and therefore that the obligation of parents to baptize them is absolute and strong. This being the case, nothing short of a divine *express warrant* should influence any christian parent to the contrary. But scripture is so far from affording any such evidence, that it abounds with corroborating proofs to the contrary. We have appealed to every successive dispensation of revealed religion, we have appealed to the language of prophecy relative to gospel times, whereby the original thesis acquired additional confirmation;

firmation; and now we chearfully appeal to the New Testament records.

§ 37. JOHN the Baptist, or the Baptizer, makes his appearance as a Jew among the Jews; in spirit, aspect and manners, another Elijah. But *whom* does he *baptize?* *Who* were the subjects of his extraordinary *purification?* " Jerusalem and all Judea, and all the region round about Jordan." Matt. iii. 5 — 7. " All the people that heard him, except the Pharisees and Lawyers." Luke vii. 29, 30. — The whole account of the subjects of his baptism is but short and general, as may be seen at one view, Chap. ii. § 2, &c. On which I remark,

TOWARDS an accurate and judicious interpretation of this concise account, in reference to the *particulars* of our present inquiry, it is necessary to keep a steady eye upon the proper and allowable *data* for that purpose. The Antipœdobaptists lay *this* down as a general rule — " If the scripture be *silent* about infants as the subject of baptism, or even not *decisively express* in their favour, we are to take it for *granted*, that they were *not* baptized." To face this cannon, however, formidable, we venture to plant another — " If the scripture be silent about infants as the subjects of baptism, or even not decisively express *against them*, we are to take it for *granted*, that they WERE baptized with their parents." The general reason of this rule has been already produced repeatedly; but with regard to its propriety and just application

tion in the cafe before us, let the following things be obferved:

1. IF John's baptifm was *beneficial* to the parents, as a *divine inflitution*, and their children were equally *capable* of being the fubjects of it with themfelves, (which our opponents in fact allow, by promifing to accede to our practice on the evidence of a clear precept or example, which they could not promife to do on fuppofition of abfolute incapability); there appears fome reafon and propriety *for* Pœdobaptifm, and nothing againft it.

2. IF we confider the conftitution, the genius, the ftate and circumftances of that church of which John lived and died a member, and the perfons who were the fubjects of his baptifm, we may fafely conclude—that infants *were* partakers of the cleanfing rite with their parents.

JOHN was a *Jew*, and fo were thofe, *all* thofe, he baptized; nor did they ceafe to be members of the Jewifh church on account of his baptifm. Their minds were indeed raifed and directed to Chrift, as one who would baptize them with the Holy Ghoft; but *that* did not change their church relation, any more than the believing lively views and longing expectations of the patriarchs, prophets and other faints, in reference to the future kingdom of the Meffiah, did change *their* church ftate.

Now what was the *nature* of that *rite* of which John was the appointed adminiftrator? I anfwer, It was a Jewifh cleanfing, or ceremonial purification. In proof of which affertion, (omitting numerous refpectable authorities that might be produced

produced, sufficient at least to exculpate from the charge of novelty) let this consideration be duly attended to — That, independent on the testimonies of the Jewish doctors concerning proselyte baptism, since we are certified by the pen of inspiration, (Heb. ix. 10.) there were *divers* BAPTISMS in use among the Jews, we *ought not* to consider John's baptizations as any other than these Jewish purifications and cleansings, any further than we are *necessitated* to do so from the New Testament records. It is therefore incumbent on those who hold that this rite was of a *different* nature, to shew clearly wherein the *difference* consisted, or else be content with the censure due to those who adopt an hypothesis without proof. Convinced, however, that these divine records favour no such discrimination as the abettors of that hypothesis contend for, we conclude that John's baptism was one of the *divers* BAPTISMS, before mentioned *.

IT

* I am not a little surprised at Dr. GILL's remarks on John's baptism (Body of Div. Vol. iii. B. iii. Ch. i.) where he attempts to prove that water-baptism is *peculiar* to the gospel dispensation. " This is opposed," says he, " to the sentiments of such " who say baptism was in use before the times of *John*, of Christ " and his apostles.—There were indeed divers washings, bathings, " or BAPTISMS, under the legal dispensation, for the purification " of persons and things unclean, by the ceremonial law; which " had a doctrine in them, called the *doctrine of baptisms*, which " taught the cleansing of sin by *the blood of Christ*; but there was " nothing similar in them to the ordinance of water-baptism, BUT " IMMERSION ONLY!" How the Dr. takes for granted, without proof or apology, that the passage referred to (Heb. ix. 10.) signifies *divers* IMMERSIONS! a passage his opponents have always pleaded as decisive *against* him! *Nothing similar to water-*BAPTISM *but* IMMERSION. That is, on his principle, which maintains that

Βαπτισμος;

IT is plain the exprefs *defign* of it was to *prepare the way* of the Lord. For, as Mofes was commiffioned *to* SANCTIFY *the people*, i. e. to prepare them by a ceremonial purification in expectation of an approaching new œconomy (Ex. xix. 10, 14.); in like manner, John was fent to the fame honoured family, the houfe of Ifrael, not only to proclaim to them that *the kingdom of heaven*, that is, a new and more excellent œconomy, was at hand, but alfo to fecond the important meffage by a general purification‖.

BUT, the queftion now returns, what was the conftitution of the Jewifh church as to *infants ?* The reply need be but fhort to fo plain a cafe: Infants fhared in the *fame rites* with their parents, even all thofe of which they were capable fubjects, were not particularly diftinguifhed and excepted.' Not more fure is it, that children oft, particularly *infant* children, were unavoidably fubjected to ceremonial *pollutions* with their parents than they were entitled to the *fame cleanfings*. Therefore, whatever was the nature of John's cleanfing rite, we may fecurely infer — parents and children partook of it in common.

3. WHEN

Βαπ7ισμος is *immerfion* — there was nothing in thofe *divers immerfions*, fimilar to the oidinance of *water-immerfion*, but *immerfion* only ! ! To fuch ridiculous inconfiftencies is that hypothefis reducible which makes the biblical ufe of the words baptifm and immerfion convertible and fynonymous! He proceeds : " John was the *firft* adminiftrator of the ordinance of baptifm."—This is flatly contradictory to the Dr's. conceffion immediately foregoing — " that there were divers *baptifms* under the legal difpenfation," and confequently *baptizers*.

‖ Vid. GROTIUS in Matth. iii. 6.

3. When we confider, in connection with thefe things, the general and *univerfal terms* made ufe of in the narration, we are rather confirmed than otherwife in favour of Pœdobaptifm, as practifed by the venerable fon of Zacharias. When we read of, *all the people—the multitude—all that heard him*, and the like, in reference to an ordinance in which infants and young children were capable of fharing as well as adults; by what equitable rule, I would fain know, are we authorized to fet up an excluding barrier? If becaufe *infants* and children are not *mentioned* particularly, by the fame rule we muft exclude *women* from the privilege of John's baptifm. But if the *filence* of the infpired narrative is no fufficient reafon for excluding the *latter*, neither is it for excluding the *former*. The very ufe of *general terms* is fufficient evidence *(cæt. par.)* for including all the fpecies to which they are applicable.

§ 38. But here I am aware of an objection that may be thought unanfwerable againft the above reafoning, viz. "That thofe who were baptized by John *confeffed their fins*, which infants could not do." To this irrefragable argument, falfely fo called, we fhall oppofe the following anfwers.

1. In all equitable and fair conftruction, nothing more can be inferred from fuch paffages as fpeak of " Jerufalem, and all Judea, and all the region round about Jordan, being baptized of John in Jordan, *confeffing their fins*," (Matt. iii. 5, 6.) than that *fuch* of them as were *actual* finners made a *general* confeffion of their fins and iniquities; whereas,

as, to serve the antipœdobaptist cause, the narration should support a proof widely different, viz. That John baptized *no others* but those who made a *personal* confession of their sins. But this, which alone would be available to our opponents, the history of John's baptism I believe will *not* support.

WHAT better clue can we fix upon towards investigating this point, than those scripture passages which treat of national and general *confessions of sin?* Thus, for instance, the Lord himself says with respect to Israel, Lev. xxvi. 40—42. *If they shall* CONFESS THEIR INIQUITY, *and the iniquity of their fathers, with their trespass which they trespassed against me, and that also they have walked against me — if then their uncircumcised hearts be humbled, and they then accept of the punishment of their iniquity; then will I remember my covenant — and I will remember the land.* Thus also Solomon, in his excellent prayer, on that memorable and eminently solemn occasion of introducing the ark of God into the new erected temple, 1 Kings, viii. 47—53. *If they shall bethink themselves — and* REPENT, *and make supplication unto thee — saying,* WE HAVE SINNED, AND HAVE DONE PERVERSELY, WE HAVE COMMITTED WICKEDNESS; *and so return unto thee with all their heart, and with all their soul — then hear thou their prayer and their supplication in heaven thy dwelling place, and maintain their cause — and give them compassion before them who carried them captive, that they may have compassion on them; for they be thy people and thine inheritance, &c.* In like manner, on another solemn

lemn occasion, when a national reformation was attempted, and a general fast observed, it is said, Neh. ix. 2. *The seed of Israel separated themselves from all strangers, and stood and* CONFESSED THEIR SINS, *and the iniquities of their fathers.*

From these and similar passages we may observe, (1) That the PEOPLE IN GENERAL, or *as a body*, are said to *confess their iniquity*, to *repent*, and to say, *We have sinned*, &c. (2) That notwithstanding, *infants* were *not capable* of these acts. But, (3) Nevertheless, there was no privilege, national or ecclesiastical, which an infant was capable of enjoying, but was participated by the child as well as the parent, as connected with, or consequent upon, such as repentance and confession of sin. And (4) We may note the *general form* of confession,—" We have sinned, and have done perversely, we have committed wickedness."—How parallel this account is with the repentance and confession of, " Jerusalem and all Judea," let the impartial reader judge. Let him reflect, particularly, that repentance and confession of sin were the prescribed *conditions* in *both* cases, and the *benefits* suspended on these conditions were, in the one case, God's remembering his covenant, and the land—maintaining their cause, and giving them compassion before their enemies;—and, in the other, the *blessing* (not the *duty*) of the ecclesiastical purifying rite, and whatever external privileges were connected with it.

Again: it is not supposeable that " Jerusalem and

Ch. 3.   *Subjects of Baptism.*   287

and all Judea," were *deemed* by John *true penitents*; and the fequel of the hiftory fhews abundantly they were not *in fact*. *All*, who did not *reject the counfel of God againſt themſelves*, (Mark i. 5. Luke vii. 30.) were baptized of him ; ALL the people but the *Pharifees* and *lawyers*. Therefore, feeing the repentance, humiliation and confeffion were of the *general nature* above defcribed, there is no fufficient reafon affignable why the infants and children *ſhould* not, or *did* not, fhare with their parents in the baptifmal *benefit*, as the confequence of thofe conditions.—It would be eafy to make the fame remarks on the humiliation of the Ninevites ; when Jonah cried in the city, as John did in the wildernefs, that deftruction and wrath awaited the impenitent, the effect was pretty much alike ; a *general humiliation* enfued, and we are fure that in the *one* inftance, *infants* fhared in the parent's confequent privilege ; therefore, fince that participation was not founded on a *pofitive grant* but the *law of nature*, we are conftrained to conclude —that the parent's privilege, in the *other* inftance, extended to his infants, and dependent family, in virtue of the fame uniform law. Befides,

2. WHEN we confider how little notice is taken of children in the fubfequent hiftory of the chriftian church, particularly that part of it which treats of the progrefs and fuccefs of the gofpel, and the evangelizing of nations, as well as in the facred records of the Old Teftament ; where yet

from

from circumstances we may gather with certainty the avowed church-memberſhip and baptiſm of infants; it is very conceiveable how the New Teſtament ſhould leave this point as we find it. The ſame remark is applicable to moſt reformations in the church, and revolutions in civil ſociety, while the memberſhip and privileges of infants in theſe caſes ſtand confeſſed in the eſtimation of their reſpective hiſtorians.

CONSIDERING, therefore, theſe things—that the ordinance *in itſelf* does not exclude infant ſubjects, but admits them not leſs than adults, as before proved;—that the conſtitution, genius, and uniform cuſtom of the Jewiſh church (of which John and his diſciples were members) included infants with their parents;—that there appears in the brief account of John's miniſtry nothing *againſt* infants, but the *general* terms uſed are rather *in favour* of them;—and that nothing can be gathered, in fairneſs and equity, of objectionable weight, from the account of the people *confeſſing their ſins* as a conditional qualification for enjoying the baptiſmal privilege; for, on ſuppoſition that infants *were baptized*, no *other* language could be reaſonably expected, as further appears from the Old Teſtament and the moſt approved eccleſiaſtical and civil records — we conclude, That John was a POEDOBAPTIST *de jure*, THEREFORE, (*cæt. par.*) that we ought to regard him ſuch *de facto*.

§ 39. WE next appeal to Chriſt's public miniſtry. Our Lord and his ſervants, we are expreſsly told,

Ch. 3.   *Subjects of Baptism.*   289

told, made and baptized *more* difciples than John, tho' the latter baptized fo great a number. How numerous then muft they be! But were they *all* confidered as *true believers,* or *real converts,* that is, juftified and fanctified perfons? Did our Lord, by his minifters, baptize the innumerable multitudes on *that fuppofition?* Nothing lefs. All that can in reafon be thought of them is, that they made a general furrender of themfelves as families and affembled crowds, after the manner of John's followers; and indeed, their fo general defection from Chrift on occafion of his fearching difcourfes, and his approaching death, renders the fact indubitable.

We may here again obferve, that *the fame reafon* remains in force, in behalf of the privileges of children, in this period as before; as there is no ground of *repeal,* we think, either expreffed or implied. But tho' we have nothing *againft* them, we have fomething *in favour* of them. What I fhall infift upon from this part of fcripture evidence, fhall be confined to two things — our Lord's confirming and decifive *fentence* concerning the *church privileges* of infants — and the fame thing *implied* in what he fays of certain towns and cities as a general body, thro' the whole courfe of his miniftry.

Let us begin with that paffage Mat. xix. 13 —15. recorded alfo, with fome variation, Mark x. 13—16. and Luke xviii. 15—17. Inftead of tranfcribing thefe paffages at length feverally, as every reader may eafily confult them, I fhall give
                                    O   them

them in one connected view from the *harmony* of the ingenious and candid Dr. DODDRIDGE. "And they brought infants and young children "to him, that he should touch them, or put "his hands on them, and pray; and when his "disciples saw it, they rebuked those that brought "them. But when Jesus saw it, he was much "displeased, and said unto them, Suffer the little "children to come unto me, and forbid them "not; for of such is the kingdom of God. Verily "I say unto you, Whosoever shall not receive the "kingdom of God as a little child, he shall in "no wise enter therein. And he called them "unto him, and took them up in his arms, "and put his hands upon them, and blessed "them; and departed thence †."—Jesus was now, it seems, at *Bethabara*, which was beyond *Jordan*, over against *Jericho*, where he tarried with his disciples some months. Hither great multitudes resorted to him to receive his instructions, spiritual blessings, and miraculous cures. During his abode at *Bethabara*, previous to his going to *Bethany*, these things are recorded particularly,—the doctrine of divorce and matrimony, in answer to the tempting Pharisees — his doctrine concerning infants and children, occasioned by the importunity of their friends and the *harsh imprudence*, or the *inconsiderate officiousness* of the disciples — the danger of riches, occasioned by the question of the young ruler — bigotry and a party spirit, a very prevailing sin of the Jewish nation,

† Fam. Expos. vol. ii. Sect. 136.

nation, reproved in the parable of the labourers. —This, I believe, is all we have recorded belonging to this period, tho' of several months continuance.

Now, let us attend to the circumstances and import of that passage relating to infants and young children, as above. On which I would offer the following reflections; which shall relate to — the children's friends — the disciples — and our Lord's doctrine on the occasion.

§ 40. 1. THE most probable motives of the children's parents or friends seem to be, that the fame of Jesus being abroad about his condescension to children and his peculiar fondness for them, as is manifest from Mat. xviii. 2, &c. they were anxious of receiving some token of his condescending notice, and important benediction. In the instance just referred to, Jesus while at *Capernaum*, had called a little child unto him, and set him in the midst of his disciples, taking him up in his arms and telling them — that they must become *like* little children — that kindness shewn to such, was like shewing it to *himself*. And, indeed, when we consider the propriety and amiableness of the thing itself, in connection with the character of Jesus, we should think too contractedly to imagine, that the few instances recorded by the Evangelists, were the *only* ones wherein he manifested a gracious regard for them. These considerations fully justified the *motives* of the persons in question, whether *they* or the *children* were baptized not, by John or any of Chrift's difciples heretofore, and without fuppofing them to have any defign of offering themfelves or theirs to be baptized at this time; and indeed, this is the more improbable, in that, moft likely, they had certain appointed opportunities for that purpofe, whereas their exprefs defign, as here recorded, was to receive his *benediction*.

2. THE next inquiry is, What could induce the difciples to *rebuke* thefe perfons? I readily agree with Dr. S. That it is not probable their conduct is chargeable with the guilt of DESPISING LITTLE CHILDREN *as fuch*, " having a far " better opinion of thofe men of God, than " to fuppofe them capable of an evil, which " very few of the moft profligate among man- " kind are chargeable with;" but is rather imputable to " their *imprudence* and *inconfidera-* " *tion*, than to any inhumanity or cruelty in " their tempers *." In fact, it feems to me pretty evident, that what gave *offence* to the difciples was, what might appear to them an UNSEASONABLE *importunity*. Every one knows how much depends upon *well timing* an application to perfons of much bufinefs of an important nature. This remark is fufficient to fhew the inconclufivenefs of Mr. B.'s reafoning on this point: " Is it not ftrange, unaccountably ftrange, " that our Lord's moft intimate friends fhould " have been *offended* with the perfons who brought " thofe children, if it had then been cuftomary
" to

---

* Anfwer to Dr. A. p. 58.

"to baptize infants †?" *Strange!* not at all; much less *unaccountably* strange. If there be any force in the reasoning it is this,—If our Lord's attendants had been Pœdobaptists, then no *ill-timed* application, no improper *manner* of applying, no *circumstance* whatever, could have been a cause of *offence* to them. I would exclaim in my turn, and with how much greater propriety let the reader judge, " Is it not strange, unac-" countably strange," that my respectable opponent should be so inattentive to logical conclusiveness, as to rest an argument on such a foundation! Suppose an opulent and generous person, distributing liberally to proper objects on convenient and seasonable opportunities, were addressed by the medium of servants or attendants *unseasonably*; and upon these giving the importunate solicitors of his charity a *short answer*, or perhaps a *reprimand*, it should be divulged — The public is mistaken in regard of the character of the person, as if generous and charitable, and particularly his attendants who are reported to be of the same disposition with himself; for else " is it not strange, unaccountably strange," that the person's most intimate friends should have been *offended* with those solicitors of their master's bounty, and should even have *rebuked* them, if it had been *customary* for him to relieve the distressed? Any one acquainted with the world, and the nature of important business, might well say, Did you apply at a

convenient

† Pædob. Exam. p. 349.

convenient time, and in a *prudent* manner? Equally futile is the inference, that Christ and his disciples were no Pœdobaptists, else the latter could not have been *offended* with the persons who brought the children.— Besides; Mr. B. seems to forget or conceal the circumstance of our Lord's being *greatly displeased* with the disciples for their conduct; which he would not have been, without any *ground* of blame. And I believe with Dr. S. that his displeasure " was " expressed with the greater warmth, in order " the more deeply to impress the minds of " spectators with the exceeding great tenderness " he felt for little children. And I imagine it " was chiefly with a view to mark this distin- " guishing feature of benevolence in our Lord's " character, and to instruct us in the duty we " owe to our children, that the evangelists have " so particularly related this pleasing story †." While all attention, perhaps, to some heavenly doctrine, the disciples inadvertently thought he ought not to be interrupted by *children*, by *infants* (Βρεφη) who are incapable of attending to and comprehending the divine lecture*. But he soon convinces them of what they ought to have had always fresh in mind—" what ex- " ceeding great tenderness he felt for little chil- " dren." But

3. WHAT

† p. 58.

* Apostoli rem minus dignam Christo putabant, contingendis pueris occupari. POLI Synops. in loc. " Si impositum ejus capiti " fuisset diadema, libenter nec sine plausu excepissent: quia propri- " um ejus munus nondum tenebant." CALV. in Matt. xix. 14.

Ch. 3.   *Subjects of Baptism.*   295

3. WHAT was our Lord's doctrine on the occasion? *Suffer the little children to come unto me, FOR of such is the kingdom of heaven.* " Hunc " clypeum Anabaptistis non *temere* opponimus ‡." This I venture to call a *decisive sentence* in favour of the *continued privilege* of the church-membership of infants under the gospel dispensation, and consequently their title to baptism; the evidence of which let us now investigate.

§ 41. From the passage under consideration we may learn,

1. " THAT these little children, being stiled " (τα βρέφη) *infants*, (Luke xviii. 15.) and taken " up in Christ's arms, (Mark x. 16.) were " children not yet come to the age of discretion: " for βρέφη, according to EUSTATHIUS and PHA- " VORINUS, is το αρτι γεγονὸς παιδιον, και τρεφομενος " απο τηθης — *a new born child, nourished from the* " *teat* *."

2. WHATEVER may be included in this blessing, *of such is the kingdom of heaven*, we are not to suppose it *confined* to those children, much less to adults. " I cannot approve of rendering τοιέτων, *such as resemble these.* It is the part of a faithful translator, not to *limit* the sense of the *original,* nor to *fix* what it leaves ambiguous ∥." And Mr. HENRY observes, that " the word ge- " nerally signifies not similitude, but *identity*; nor " can any one instance be found where it excludes

                                              " the

‡ CALVIN *in loc.*   * WHITBY *in loc.*
∥ DODDR. Fam. Expos. vol. ii. Sect. 136.

" the perſon or thing mentioned ‡." " Horum
" et ſimilium: puerorum ut ætate, ita et mori-
" bus: non excludit pueros, a quibus facit ini-
" tium, ſed includit adultos eis ſimiles; q. d.
" Pueri, a me jam benedicti, jam nunc idonei
" ſunt regno cœlorum: vos adulti qui diu mea
" preſentia & benedictione fruimini, nondum ido-
" nei eſtis, &, ut idonei fiatis, reddamini oportet
" illis ſimiles quos contemnitis, a faſtu alieni,
" &c. *" " Hac voce tam parvulos quam eorum
" ſimiles comprehendit. Inſulſe enim Anabaptiſtæ
" pueros excludunt, a quibus *initium* fieri debe-
" bat †." And Dr. S. underſtands Τοιѕ́των,—
" *of ſuch little children*, LITTLE CHILDREN IN
" GENERAL §;" which I am by no means inclined to diſpute.

YET afterwards he qualifies this univerſality
thus: " All little children WHO DIE IN THEIR
" INFANCY. And this," ſays he, " I take to
" be our Lord's meaning, *Of ſuch*, of little chil-
" dren PASSING OUT OF LIFE IN THEIR IN-
" FANCY, *is the kingdom of heaven*. And con-
" ſidering what prodigious numbers, out of all
" kindreds, nations and tongues, are removed
" hence at that early period, heaven may very
" properly be ſaid, a great part of it, to conſiſt
" of them." Yet our author adds, " There is
" no way by which it can be credibly known,
" which

---

‡ Treatiſe on Baptiſm, p. 104.

* MALDONAT. ex ORIG. HIERON. AUGUST. &c. et LUC. BRUGEN. ap. POLI Synopſ. in loc.

† CALV. *in loc.*   § Anſwer to Dr. A. p. 61.

"which of them do poffefs fuch title to the "kingdom of heaven, till they die ‖." Hence he concludes, that becaufe we cannot certainly or credibly know which of them fhall *die* in their infancy—we are to regard NONE of them, while they live, as *fubjects of the kingdom of heaven*; except we reft our judgment "upon a prefump- "tion of their dying."

BUT what fays Mr. B. on this head? " That "it is *lawful* for a parent, or a *minifter*, to GIVE "UP INFANTS to God by folemn prayer, which "is a moral duty, we readily allow; and that "the conduct of Chrift, on this occafion, mani- "fefted his regard for *little children*, is beyond a "doubt; at the thought of which, we are fo "far from being pained, that we rejoice. Yes, "it is a matter of joy; becaufe, in our view, it "wears a *fmiling afpect* on the *final ftate* of fuch "as *die* in their infancy; and that without "any reftriction, in reference to *carnal defcent*, "which limitation has the appearance of a Jewifh "tenet †." Mr. JAMES RUTHERFORD is ftill more explicit: " As I cautioned my hearers, in "like manner let me intreat my readers, not to "entertain the *leaft fufpicion* that my fentiments "are harfh and uncharitable, refpecting the hap- "py ftate of children who die in infancy; for "tho' my conclufions fo peremptorily exclude "them from any part in the outward church "ftate, and deny their right to every ordinance "thereof, yet I dare not affirm they are incapa- "ble

‖ Ibid. p. 64. † Padob. Exam, p. 350.

"ble of internal washing, or without a part in eternal glory: For altho' I have not met with one word, either in the Old or New Testament, from which the *final state* of those who die in infancy can be *inferred*, yet where the matter is so liable to *dispute* among men, and the scriptures so *silent* about it, always choose to take the *most charitable* side; on which account, I am inclined to *believe* the salvation of ALL who *die in infancy* *." After all, according to Mr. B. the conduct of Christ manifesting his condescending regard for little children, without baptizing them, makes nothing for infant baptism. "He who can fairly prove the point, or make any advances towards it, from such premises, must be a wonderful proficient in the art of syllogizing †." On the contrary, we cannot help thinking, that "he who can interpret these words, "suffer little children, &c." to the denial of infants', *all* infants', church-membership and consequent right to baptism, is no mean proficient in the art of evading evidence. However, let us examine this matter a little more closely.

These authors unanimously agree, that the phrase, "of such," includes, "little children in "general'

---

* Thoughts on Believers' Bapt. p. 15. See, also, GILLARD's *Probability of the future state of infants, who die in infancy, stated and considered.* The Author, who is an Antipædobaptist, says of his design: "The idea pursued in this Treatise is, the probability "that ALL who die in a state of infancy, are *elected* and there- "fore certainly saved." p. 9.

† Pædob. Exam. p. 351.

"general, without any reftriction, in reference to
"carnal defcent." They alfo unite in fuppofing
the falvation of ALL fuch as *die in their infancy.*" Yet, if Mr. RUTHERFORD's opinion be
admitted,—" that there is not *one word*, either
"in the Old or New Teftament, from which
"the final ftate of thofe who die in infancy can
"be INFERRED"—the above conceffions (for fo
I may call them) come from Antipœdobaptifts
with a very ill grace. However, tho' I cannot
admit of Mr. RUTHERFORD's premifes, I can eafily
fall in with the general conclufion, for reafons
that need not be here produced, (See § 6.)
But tho' our opponents be thus unanimous in
allowing children, dying in their infancy, a place
in the church *above*, they are not lefs fo in
denying them a place in the church *below*; for
were they to grant them the *latter* privilege,
their obligation to *baptize* them, as belonging to,
or members of, the church of Chrift, could not
be difputed. Here I would afk our opponents,

§ 42. CAN they coolly and impartially believe,
that thofe very children whom Chrift *actually
bleffed*, to the joy of their parents, and the in-
ftruction of his miniftring fervants, were NOT
members of the gofpel church, in the fame fenfe
as their parents or any other difciples were, at
leaft AFTER this benediction * ?

As

* " Certe non luforium nec inane fymbolum erat manuum im-
" pofitio, nec fruftra preces in aerem Chriftus effudit ; folenniter
" autem offerre Deo non potuit quin puritate donaret. Quid
" vero

As Jews, they were members of the church of God, as well as their parents. But when a Jew believed Jesus to be the Messiah, and professed attachment to him, was he required to *renounce* his former religion, in like manner as a heathen was required to renounce his? Or, was there any thing whatever required of a Jew, but to *believe* what Christ *taught*, and to *observe* what he *commanded?* But believing what he taught, and observing what he commanded, no way interfered with the continued and uninterrupted church-membership of his children. Nay, his *own* church-membership was not *changed* but *improved* by confessing Christ. Therefore, for such a parent to treat his children as *dispossessed* of their church-membership, when he himself was not, and without any pretence of necessity from any thing which Christ taught or commanded, must be evidently unjustifiable. Consequently, in proportion as these parents judged and acted agreeably to *truth*, they must have conducted themselves towards their children, as *actual members* of the church of God.

But since it appears that not only the less instructed among the Jews, but our Lord's disciples

---

" vero illis precatus est, nisi ut reciperentur *inter Dei filios?*
" Unde sequitur regenitos Spiritu fuisse in spem salutis. Ipse
" denique amplexus testis fuit censeri ipsos a Christo in *suo grege*,
" Quod si donorum spiritualium quæ figurat baptismus, compotes
" fuerunt, *externo signo* privari absurdum est. Sacrilega vero au-
" dacia est, abigere procul ab *ovili Christi* quos ipse in *sinu suo*
" fovet, & quasi extraneos clausa janua rejicere quos prohiberi
" non vult." CALV. in Matt. xix. 14.

ciples who constantly attended him, formed very wrong conceptions of the nature of the Messiah's kingdom, which they called *the kingdom of heaven*, (See Mat. xviii. 1—4.) what can be more natural than to consider our Lord's declaration in the text, as a direct answer to such a mistake? Why should we not, therefore, interpret, " the " kingdom of heaven," of the Messiah's kingdom? In the last mentioned text, the disciples, labouring under this common prejudice, inquire of their Lord, " Who should be greatest in *the* " *kingdom of heaven?*" His answer to their question was, by an action similar to that we are considering; and (except we suppose the answer *foreign* to the question) in the *former* instance, the requisition for membership in the gospel church, or for subjects in the Messiah's kingdom, was— *conformity* to a little child, which he proposed to them as a model; in the *latter*, he seems to cut off all occasion of the absurdity of *confining* his doctrine to the case of adults, whose excellency consisted in likeness to infants, to the exclusion of infants themselves. Therefore, the *kingdom of heaven*, i. e. the *gospel church*, is made up, as to the true character of its subjects, not only of those who are *like* little children, but of little children *themselves*. Not only such adults as *resemble* these, but *these*, and *such as these*, in the strictest sense, belong to my kingdom now about to be established.

To this Dr. S. objects: " That he means " the *world of glory*, and not his kingdom on " earth, appears plain to me from the words
" immediately

" immediately following, as reported by Luke,
" *Whofoever shall not receive the kingdom of God
" as a little child, shall in no wife enter therein,*
" that is, Whofoever fhall not receive the gofpel
" with the fimplicity and teachablenefs [*teach-
" ablenefs!**] of a little child, he fhall in no wife
" enter into the world of glory — not furely he
" fhall in no wife enter into the vifible church,
" for into that fome of the vileft hypocrites have
" entered †." If this be a juft account of the
pre-requifites for glory, what becomes of infants,
who do not receive the gofpel at all? Our refpectable author feems to forget, that fimplicity and teachablenefs are not *univerfally neceffary* for entrance into the kingdom of glory, which he muft allow in granting the falvation of dying infants. Paffing by this, let us attend to his main argument: " Not the vifible church, for into that fome of
" the vileft hypocrites have entered." But if this proves any thing, I fear it will prove too much. On other occafions we are told, " He that forfaketh not all to follow Chrift, — and hateth not father and mother, &c. for his fake, cannot be *his difciple*, i. e. cannot be a *fubject of his kingdom*." But who fees not that in fuch paffages we are to underftand the term *difciple*, not as implying mere *profeffion*, but the *poffeffion* alfo of what is profeffed? In like manner,

entering

" * When Mr. —— makes their *deciblenefs* the thing intended by
" Chrift, he forgot that he judged them uncapable of being *difciples.*
" Why may not thofe be *difciples*, who are not only *decible*, but
" *exemplary* for their teachablenefs?" Baxter's Plain Script.
Proof, p. 105.

‡ Anfwer to Dr. A. p. 65.

entering into the kingdom of heaven, or the church of Chrift, is twofold; either into the *number* of fubjects *externally*, or into the real *fpiritual happinefs* it exhibits. And in this view the impartial Dr. DODDRIDGE paraphrafes the paffage in queftion, Mark x. 15. and Luke xviii. 17. " *Who-* " *foever fhall not* be willing to *receive the kingdom* " *of God*, or the GOSPEL DISPENSATION and the " HAPPINESS IT PROMISES, *as a little child*, " divefting himfelf of thofe prejudices, and thofe " fecular views which men contract in their riper " years — *he fhall not in any wife*, or on any " terms, *enter into it*, be his genius ever fo fub- " lime, or his circumftances in life ever fo confi- " derable †." This I believe is a plain, natural and confiftent interpretation of the text; and avoids *five* great inconveniences with which the other appears clogged.

(1) THE confined fenfe of the words, for which our opponents contend, referring them exclufively to the *world of glory*, labours under this inconvenience, viz. That then they are *not fo direct* and full an anfwer to the reigning prejudice of the perfons addreffed, particularly the difciples, whofe wrong views of the Meffiah's kingdom are here, it feems, intentionally rectified. (See Matt. xviii. 1—4.)

(2) IT labours under another difadvantage, viz. It virtually renounces that well known fcriptural diftinction of a *twofold* entering into the kingdom of Chrift; into its *external privileges*, and its *internal bleffings*: as if thefe words, " Whofoever fhall

---

† Family Expof. vol. ii. Sect. 136.

shall not receive the kingdom of God as a little child, shall in no wise enter therein," must *needs* refer either to a mere external relation to Christ and his people, or to heavenly glory. Whereas it is equally true, that the worldly minded miser, or the self-righteous pharisee, can not enter into the *happiness* of the gospel dispensation, as that they can not enter into *glory*.

(3) It seems to deny, that the *state of grace* as well as the *state of glory*, may be called the *kingdom of heaven*. Nothing is more evident, or more universally acknowledged, than that the gospel dispensation, in its external aspect, is so called. Nor is it much less evident, that the *spiritual œconomy* of the gospel is so denominated in the following places. Matt. iii. 2. iv. 17. x. 7. xii. 28. xvi. 28. &c. &c.†

(4) It excludes these very infants from *present* interest in the blessing pronounced concerning them. Is it supposeable that they have no real privilege either confirmed or conferred? Was our Lord's laying his hands on them, and reproving his disciples for their sakes, expressive of no favour towards them, but a mere empty sign? But if this wonderful condescension and loving regard to them was attended with any benefit to them, are we at liberty to fix on any which fancy dictates, to the exclusion of what the words plainly express? *Of such* is *the kingdom of heaven.* The benefit here pronounced on them, (if at all here included, which cannot reasonably be denied,

as

---

† For a large collection of such passages, see WHITBY on Matt. iii. 2.

as before shewn) was a *present* benefit, whether now conferred or only asserted and confirmed. And to deny this will be attended with another inconvenience, viz.

(5) If they were at all included, it must either make the plainest language of the time present refer to time *future*; or, convert the declaration, " of such is the kingdom of heaven," into a *prophecy* concerning their eternal state—both which will be thought sufficiently improbable; and the more so, when we reflect, that there is not the least necessity of running into such extremes.— I would again inquire,

§ 43. Have we any ground to suppose, that our Lord would have denied the privilege here expressed, to any *other* infants or little children, had they been brought to him? Was not his declaration, " of such," abundantly encouraging on behalf of *any such* that should be brought to him? Or must we interpret what is expressed in terms so general, as exclusive of *all the infants and little children* in the world? Strange interpretation! For, then, what encouragement or even propriety can there be in the preceding gracious declaration, " Suffer them to come unto me, and forbid them not?" How could this be *founded* on the general doctrine, " Of such is the kingdom of heaven? Or must we say, in compliance with our opponents' interpretation, — " Such as DIE in their infancy go to glory, THEREFORE let these which are ALIVE, and SUCH as these, be brought unto me!"

AGAIN

AGAIN: Seeing what was done to thefe children was not of a miraculous nature, have we any authority to affert, that parents *in the prefent day* are debarred from every privilege tantamount to this with refpect to their children? Yet, on Antipœdobaptift principles, which deny their church-memberfhip and baptifm, this is the cafe! For, according to them, we cannot conclude, that " theirs is the kingdom of heaven," but on fuppofition of their *dying*. But our Lord's gracious mandate, " Suffer them, &c." was not *that they may* partake of the kingdom of heaven, but *becaufe* of thefe, and fuch as thefe, is the kingdom of heaven.

MOREOVER: How can parents bring their children to Chrift, in the Antipœdobaptift fenfe of bringing them, *becaufe* theirs is the kingdom of heaven? Or were it further granted, that our Lord meant, heaven above was in a great meafure peopled with fuch infants, *therefore* thefe were welcome; will it not ftill follow, that *ours* are welcome in the fame fenfe and for the fame reafon? And if *bringing them to him* be followed with no church privilege, if no poffible difpofition or conduct of a parent be attended with prefent advantage, and if the children of heathens (as my opponents hold) be equally admitted to heaven with thofe of believers, dying in their infancy,— what poffible advantage can there be to our offspring, or encouragement to ourfelves, from *thefe words* of our Lord?

ONCE more: if parents or minifters may now lawfully

lawfully, in the language of Mr. B. " GIVE UP INFANTS TO GOD by folemn prayer," *becaufe* there *are* infants in glory, it ftill follows — that we may lawfully *give up infants to the church* of God, becaufe there are fuch in glory. For to hold, that they may be *given up* to God with the view of their obtaining the *grace* of the covenant, and yet debarred from the *means* of the covenant, without any perfonal forfeiture, is abfurd. Nor can it be maintained, with any fhew of reafon, that our Lord's words, " Suffer them to come, and forbid them not," are the fame in meaning as — " Do not hinder parents to *pray* for their children ;" for *this* neither the difciples nor any other perfon who would permit a *parent* to pray at all, would once think to *forbid*.

BUT fuppofing, for argument fake, fo unnatural and forced an interpretation were allowed, which grounds the reproof of the difciples, and the encouragement of parents to bring *living* infants to him, on the happinefs of the *dying*, and of *theirs* if they die while infants —— ftill, I fay, if I am not greatly miftaken, we ought to regard infants as parts of the *vifible church*. For, if Mr. TOWGOOD's calculation be juft, viz. That " from the exacteft obfervations, it appears, that of thofe who are born into the world, fcarce a *third part* attain to the age of *one year* † :" nay, upon a more moderate calculation, if, inftead of a " third part," we fay *one half* attain to the age of *two years :* —— there is not a new born infant in the world, our

opponents

‡ Baptifm of Inf. Reafon, Serv. p. 1.

opponents being judges, but of that it may be faid —— it *more probably* is an heir of glory than of woe. And, tho' the matter were not quite fo clear, Mr. RUTHERFORD candidly obferves, " we " fhould always choofe the *moſt charitable* fide." Hence it follows, that tho' none were to be vifibly brought to Chriſt, or admitted to church-memberſhip, but thofe whom we charitably judge to be heirs of glory, we ought, on the conceffions of our opponents, to treat our new born infants as thofe who are vifibly related to Chriſt, or church members. For a *probable* vifible relation to the kingdom of glory, includes a *certain* vifible relation to the church militant. If we have any charitable probable ground of judging—" the king-
" dom of heaven belongs to fuch, *much more* a
" ſtanding as members in the vifible church: for
" what is it to be a member of the church vifible,
" but to be one that in feeming, or appearance,
" or to the judgment of man, doth belong to
" the invifible church, or the kingdom of hea-
" ven? For the church is but one, and the dif-
" ference refpective—Therefore, both vifible and
" invifible, both military and triumphant, are called
" in fcripture, The kingdom of heaven, or of God.
" If a man be [but probably] *known*, or any fort
" of men, to belong to the church invifible, then
" they *vifibly* belong to it; and then they are vifible
" members of the church. So that this proof
" [founded on our opponents' conceffions ‖] is
" more full for infants' church-memberſhip, than
" if

‖ See § 41.

"if it had been laid, They may be visible church members: for it faith much more of them, which *includeth* that *."

BESIDES: have our antagonists any thing more than *probability* to influence their determinations with respect to adults? *Infallibility*, we know, they disclaim; and a *medium* between both, will not be pretended. Now if a visible probability of relation to the kingdom of glory be, according to our Lord, a reason of a visible access to him; and if he says " of such" (understanding thereby with our opposers, the *species* of infants dying in their infancy) " is the kingdom of heaven," or heavenly glory; it follows, that we have a *stronger reason* for concluding that any child whatever belongs to the visible church, than any can have respecting any adult. In the latter we *may* be deceived, in the former we *cannot*. The premises duly weighed, we dare not hesitate to conclude, —that the balance evidently turns in favour of Pœdobaptism.

SHOULD any object, that to acknowledge the church-membership of infants would not amount to a concession to justify Pœdobaptism;—I answer, If baptism be the only regular way and manner of solemn admission into the gospel church (as the learned Mr. TOMBES allows†, and if I mistake not the generality of Antipœdobaptists); it will be time enough to prove the certain *connection* between church-membership and baptism, when our opponents enter their protest against it.

BEFORE

* See BAXTER's Plain Script. Proof. p. 105.
† Apology. p. 54. See BAXT. Plain Script. Proof. p. 24.

Before I dismiss this branch of our subject, the length of which has been occasioned by the subtle evasions of our adversaries, I would present the reader with the following words of Mr. Richard Baxter: " Doth Christ take them
" [infants] in his *arms*, and would he have them
" *all* put out of his *visible church?* Would he have
" us receive them *in his name*, and yet not receive
" them into his church, nor as his disciples? How
" *can* infants be received in Christ's name, if they
" belong not visibly to him and his church? Nay,
" doth Christ account it a receiving of himself,
" and shall I then refuse to receive them, or ac-
" knowledge them, the subjects of his visible king-
" dom?— For my part, seeing—Christ hath given
" me so full a discovery of his will in this point,
" I will boldly adventure to follow his rule, and
" had rather answer him, upon his own encou-
" ragement, for ADMITTING A HUNDRED IN-
" FANTS into his church, than answer for KEEP-
" ING OUT OF ONE ‖." " I desire any tender
" conscienced christian, that is in doubt, whether
" infants should be admitted members of the visible
" church, and would fain know what is the plea-
" sure of Christ in this thing, to — bethink himself,
" Whether it be more likely that it will *please*
" *Christ better* to bring, or solemnly admit, in-
" fants into the church, or to shut them out?
" And whether *these words* of Christ, so plain and
" earnest, will not be a *better plea* at judgment for
" our admitting infants, than any that ever they
" [Antipœdobaptists] brought, will be to them
" for

‖ Plain Script. Proof. p. 103.

"for refusing them *?" "I bless the Lord Jesus, the King of the church, for having so great a tenderness to the infants themselves, and so great a care of the information of his church concerning his will, as to speak it thus *plainly*, that plain meaning men may well see his mind: even as if he had therefore done this because he foresaw, that in these latter days some would arise that would *renew the disciples' mistake* in this point ‡."

§ 44. HAVING, as proposed, (§ 31.) considered our Lord's confirming and decisive *sentence* concerning the church privileges of infants; we proceed to consider more briefly, the same thing *implied* in what he says of Israel and certain towns and cities, through the whole course of his ministry.

1. IT is well known, that the mission and ministry of Christ were primarily intended for the use of the Jews, Matt. xv. 24. with which coincides his commission to the seventy, Matt. x. 6. Now if our Lord by his ministry addressed *Israel* as a *body of people*, even as they were wont to be addressed by the former prophets; and the same was given, in commission to the seventy disciples, that they should " *go to the lost sheep of the house of Israel*, preaching, and saying, " the kingdom of heaven is at hand"—it follows, that their *national conversion* was proposed, and but for their unbelief, and general rejection of the Messiah, would

* Ibid. p. 106.

‡ Ibid. p. 107.—See also Dr. DODDRIDGE's excellent Improvement of the sacred story, Fam. Expos. Sect. 136.

would have been effected. Therefore, it was œconomically and ministerially *intended* that the Jewish *infants* should be among the converted, or subjects of the Messiah's kingdom. Consequently, it would be absurd to suppose, that those who *did receive* him were not favoured in regard to their children, as they would have been on the general conversion of their countrymen, except obliged thereto by a revealed fact. But no such revealed fact exists. Hence we conclude, that the infants and dependents of converted Jews were *de jure* members of the gospel church, and, for aught appears to the contrary, *de facto* likewise.

2. THE same thing is implied in our Lord's instructions to his disciples Luke x. 5—15. They were instructed to direct their message to *families* and *cities*; the family was blessed, proselyted or *discipled* if the *son of peace* was there; and in proportion as a *city* gave reception to them and their message, it was *discipled* in like manner. But if they and their message were despised and rejected, an awful curse was denounced. The threatened woe was levelled against the inhabitants of a place, *collectively*; in which the parents and children shared alike, at least externally; which implies, that the contrary blessings would have been shared in common, on supposition of the parents receiving the gospel. Now it appears, that what was required of these families and cities for the continuance and extension of their religious privileges, was their *not rejecting* the gospel message; but

but perfonally to *repent* and *believe* in fuch a fenfe as is peculiar to the regenerate, cannot be fuppofed to be that, and that alone, which entitled whole *families* and *cities* to difciplefhip and gofpel privileges.

3. WHAT our Lord fays in his lamentation over Jerufalem, Luke xiii. 34, 35. and chap. xix. 41 —44. and Matt. xxiii. 37, 38. implies, that, had it not been for its ingratitude and unbelief, in that *general* fenfe before mentioned, its religious privileges would have been continued, confirmed and enlarged, as well as its temporal calamities averted. " How often (fays the compaffionate Saviour) would I have gathered thy children together, as a hen doth gather her brood under her wings, and ye would not?" Again, " He beheld the city, and wept over it, faying, If thou hadft, (or Oh! that thou hadft) known, even thou, at leaft in this thy day, the things which belong unto thy peace! but now they are hid from thine eyes —— BECAUSE thou kneweft not the time of thy vifitation." Is it not here *implied*, that the genuine tendency and exprefs defign of our Lord's miniftry complied with, would have prevented their awful doom? But what was that doom? Did it not include a diffolution, not merely of their civil polity but of their *religious privileges* alfo? And did not thefe include the *church-memberfhip* of their infant children, which we have feen was by no means *peculiar* to the mofaic difpenfation, and therefore

P would

would not have been abrogated with the mosaic ritual?

4. The same conclusion is evidently inferable from Matt. xi. 20—24. where our Lord *upbraids* the cities wherein most of his mighty works were done, because they *repented* not; and the kind of repentance that would have been available, for the purpose of admission into the gospel dispensation, is mentioned ver. 21. " a repenting in sackcloth and ashes;" in the same manner as Nineveh; (compare Matt. xii. 41.) From whence, and from the foregoing passages, we infer,——That the whole tendency, and express design, of our Lord's ministry and that of his disciples, *implied*, that the church-membership and religious privileges of parents were to be extended to their children under the gospel. Consequently, the Antipœdobaptist plan of evangelizing and discipling the *nations*, which admits none to the christian church, in its more universal form, *but* on personal profession of what is deemed saving faith and repentance, differs essentially from that of Christ through the whole course of his ministry.—Should it be said, that we ought to distinguish between the averting of judgment from a people, and their partaking of religious privileges and rites; I answer, it is true these are *distinguishable*, but it is equally true, that no such distinction can be of any real service to the Antipœdobaptist cause. For, being *Jewish* towns and cities, families and people—the *mode* of their conversion is to be sought from their *own*, history

history, and the former revolutions that *had before* obtained in the church of God; except a different manner be *expressly* specified. Whatever hypothesis is erected in defiance of this fundamental rule, must be necessarily a *baseless* fabrick. Or, we may as soon contrive an even balance possessed of the wonderful property of outweighing *something* with *nothing!* as to contrive a rule for excluding infants from the church of the New Testament, without an *express* injunction for so doing.

§ 45. IN confirmation of our general argument, that it is the WILL OF CHRIST infants should partake of all their parents' privileges, and consequently that of baptism, we next appeal to that capital text, Matt. xxviii. 19. *Go ye, therefore, and teach all nations, baptizing them,* and so on*. " The whole tenour of the succeeding books

* Mr. BOOTH says, this " is not a mere *allusion* to baptism, nor an *incidental* use of the term,—but it is *the institution* of that ordinance." But what *proof* does he offer in support of this assertion? Why, " It is the first appointment of baptism for the use of the *Gentiles*;" and " Jesus Christ, on this occasion, expressly claims *all authority in heaven and on earth.*" (Pœdob. Exam. p. 322.) But how can the fact of its being now first appointed *for the use of the Gentiles*, disprove its being before appointed *for the use of the Jews?* With as great propriety may it be inferred, that because in this commission we have the first appointment of *preaching the gospel* to the *Gentiles*, therefore the gospel was not preached before to the Jews!—Did not the disciples baptize *before* this period? And was not that done *by commission* from Christ? Had he not *authority*, divine authority, to commission? Or was it now his kingly office commenced?—" *He plainly appears as King of Zion, and Sovereign of the world.*" But will Mr. B. say, that he was not so *prior* to this period? If not, how does this shew that baptism was not before instituted?

" books of the New Teſtament ſhews, that Chriſt
" deſigned by this commiſſion, that the goſpel ſhould
" be preached to *all nations* without exception, not
" only to the Jews, but to all the idolatrous
" gentiles: but the *prejudices* of the Apoſtles led
" them at firſt to *miſtake the ſenſe*, and to ima-
" gine, that it referred only to their going to
" preach the goſpel to the Jews among all nations,
" or to thoſe who ſhould be willing to become
" Jews*." It is, I believe, generally agreed,
that by *all nations* (πανla τα εθνη) is intended, the
Gentile world at large, together with the Jewiſh
nation. They were no longer to *confine* their labours among the loſt ſheep of Iſrael. The middle wall of partition being taken down, their commiſſion is unlimited. The whole habitable globe
is their dioceſe, in which they were to employ
their extraordinary talents, and ſeraphic zeal,
without any official ſuperiority.

In our inquiry into the *controverted* part of this
important paſſage, it will be neceſſary to premiſe,
what is properly the point contended for from
theſe words? And this is the rather neceſſary, on
account of the following remarkable declaration:
" Could it be proved, that μαθητευσατε, ſometimes
" conveys the idea of making diſciples, where
" there is *no teaching*; and that βαπτιζοντες, is
" occaſionally uſed for pouring or ſprinkling, where
" there is *no immerſion*; yet the diſpute between
" us and our brethren would not be decided:
" becauſe this queſtion would ſtill remain for
" diſcuſſion;

* Doddr. Fam. Expoſ. *in loc,* *Note,*

" difcuflion ; Is making a difciple *without in-*
" *ſtruction,* in the onè cafe; and *pouring* or *ſprink-*
" *ling,* in the other; the NATURAL and PRI-
" MARY fignification of thofe Greek words*;"
In fettling this point, if we wifh not to confound,
it will be neceſſary to diftinguifh.—*Still the difpute
would not be decided*; *becauſe of the* NATURAL and
PRIMARY *ſignification.* Here let the following
things be confidered.

1. THERE is an important difference between a
primary PHILOLOGICAL or ETYMOLOGICAL, and
a *primary* LEGAL fenfe of terms; founded on this
ground—That terms acquire different acceptations according to the pofitions in which they
ftand. There is hardly any law, facred or civil,
but may furnifh a confirmation of this neceſſary
diftinction †.

2. IT follows, that a term, in its primary *legal*
fenfe, · may have one acceptation; while, in its
primary *philological* fenfe it occupies another.
And this, we contend, is the cafe here, even on
fuppofition—that μαθητευω (referring the *other*
term to its proper place) fignifies, in its primary

philological

* Pœdob. Exam. p. 322.

† " It muft be obferved, that in tranflating, we are not to render
" *word* for *word*, but *ſenſe* for *ſenſe*, and that the moft *literal verſions*
" are not always the moft *faithful.* There is a great deal of differ-
" ence between the *letter* and the *literal ſenſe.* The *letter* is the
" *word* explained according to its *etymology.* The *literal ſenſe* is the
" *meaning* of the author, which is frequently quite different from
" the *grammatical* fignification of the words." BEAUSOBRE and
L'ENFANT's Introduction to the reading of the Holy Scriptures,
a p. Bp. WATSON's Collect. of Theol. Tracts, Vol, iii. p. 103.

philological meaning, and in certain pofitions, what Mr. B. contends for.

3. Nothing is capable of fixing the exact *legiflative force* of a word or phrafe, but a careful and impartial attention to circumftances; and thefe refer either to the Sovereign or the fubject. For, if we overlook relations, time, place, cuftoms, laws already in force, and the like, what fuccefs can be expected in afcertaining the fenfe?

4. That muft needs be the moft *natural* fignification, which refults from a due weighing of all circumftances. Should not the force and comparative influence of terms be fought in connection with the conftitution and genius, and efpecially the former ftatutes of any ftate? And is not this rule equally applicable to that kingdom which is not of this world?

These things confidered, then, may we not juftly expoftulate—How was it poffible for the difciples,— who were native Jews, and brought up in the bofom of the Jewifh church, receiving inftructions from the Meffiah who was alike circumftanced,—to underftand the terms employed in this text, in any other fenfe than that which includes infants with their parents? Would they underftand their commiffion in a fenfe to which they never had been accuftomed? take words *capable* of *two* conftructions in that fenfe which excluded infants from their parents' privileges? A fenfe, I will add, they never heard of; nay, that NEVER HAD BEEN HEARD OF SINCE THE WORLD BEGAN? Or, had they been previoufly verfed in our opponents' notions about

pofitive

positive rites? These we have seen, and seen I think demonstrated, to be inconsistent with truth; and therefore, may boldly affirm, they were governed by no such maxims. Moreover; could they so easily forget, in the interpretation and execution of their commission, their Lord's repeated declarations, that " of infants was the kingdom of heaven?" Could they forget his being *greatly displeased* with them, for their not paying infants that attention which was their due, and to which culpable neglect their ambitious and erroneous views of the gospel kingdom had betrayed them? Had they not just reason ever after to fear adopting any sentiment or practice which would exclude infants from a visible access to their Divine Friend and Saviour; by whom their privileges, as visible church-members, had been so expresly asserted and confirmed? (See § 39—43.)

" Are these the senses of those terms, says Mr. B. that would naturally *first* occur to the mind of a wise and impartial person, on reading or hearing this law of baptism?" and again; " each of these emphatical words, making a capital figure in the heavenly edict, should be understood in its *most plain*, and *common*, and *expressive signification*: for, as to any *absurdity* following upon it, our opponents pretend none, but what implies a begging of the question†." We answer, that in connection with all those circumstances of legal interpretation which *ought* to be taken into the account, the sense which includes infants with their

† Pædob. Exam. p. 322."

their parents, in this phrase —— μαθητευσατε παντα τα εθνη βαπτιζοντες αυτες —— is not only the *first* that would occur to the mind of the disciples, but we maintain that there is the " highest evidence" the Legislator did *intend* that sense. Nay further, we insist that it is " highly absurd" to interpret them otherwise than what we contend for, and that without " begging of the question disputed." For, is it to " beg the question," to take into the account the circumstances of legislation? And were not the disciples always accustomed, as Jews and as the disciples of Jesus, to reckon infants as members of the church with their parents, in every preceding dispensation? Besides; on supposition that our Lord intended, in so many words, to establish our sense of the text, how could it be more properly expressed, or more effectually established? And though designed for all ages and nations, that does not hinder their being adapted to the circumstances of the persons first addressed. Upon the most equitable ground, therefore, it would be *absurd* to suppose the disciples understood them of adults *only*. This being the case, nothing can be admissible in evidence against Pædobaptist principles, from this or any other text, which does not reject and excommunicate infants in the most express and unequivocal manner. I say *excommunicate*; for can it be any thing short of this, when the whole *species* of infants is *cut off* from the church militant at one blow? Before we accede to such a step, is it not proper to pause—to pause again—

and

Ch. 3.   Subjects of Baptism.   321

and to inquire with holy alarm;—On what ground are *they* excluded from the church on earth, who are confessedly admitted to glory, dying in their infant state? The Jews were *cut off* for *unbelief*; but this is no adequate cause in the case of infants born in the city of God. Is the species of infants *more wicked* now, than before and after the deluge, that they should be debarred from their parents' privileges? Where is the broad seal of heaven to ratify that absolute authority which puts an end to all strife? I must ingenuously confess, that, with all the *light* Mr. B. has thrown upon the point, I can discover no such authority. But I see, or think I see, every part of the divine dispensations, and the whole of the sacred oracles, perfectly consistent with Pœdobaptism, and delivering a verdict not a little favourable to it.

§ 46. But Mr. B.'s most formidable objection, and that on which he seems to lay the principal stress, is still behind. Its figure is that of a horned dilemma. " If this law of the
" Lord have any regard to instruction, as a pre-
" requisite for baptism; that instruction must be
" required, either of *all* or only of *some*. To
" affirm the *latter*, there is not the least ground
" in this divine canon; because it makes no dis-
" tinction between what is required of some, and
" what is demanded of others.——It remains,
" then, that *all* must be taught, that *all* must
" become disciples, before they are baptized*."
This does not appear to me consequential and solid, though subtil. I would, therefore, propose
what

* Ibid. p. 325.

what, to my apprehenſion, ſeems to be the preciſe meaning of our Lord in the text, viz. That goſpel miniſters ſhould *proſelyte*, *diſciple*, or *teach*, and *baptize* ALL PROPER SUBJECTS in all nations, introducing them thereby into the goſpel kingdom, and exerciſing their commiſſion diſ-cretionally, *pro captu ſingulorum et inſtantium rerum*. And not only do I think this to be the genuine intent of the commiſſion, but apprehend that, by fair criticiſm and argument, it is *im-poſſible* to ſettle the meaning of the text, by any other interpretation †. For, if it be ſaid, that παντα τα εθνη muſt be taken *ſtrictly* and without any ſuch qualification—if μαθητευσατε be underſtood in that ſenſe of proſelyting which may be done *without inſtruction*, abſolutely and unconditionally—if we ſay that *all who are taught* may be baptized with-out diſtinction—they all lie equally expoſed to exception, uncertainty and error.

BUT

† "It ſeems to me (ſays the judicious Dr. GUYSE), that "μαθητευσατε παντα τα εθνη, *Diſciple all nations*, relates to "the WHOLE DESIGN of Chriſt's commiſſion for making diſci-"ples to him; and that βαπτιζοντες, and διδασκοντες αυτες, "*baptizing* and *teaching them*, are mentioned, as PARTICULAR "BRANCHES of that general deſign, the order of which was to be "determined by the *circumſtances of things*. And *theſe* indeed made "it neceſſary, that in diſcipling ADULT *Jews* and *Heathens*, they "ſhould be taught *before* they were baptized; but *other* circum-"ſtances, in the ſettled ſtate of the goſpel kingdom, make it *as* "*neceſſary*, that in diſcipling the children of believers [i. e. of "Chriſtians] they ſhould be *firſt baptized* and *afterwards taught*, "as the CHILDREN of Jews, and of proſelytes to their religion, "were *firſt circumciſed*, and when they grew up were inſtructed "in the faith of the God of *Iſrael*." Note *in loc*.

But here it is obfervable, that what Mr. B. cites as *conceffions* from HOORNBECKIUS, RIDGELEY, CALVIN, POOLE, BECKMANUS, BARROW, MASTRICHT, BURNET, WHITBY, VENEMA, &c. who were profeffed Pædobaptifts, fhould be underftood in the fenfe juft propofed; and what thofe paffages fairly imply is—that it would be an abufe of the term μαθητευσαῖε to plead from it the mode of difcipling which the church of Rome has fometimes adopted, to the difgrace of the chriftian religion. It is extremely improbable, nay highly uncharitable to fuppofe, that thefe eminent characters fhould be capable of fo glaring a contradiction, as to hold any fenfe of the word μαθηΐευω incompatible with infant difciplefhip and baptifm. However that be, my bufinefs is not to vindicate characters, but to inveftigate truth.—In fact, the text is capable of abufe in two oppofite extremes: the one ftrains them into a fenfe *too general*; the other into a fenfe *too particular*, or unreafonably contracted. But if repentance and faith be required ONLY of adults, as conditions, *fine qua non*, of *falvation;* for the very fame reafon—teaching is required ONLY of adults, as a condition, *fine qua non*, of *baptifm*. Here the hackneyed diftinction between the different kinds of evidence required in moral duties and pofitive rites, is ufelefs. For, is it not an act equally fovereign, to prefcribe the conditions of falvation and the qualifications for baptifm? And is not the *former* as much included in Mr. B.'s definition of pofitive abfolute authority as the *latter* can be? Besides, are not these qualifications for salvation and baptism, respectively, delivered in the *same commission?* It follows, therefore, inevitably, that if this commission (see Mark xvi. 15, 16.) excludes infants from baptism, it must on the same principle exclude them from salvation and glory, contrary to our opponents' declarations. Nor will it ever be in their power, I scruple not to affirm it, to prove the greater probability of dying infants' salvation than their perdition, without at the same time furnishing us with premises from which we may fairly conclude they may be baptized while living. For if it be said, that their *salvation* may be gathered from *other* considerations; so may the duty of parents and ministers to baptize them. But this I hope has been sufficiently established before.

"Here one can hardly forbear to remark," says Mr. B. "in what *opposite* ways this capital text is interpreted, to make it agree with different hypotheses †." True: And we claim the liberty, in turn, to class his interpretation among those which are so *different* and *opposite*. Or can he suppose, that *his* hypothesis must needs pass for true, because he finds a disagreement among other authors? Were this mode of arguing admitted, with what ease might the Quakers confute the Pœdobaptists and Antipœdobaptists alike; the Papists our Protestant principles; and Deists our common christianity!

§ 47. It

† p. 330.

§ 47. It would be eafy to produce a long lift of eminent authors, ancient and modern, who render the word μαθητευειν, by TO PROSELYTE, TO DISCIPLE, or TO MAKE DISCIPLES, as well as by *to teach.* Let the few following fuffice. Thus LEIGH, in his *Critica Sacra:* " μαθητευσατε, *Go and teach all nations*; or word for word from the Greek, GO MAKE THEM DISCIPLES, as it is expounded, John iv. 1." BULLINGER: " DISCIPULATE, five, facite mihi difcipulos †." DUTCH ANNOTATORS: " Inftit... all the nations; or MAKE DISCIPLES among all nations, as the word is alfo taken, Acts xiv. 21. Mark xvi. 15." POOLE'S CONTINUATORS: " The Greek is, μαθητευσατε, MAKE DISCIPLES all nations." DODDRIDGE: " Go forth therefore and PROSELYTE all the nations of the earth ‖." Turretine " Vox μαθητευειν, qua Chriftus utitur, proprie non tam eft docere per predicatiqnem quam DISCIPULOS FACERE, quod fit etiam adminiftratione baptifmi, qui eft facramentum initiationis, & primus in ecclefiam & familiam Chrifti introitus *." STOCKIUS: " Μαθητευω, FACIO DISCIPULUM. Proprie difcipulatum innuit, & *tranfitive*, notans, DISCIPULUM FACERE §." BEZA: " μαθητευειν hic non neutropafiive pro, *difcipulum effe*, fed *active* accipitur; q. d. DISCIPULATE." GATAKER: " *Difcipulos facite.*" LIGHTFOOT : " Introducite

per

‡ Crit. Sacr. ad verb. ‖ Fam. Expof. vol. ii. § 202.
* Inftit. Theol. Loc. xix. Quæft. xx. § 4.
§ Clav. Nov. Teft. in voce.

per baptismum, ut doceantur.—Errant qui hinc colligunt, necessario docendos qui baptizandi sunt.—Dixit ethnicus ad Hilelem, *proselytum me fac, ut me doceas**." HAMMOND: "Mat. xxviii. 19.—The phrase which is there used in the original is a singular one, not duly expressed by our english, *teach*. It is μαθητευσατε, MAKE DISCIPLES, or *receive into discipleship*, all nations, baptizing them in the name, &c. making this form of baptism their ceremony, of receiving them.—John iv. 1. μαθητας ποιει, και βαπτιζει, is all one with μαθητευσατε βαπτιζοντες.—Διδασκοντες, *teaching*, follows after βαπτισοντες, *baptizing:* all that are thus brought and received *ad discipulatum*, to be for the future instructed, and instituted in the christian faith, may surely be received in baptism, the ceremony which is there prescribed by Christ, with which to receive disciples †." WITSIUS: " Mat. xxviii. *Go ye, therefore, and* μαθητευσατε, DISCIPLE *all nations, baptizing them*, &c. There Christ commands that disciples be gathered into his school, and, as persons in covenant with him, sealed with the seal of baptism. But it is evident, that when parents become disciples of Christ, their *children* likewise are reckoned in the number of *disciples*. Just as among the Jews, together with the proselyte parents their infants were initiated in the Jewish rites. It was needless therefore that Christ should make express mention of infants as the subjects of baptism ‖."

To

---

* PoLI Synops. in loc. † Six Querics. Quer. iv. § 25.
‖ WITS, Oecon. Foed. Lib. iv, cap, xvi. § 41.

Ch. 3.   *Subjects of Baptism.*   327

To thefe refpectable authorities many more might be added, were it neceffary; in whom we find μαθητευω is expreffive of fuch *difciplefhip* as includes infants and young children, no lefs than adults; and confequently, that previous teaching is by no means *effential* to difciplefhip. Therefore, the word muft be a *general term*, which does not, nor is intended, to exprefs the *fpecific mode* of difcipling. The *manner* of executing the command depends, entirely depends, on the capacities and circumftances of the perfons to be difcipled. And this difcretionary nature of the commiffion, well attended to, is the only preventive againft abufes.

AGAIN; if infants and children cannot be *difciples*, they cannot be *chriftians*, for thefe terms are convertible, and ufed fynonymoufly (Acts xi. 26.); and if not chriftians, they cannot belong to Chrift; but there are many fuch, our opponents grant, who belong to Chrift (fee alfo Mark ix. 41.); therefore infants *may* be *difciples*, except it be faid, they may be admitted to glory without belonging to Chrift, which is abfurd. And if fo, they may be *difciples* without human teaching, in the New Teftament fenfe of difciplefhip.

BESIDES; if παντα τα εθνη be the object of the command, μαθητευσατε; we infift that the rendering, DISCIPLE, is more *obvious* and *natural*, than the other, *teach*. For *difcipling*, in the fenfe now explained, may naturally and ftrictly belong to *a nation*, to *all the nations*; but not teaching.

Hence

Hence we further argue—if the *difcipling* in the text be fuch as *may* comprehend *a nation*, nay, *all the nations*, as it certainly is (except Chrift commands an impoffibility), then it is fuch as *cannot* agree to that fpecific mode of difcipling which is effected by *teaching*, *exclufively*. For, on Antipœdobaptift principles, what tolerable propriety can there be in making *all nations* the objects of difciplefhip! According to them, the term *nation* muft have a very fingular acceptation indeed; for, in the firft place, they muft exclude from it *all infants* and young children; and, in the next place, they would exclude all adults, except the *few*, comparatively *very few*, who are deemed by them fit fubjects of baptifm. Well, when they have *taught* them, few as they may be, they muft fay—that the *nation!* is difcipled. Does not fuch an interpretation militate againft the plain and natural ufe of terms, and bid defiance to the force of language? On our principles, it may be fome time firft before *a nation* be difcipled; but on our opponents', no nation *ever can* be. How much more rational, and agreeable to the language of prophecy; and how much more worthy of the nature of the Meffiah's vifible kingdom, the following words of the judicious and venerable TURRETINE? " μαθητας ποιειν non eft fimpliciter docere, fed *difcipulos facere.*—[Mat. xxviii. 19. Probatur Pœdobaptifmus ex hoc mandato] ab antithefi nam *omnes gentes* opponuntur omnibus & folis Judæis, ut poftulat difcrimen Veteris & Novi

Novi Teſtamenti.—Qui præcipit *omnes gentes* baptizari, is etiam præcipit baptizari *infantes*, præceptum enim de genere includit *omnes ſpecies*‡." To this let me add the following words of Biſhop BEVERIDGE: " Our Lord Chriſt, a little before his aſcenſion into heaven, left orders with his apoſtles, and in them with all that ſhould ſucceed in the miniſtry of the church to the end of the world, to make *all nations* his diſciples, *by baptizing* them in the name, &c. as the original words plainly import Mat. xxviii. 19.—It is to be further obſerved, that when our Saviour ordained baptiſm to be the way or means of admitting perſons into his church, or the congregation of his diſciples; leſt we ſhould think, as ſome have done, that he meant it only of thoſe who are of riper years, he uſed the *moſt* GENERAL TERMS *that could be invented*, requiring that *all nations* ſhould be baptized; and if *all nations*, then children alſo, which are a great, if not the greateſt part of every nation ||."

MOREOVER: There ſeems to me a peculiar propriety in our Lord's uſing terms of ſuch *general import*; for had it been inſtead of μαθητευ- σατε any term which *excludes* teaching as a mode of diſcipling, what a handle muſt ignorant and cruel bigots make of it in ſubjecting nations to the chriſtian faith! Ambitious miſſionaries might then juſtify their cruelties with ſpecious arguments

‡ Inſtit. Theol. Loc. xix. Queſt. xx. § 4.
|| Priv. Thoughts, Part ii. On Chriſtian Education, p. 6.

arguments, and abuse their commission by pretending to divine credentials. Would not *any other* term be liable to greater abuses and stronger objections than that which is wisely chosen? For instance, had διδασκω or παιδευω been adopted as terms *less general* to express the pre-requisition for baptism, it would have weakened what we apprehend our Lord meant to countenance, viz. our obligation to receive children together with their parents into the visible church, by the initiatory rite of baptism. On the other hand, had μυεω or τελεω been substituted for μαθητευω, the same inconvenience would have followed. For tho' the two former, I presume, might have conveyed the main idea contained in the latter (and accordingly some of the greek fathers seem to use them synonymously, see Isidore of *Pellusium* Lib. ii. Ep. 37. &c.) yet they would have been on many accounts less eligible.

Once more: Why, we wish to know, must we put a construction so unfavourable to infants (when no necessity requires it), upon every clause of the law which is deemed the rule of entrance into the church militant; while our opponents themselves assume, and justly assume, the liberty of giving an *apparently opposite* construction to that law which refers to their admission to the church triumphant? " He that *believeth not* shall be damned." Nay, we may add, we have greater apparent reason, from this very commission (Mark xvi. 15, 16.) for excluding infants from salvation, than from baptism.

For

For we contend that it is a law of nature, that children should partake of all the external rites and privileges of religion they are capable of, and therefore baptism, together with their parents; which cannot be said of their salvation.

To conclude: If infants were deemed, and justly deemed, *proselytes**; they may in like manner,

---

* Dr. STENNETT, indeed, seems to deny this, when he says, "Is it proper to say of persons, that they may be *proselyted* or discipled without any previous instruction, conviction or persuasion?" (Ans. to Dr. A. p. 133.) To this I reply,

1. If it was *customary* among the Jews to call those who were translated from Heathenism to the true religion, or the kingdom of God among them, GERIM, *foreigners* or *inmates*; and if it was customary for the Greeks to call these Προσελυτοι, *proselytes*, απο τȣ προσεληλυθεναι; and if it be FACT that *infants* were always reckoned, and by divine appointment, (Exod. x.i. 48, and Numb. xv. 14, 15.) among these *inmates* — We may well ask, what impropriety is there in calling an infant a *proselyte ?*

2. It is an *incontestible fact* that the Jewish writers, speak of *infants* and little children, as *proselytes*. 'Tis not only the *Gemara*, but the text of the *Misna* itself, both in the *Babylonian* and *Jerusalem Talmud*, which speaks of a *child* becoming or being made, *a proselyte.* — And the *Gemara* speaks expressly of " *a proselyte in infancy.*" And MAIMONIDES calls a little child or an *infant* " *a proselyte.*" (See Dr. WALL's History of Infant Baptism; Introd. § 3, 4, with the Authors there referred to.) This, Dr. GILL himself could not gainsay, and therefore gives it up. Body of Div. vol. iii. 486.

3. If a *proselyte* be *advena*, a *stranger*, one come over from one place or relation to another, as the term imports; what impropriety is there in applying it to infants? When we say " *strangers are come* to a place," is there any impropriety in our including *infants*, because *these* are strictly *brought ?*

4. When our Lord says of *infants* (Matt. xix. 14.) " Suffer them, and forbid them not ελθειν πρoς με," is there not the strictest propriety in calling *infants* when brought, PROSELYTES?

ner, be deemed *difciples:* for, (as a great critick obferves) " a difciple and a profelyte being perfectly all one, fave only that the latter denotes a *coming* from fome *other nation* or country, which difference hath no place in this matter, where the difciples are fpecified to be received from *all nations* †." And if *difciples*, they ought to be *baptized*; for the text in difpute affords no ground of exception againft any who are *difciples*. " Nor ought that hoary maxim of legal interpretation to be haftily caft afide;—*We muft not diftinguifh, where the law does not diftinguifh.*"—And fhould it be objected, that infants are not *made* difciples, and therefore fhould not be baptized; we anfwer, if they *are* difciples, they muft be *conftituted* fuch; and whether that conftitution be derived from a divine appointment in favour of the *fpecies*, from a minifterial act whereby they are profelyted to the chriftian religion (as heathen families were profelyted to the Jewifh religion) or from any other caufe, is perfectly immaterial in the prefent argument.—As to the trite objection urged from the *order* of the words, " *teach—baptizing them,*" I anfwer with Dr. ADDINGTON; " It is, in every view, indefenfible and ill-grounded. It is a *mere englifh* criticifm ‖." And with Dr. HAMMOND; " The phrafe which is there ufed in the *original*, is a fingular one, not duly expreffed by our Englifh *." But, even in *our tranflation*

† Dr. HAMMOND's Six Quer. Q. iv. § 27.
‖ Chriftian Minifter's Reaf. p. 112.   * Ut fupra, § 25.

tranflation, there is no *conjunction* to denote a diverfity of acts: for it is not " *teach AND baptize*," but " *teach, baptizing them*." Hence the author laſt quoted fays, " We know from that place of Mat. xxviii. that baptifm is the folemn ceremony of receiving into Chriſt's fchool the church ‖."

AND, indeed, were our oppofers indulged with their favourite rendering, *teach*, they muſt either renounce their fingular notion of *pofitive inſtitutions*, as utterly excluding all analogy and inferential reafoning, or find themfelves involved in endlefs uncertainty; for on what authority can they deny baptifm to *any* who are *taught?* And yet, how very unfit for baptifm, our opponents being judges, are numbers who *are taught*, and who *profefs* that Jefus is the fon of God and the only Saviour? But if " *we* muſt not diſtinguiſh where *this law* does not diſtinguiſh," what grofs abfurdities would follow? Not more oppofite is the Antipædobaptiſt hypothefis to the *truth*, than fubverfive of *itfelf!*

§ 48. LET us next inquire, In what fenfe the Apoſtles underſtood their commiffion? And particularly, whether they did not underſtand it to include the difciplefhip and baptifm of infants with their parents? But here it is neceffary to prefcribe the limits of our inquiry. Now fince the *pofitive part* of the evidence has been already eſtabliſhed, it would be fufficient for us, in point of ſtrict argument, to act henceforth only on the

defenfive

‖ Ibid. § 26.

defensive; for until that part be difproved (which, I prefume, will not be done in a hurry) the fmalleft probability will be a corroborating-addition. We fhall therefore attend, in the remaining part of this chapter, to what we apprehend to be, in connection with the premifes, *additional* evidence; referving for another place an examination of thofe paffages in the apoftolic writings, which are fuppofed by our oppofers to be inimical to Pœdobaptifm.

LET us begin with Acts ii. 39. For *The* PROMISE *is to you, and to your* CHILDREN, *and to all that are afar off, even to as many as the Lord our God fhall* CALL.—There are three terms in this paffage,—*promife, children, call*—the exact meaning of which it is neceffary to afcertain before any deduction be attempted.

1. WHAT are we to underftand by *the* PROMISE?—A fatisfactory anfwer to this queftion requires, that we fhould fix the meaning of the term (ἐπαγγελία) *promife,*—and determine what is the *matter promifed*; for every promife is *of fomething.* Refpecting the word ἐπαγγελία, STOCKIUS remarks: "Generatim et vi originis ANNUNCIATIONEM " fignificat. Speciatim autem notat *promiffionem.* " In hac fignificatione adhibetur nunc *proprie,* " nunc *improprie* et *metonymice.* *Proprie* fi " adhibetur, denotat *actum voluntatis,* quo pro- " mittens fe aliquid alteri daturum, vel facturum " indicat ac denuntiat.—*Improprie* et *metonymice* " fignificat *rem promiffam.*—— *Complementum et* " *eventum*

"*eventum promissionis*, &c.‡" The word often occurs in the New Testament, and is variously rendered by Latin interpreters; as, *Promissum, promissio, pollicitatio, repromissio, nuncium,* &c. And BEZA observes: " Est autem notanda hæc pro-
" pria significatio επαγγελίας a doctissimo BUDÆO
" observata, quæ *gratuitum esse Dei promissum* de-
" clarat *." In our translation, it is generally rendered, *promise*. But in 1 John i. 5. *Message.*
—The passage we are upon, seems to be of the same import with Acts xiii. 26. *Men and brethren, children of the stock of Abraham, and whosoever among you that feareth God,* TO YOU IS THE WORD OF THIS SALVATION *sent.* ver. 32, 33. *And* WE DECLARE UNTO YOU GLAD TIDINGS, *how that the* PROMISE *which was made unto the fathers, God hath fulfilled the same unto us their children, in that he hath raised Jesus again.* Or,
" And we *evangelize unto you that promise* which was made unto the fathers, how that God, &c."

Now, whether the term *promise*, in Peter's address, signifies strictly, according to the force of the original (ab επι et αγγελος, Denunciatio divinæ voluntatis et beneficentiæ†) *declaration, proclamation, annunciation, denunciation,* of the divine will and pleasure, a *message,* &c: or, more particularly denotes " an *act of the will,* whereby the promiser *shews* and *delares,* that something shall be given to another, or done for him," it amounts in fact to the same thing, the difference being only circumstantial. For in this they both
agree

‡ STOCKII Clav. Nov. Test. sub voc   * Annot. in loc.
† Vid LEIGH Crit. Sac.

agree, that the *will* of the promiser muſt be *announced* to conſtitute either; and therefore muſt imply—" A DECLARATION OF GOD'S WILL concerning ſomething." Nor is it again material whether it be taken *properly*, or *metonymically* for the *thing promiſed*; becauſe, in the preſent caſe, " *the promiſe* OF A THING" is tantamount with " *the thing promiſed*." No difficulty therefore remains but what lies in aſcertaining the *contents* of the promiſe, or *that* of which the promiſe is made.

SOME ſeek the Apoſtle's meaning from ver. 21. " *And it ſhall come to paſs that whoſoever ſhall call on the name of the Lord* SHALL BE SAVED." Some ſeek it from ver. 38. where " *the* REMISSION OF SIN" is promiſed. Others, from the laſt clauſe of the ſame verſe, " *and ye ſhall receive the* GIFT OF THE HOLY GHOST;" and the rather becauſe this *immediately precedes* the controverted text. And others ſuppoſe, that Peter here uſes the phraſe, " *The promiſe*," by way of eminence and diſtinction. " The word [*promiſe*] in the New Teſtament," ſays Mr. CRUDEN, " is *often* " taken for thoſe promiſes that God heretofore " made to Abraham, and the other Patri- " archs, of ſending the *Meſſiah:* It is in this " ſenſe that the Apoſtle Paul *commonly* uſes the " word promiſe.‡" This uſe of the word in the text before us implies; The aſpect of the promiſe in its preſent accompliſhment in Jeſus Chriſt, is towards you and your children. In vindication of this ſenſe, ſeveral Expoſitors diſtinguiſh between the

‡ Concord. under the word *Promiſe*.

Ch. 3.   *Subjects of Baptism.*   337

the Apoſtle's *advice,* and his *encouragement.* His *advice*—(1) Repent, (2) Be baptized, (3) Every one of you. His *encouragement*—(1) The remiſſion of ſins, (2) The gift of the Holy Ghoſt, (3) The well known promiſe refers to you and yours, notwithſtanding your ungrateful and cruel treatment of the Meſſiah, who was the end and ſum thereof. Thus BENEDICTUS ARETIUS:
" Conſilium Petri duas complectitur partes.
" Prior monſtrat facienda : Poſterior addit rationes.
" Nam fine rationibus aliquid jubere rebus afflictis
" non ſatis eſt prudentis oratoris. Itaque orator
" apoſtolicus perſpicuitati ſtudet. Jubet faci-
" enda, ac conſilii ſubnectit admodum perſpi-
" cuas rationes. — *Primum* a fine rem commen-
" dat: In REMISSIONEM PECATORUM — *Alia*
" *ratio* eſt, QUIA ACCIPIETIS DONUM SPIRI-
" TUS *ſancti.*—*Tertio,* VOBIS ENIM eſt PROMIS-
" SIO FACTA ET LIBERIS VESTRIS, h. e. de
" Meſſia, et illius beneficiis, promiſſiones in pri-
" mis ſpectant ad vos. — *Quarto,* declarat perſo-
" nas, ad quas ſpectant promiſſiones. VOBIS &
" LIBERIS VESTRIS, ET QUI LONGE SUNT *."

THIS view of the paſſage appears to me moſt agreeable to the ſcope and occaſion of it. For the Apoſtle's reply and encouragement muſt be ſuppoſed *anſwerable* to the ſolicitude and enquiry of the awakened multitude. What particularly ſtruck them, it ſeems, was, " the evidence with which the Apoſtle urged the *Meſſiahſhip* of *Jeſus*
Q   from

* BENED. ARET. Comment. in Act. ii. See alſo CALVIN's admirable Notes on the text in queſtion.

from the Jewish writings, and the miraculous gifts which were now visible and astonishing."— This was the great design of those miraculous effusions, " to reprove the world of sin, of righteousness and of judgment;" that is, to be an unparalleled and invincible demonstration of the Messiahship of Jesus Christ. This is what he *principally* aimed at, and this idea he fixes in their minds, " as a nail fastened in a sure place," by concluding in these pungent and persuasive expressions—ver. 36 " *Therefore let all the house of Israel know assuredly that God hath made that same Jesus, whom ye have crucified, both Lord and Christ.*" The historian adds, " *Now when they heard this, they were pricked in their heart, and said unto Peter, and to the rest of the Apostles, Men and brethren what shall we do?*" Peter replies, " Repent; and your sins, particularly your rejection and crucifixion of the Messiah, shall be remitted. Be baptized, every one of you; submit to this initiatory ordinance of his kingdom, which exhibits the influences of the Holy Spirit; and Christ shall baptize you, as John his forerunner has often declared, with the Holy Ghost; at least this is your path of duty, — he has the residue of the Spirit, — and do not imagine that the *grace of Christ*, or the blessings of his kingdom, are *peculiar* to *us*. For the well-known promise, grant, covenant, or EXHIBITION *of mercy and grace*, is common to us all. Do not suppose that *we* have any *other* divine charter, whereby we are entitled to these unspeakable blessings,

blessings, than what was granted of old to our forefathers: and this, you may be sure, is no less open to you, as a ground of application for the blessings of the Messiah's kingdom, than to us. And, according to what was said of old, that in HIM all the families of the earth were to be blessed, the time is come that the *gentile* nations, as well as our own, are to be called to him."

To *confine* the promise to the *miraculous* gifts of the Spirit, would be unworthy of an apostle; for it would be prescribing a remedy to the multitude, cut to the heart with remorse for their cruel treatment of Jesus, inadequate to the disease. When he speaks of *the promise*, it must be as a *ground* of their faith and their access to God; but nothing can be so to fallen man but a dispensation of mercy, a sacred warrant, salvation thro' a Redeemer, the ministry of reconciliation, in a word, the *covenant of grace* in its exhibition and direction to him. I say in its EXHIBITION or external form, for this, and this *alone*, properly speaking, is the ground of a sinner's approach to God. " *To us are given*, that is, EXHIBITED for our use and encouragement, *exceeding great and precious* PROMISES, *that by these we might be partakers of the divine nature.* (2 Pet. i. 4.) For the apostle to assure his hearers, that *the promise was to them*, in their present circumstances, was the same as to *preach the gospel to them.* And these are used synonymously. (See Gal. iii. 8 and 18.) For, *to give Abraham*

Q 2 *a divine*

a divine PROMISE, is the same as, *to preach the* GOSPEL *to him.*

BESIDES: Is there any probability *in fact,* that ALL who complied with this exhortation received *the promise,* if the *miraculous gifts* of the Spirit as about to be conferred upon them, be thereby intended? Or was *this* promise made to the mixed multitude; to their children *as such,* whether their immediate offspring or posterity; to *all* afar off, whether Jews or Gentiles, that the Lord should *call?* If this interpretation were admitted, would it not follow, that we sinners of the Gentiles, being some of the ALL *that were afar off,* upon being *called* of the Lord, upon *repentance* and *baptism,* may expect from *the promise,* the *miraculous gifts* of the Holy Ghost? In my opinion, it could be *then* no *just motive* either to repentance, to be baptized, or to any christian duty, *of itself*; and to us who are called and afar off, it can be *no motive at all.* And, indeed, had any complied from such an expectation of miraculous endowments, except in subordination to a *more important* promise, their mercenary motive must stand condemned as unworthy of christianity, and therefore unworthy of an inspired teacher of it to recommend. — But should any contend, that the *promise* refers to the Holy Ghost in his ordinary gracious influences, and not merely those which were miraculous, this is virtually to admit that sense of the passage for which I plead; for it implies and eminently contains what the scriptures

Ch. 3. *Subjects of Baptism.* 341

scriptures term, καῦ' ἐξοχην, *the promise*. "To conclude this point, the apoſtle himſelf has plainly informed us, in another place, what he here intends by the promiſe; ſee Acts iii. 25. where, urging much the ſame exhortation upon his Jewiſh hearers, as he does here, he enforces it with this argument: "Ye are the children of the covenant," [or promiſe, according to Gal. iii. 18.] "which God made with our fathers" [or granted to our fathers; ἧς διεθέλο ὅ Θεος προς τες πατερας ἡμων,] "ſaying unto Abraham, and in thy ſeed ſhall all the kindreds of the earth be bleſſed; unto you *firſt* [or *primarily* for your ſake,] God hath raiſed up his ſon Jeſus, and ſent him to bleſs you, &c. †"

§ 49. 2. Who are the *perſons to whom* the promiſe is made? "The promiſe is *unto* YOU, *and to your* CHILDREN, *and to* ALL *that are* AFAR OFF, *even* AS MANY *as the Lord our God* SHALL CALL." *The promiſe is unto* YOU, ſays the apoſtle; *you* who now hear me; *you* who compoſe this vaſt aſſembly, of every nation, rank or age. *You* does the Lord our God *call to repentance*, who have rejected and murdered the Prince of Life; on whom the guilt of the horrid deed, ſo impiouſly imprecated on yourſelves and children, muſt otherwiſe abide. *You*, without exception, who are *capable* of remorſe, does the Lord our God *call to repentance*, in as much as all of you have ſins to repent of; and a

Q 3 ſtate

† Bostwick's Fair and Rational Vindication of Inf. Bapt. p. 9.

state to be changed for the better. And to *each one* of you, without the least exception, is the *promise*, the glad tidings of mercy, made. And as *baptism* is the instituted *seal* of that promise, you may be sure that if the one belongs to you, the other does of course; for if the testamentary grant be yours, it follows that every confirmation of that grant is yours, of which nature baptism is. Here we might ask, Is it not reasonable to suppose, that among so great a multitude there were some children and infants in arms before the apostle; and if so, by what rule were such excepted from being included in this declaration —the promise is unto *you?* Were they not addressed as a body? Or, will it be said, "All who are capable of *repentance* were addressed?" Nay, rather, all who were capable of repentance were called to repent; and all who were capable of the promise or divine grant, and its seal, were included therein. And no one can deny that infants are capable of bequeathments and grants (and consequently the *sealing* of them) in their favour.

But to put this matter further out of doubt, the apostle adds, " *the promise*, or grant, *is to your* CHILDREN, τοις τεκνοις." It appears to me a matter of no great moment, in this controversy, whether we understand by the term *children*, sons and daughters, seed, offspring, descendants, posterity, or any other the like; for none of these expressions *exclude* infants, which is sufficient for our purpose. If there be any *exclu-*
sion

sion in the cafe, it muft be fought, not from *thefe terms*, but fome other confiderations; which is foreign to the prefent point. Suppofe, for inftance, our opponents attempt the exclufion of infants, by adopting the term, *pofterity.*; it will not ferve their turn: for who can we underftand by the *pofterity* of a perfon or perfons, but thofe who lineally come after, or defcend from fuch? And is not the term applicable to them, as foon as they exift? Are they not fuch in every ftage of life? Befides: Were that interpretation allowed, which excludes all from pofterity but adults, what would it prove? Why, that the *promife* is to the adult *pofterity* of this audience, tho' they were Jews or Mahometans, but *not* to the infant offspring of any Chriftian. But muft we regard our infant children, tho' born in fin, *in a lefs favourable condition*, as to any merciful grant, than the obftinate Jew, and the deluded Turk? He that *can* believe it, let him.

Nor is it material, whether the phrafe, " *all that are afar off*," refer to diftant Jews or Gentiles; diftant as to place or time. From this phrafe infants are not excluded, nay are clearly implied.

But, fays Mr. B. " There is nothing faid about the promife refpecting any, befides thofe whom *the Lord our God fhall* CALL. Yes, whether they be Jews or Gentiles, whether they be parents or children, they muft be *called*, before this text will permit us to view them as interefted in that promise of which it speaks †." To this we readily subscribe; but deny what he immediately subjoins: "which intirely excludes infants from all consideration here." This will lead us to inquire,

§ 50. 3. WHAT are we to understand by the term, προσκαλεσηlαι, CALL? The word Προσκαλιομαι, which often occurs in the New Testament, (tho' never I believe in its active form,) plainly and properly signifies, *advoco, accerso, adcisco, arcesso,* &c. LEIGH: "Utrumque significat, & *convocare* & *ad se vocare,* Mat. x. 1, &c. *" STOCKIUS: "Generatim notat *advocare,* connotato termino ad quem, sive hic sit persona sive res personæ opposita.—Est *vocare gentes* AD ECCLESIAM, per predicationem evangelii, Act. ii. 39 ||." But here we should carefully distinguish between *God's call* and *men's compliance* with it. The *latter* of these ideas is out of the present question; being excluded by the nature of the subject, and the proper force of the term. Nor should we confound the CALL *of the gospel,* with God's *secret* choice of individuals, or his *efficacious* drawing of them to himself to love and serve him in spirit and in truth. These things belong to a sovereign invisible dispensation; a dispensation of quite a different nature from what our apostle mainly intends. And indeed, with regard to what is termed *effectual calling,* which Mr. B. seems to take for granted is here intended, the
call

† Pædob. Exam. p. 362. * Critica Sacra, sub voce.
|| Clav. Nov. Test, sub voce.

call muſt not be confounded with the *effect* of it. In my apprehenſion, the ſecret and efficacious influence of God on the ſinner's mind, whereby it is difpoſed to receive the truth, is very improperly termed God's *call*. For his *calling* of them, properly ſpeaking, is by his *word*, his will *revealed*, the *miniſtry* of reconciliation, &c. but what renders this calling *effectual*, is the imparted influence or powerful operation of the Spirit on the mind, and thereby a difpoſition, inclination, or moral ability, is produced, to *comply* with the call. Hence *many* are *called*, but *few* are *choſen**.

BESIDES: The promiſe, or goſpel grant, is not any bleſſing conferred *in* CONSEQUENCE *of effectual calling*, but in *ſubſerviency* to it. For the promiſe is the *foundation* of our acceſs to God, and our *encouragement* to repentance, and not a bleſſing conſequent upon either. Repenting, complying, coming to God, &c. are *our* acts and exerciſes; but without a promiſe they have no ground, no motive, no exiſtence. Perſons, families, and nations, are *called* THAT THEY MAY COMPLY, and the promiſe is given them as the *inducement*. When any *actually comply* with the purport of the call, we are taught and obliged to aſcribe that efficiency, not to our own diſtinguiſhing worthineſs and ability, but to the power of God, executing the plan of ſovereign diſtinguiſhing love. Thus God *calls*, but man, through the ſtupifying effect of ſin, refuſes; yet when

* Matt. xx. 16. xxii. 14.

when God *works* in us both to will and to do of his good pleasure, who can let? Neverthelefs, the bleffings promifed, or exhibited in the promife, become actually ours in confequence of our anfwering the divine requifition or *call*.

ON the whole: As the apoftle has no reference to the *internal* power of grace, we are conftrained to feek his meaning in the *external* call of the gofpel. Into whatever part of the gentile world, as if he had faid, the cloud of divine providence moves, from henceforth, the miniftry of reconciliation, or God's *call* to men by the Gofpel, is defigned to follow it. Our call has no limitation but what arifes in the courfe of providential conduct. If *all* the gentile nations are not actually evangelized, fuch confinement and feeming partiality is not owing to any limiting claufe in our commiffion, but to the all-wife conduct of providence, while it opens a door of entrance to fome nations, and leaves others for a time fhut. But no fooner is a perfon, a family, a nation, or a people, *evangelized*, or addreffed by a gofpel miniftry, than we can affure them, that the promife is to *them and theirs*. If they *reject* the call, they reject alfo the promife; and if they *reject* the promife, grant, or covenant, they have no right to the *feal*; for the inftrument and the feal muft not be feparated. *External* compliance is fufficient to fecure whatever is in the covenant of an *external nature*; and baptifm, the initiating feal, being *fuch*, by that compliance it is fecured. But an *internal* and fpiritual compliance, and that alone

alone, secures to us whatever is in the covenant of an *internal* and spiritual *nature*. And whence the ability to comply, as before observed, belongs to another question, and flows from the covenant of redemption, well ordered in all things and sure, in its *internal form*.

WE might again ask : Are any individuals, families, tribes, or nations, *proselyted* to the visible church of God, without being *called?* Does not *proselyting* of necessity imply *calling?* Yet infants may be *proselyted* with their parents, as parts of themselves, as members of families, and as making a very considerable part of those *nations* that may be *joined to the Lord*; and therefore such infants should be reckoned among the *called*. On the whole, the following remark of CALVIN on the place, appears very just and comprehensive. " Christus diruta maceria, utrosque reconciliavit " Patri, & veniens annunciavit pacem his qui " *prope* erant, & his qui *procul*. Nunc tenemus " Petri mentem. Nam ut Christi gratiam am- " plificet, eam Judeis sic proponit, ut Gentes " quoque fore consortes dicat. Ideo utitur *verbo* " *advocandi :* acsi diceret, Quemadmodum vos " prius in unum populum sua voce collegit Deus, " ita vox eadem ubique personabit, ut qui remoti " sunt, ad vos accedant, ubi novo Dei edicto " fuerint accersiti †."

Now if this be the meaning of the text, it appears — (1) That wherever the *dispensation* of the gospel comes, there the *promise* comes. For

† CALVINI Comment. in Act. ii. 39.

to be *called* is to be " *invited* to the honours and privileges of the visible church;" and to be *the called*, as expressive of a continued state, in the scripture style, is to be actually possessed of such privileges. Thus Isa. lxviii. 12. *Hearken unto me, O Jacob, and Israel* MY CALLED. Rom. i. 6. *Among whom are ye also* THE CALLED *of Jesus Christ.* ver. 7. *To* ALL *that be in Rome, beloved of God,* CALLED *to be saints,* &c. (2) That no people are actually *the called* of God, in a state of gospel privileges, but their children, *as theirs*, or in virtue of their right in them, are included with them. (3) When we consider this, in connection with preceding revelations, we cannot say, properly, that infants' *right* to their parents' privileges, inclusive of the promise and initiatory seal, is *founded* here, but *confirmed:* rather, what is *founded* in the law of nature, what is *implied* in every dispensation, and what has been in many instances explicitly *ratified*, is here *asserted* and *confirmed* against all suspicion to the contrary, viz. That the promise, covenant, or grant of mercy, is not more to the parents than to their children; and consequently the initiating and confirming seal of that grant, baptism*."

§ 51. WE come now to inquire what *additional* evidence we have from the account given us of HOUSEHOLDS, from Acts xvi. 15. *When she*

---

* It may be here remarked, that the interpretations of Dr. OWEN and WITSIUS, of HAMMOND and LIMBORCH, are not at all inconsistent with Pædobaptist principles as here stated, tho' produced by Mr. B. in favour of Antipædobaptism; and the same remark is applicable to numerous other instances, in the work I am examining.

she was baptized and her HOUSEHOLD. — Acts xvi. 33. *And was baptized, he and* ALL HIS, *straightway.* — 1 Cor. i. 16. *I baptized also the* HOUSEHOLD *of Stephanus.* But here it is necessary to premise what is the just use and real importance of these passages in the controversy. Our opponents would fain insinuate, that if we cannot demonstrate hence there actually were infants in these families, and that these were baptized, the texts in question are of *no use* to the Pœdobaptist cause. But this is a great mistake. We insist, from *other* premises, that parents *ought* to baptize their children; therefore we do not urge these texts to *prove their right*, but to *increase the probability* that they were *de facto* baptized. I say, to increase the *probability*; for it is evident from the nature of the controversy, that these texts, which refer to a case of *fact*, should be weighed only in the scales of *right*; and that the balance of probability will preponderate according as the previous right is proved or disproved.

WE have insisted from various topicks — the law of nature — the divine dispensations — prophetick language — our Lord's ministry and commission, &c. — that religion, that is, Christianity, (for the *nature* of it does not alter the case) is a *family* concern. In other words, a man's children, and non-opposing domesticks, are not only to be *denominated* from his religious profession, as the head of the family, but are entitled to all the external *privileges* of that religion, as instituted means of grace and godliness, according to their respective capacities. When therefore we

hear

hear of a man who has a family, that he became a believer, a disciple, or a christian, we infer (and the more excellent the nature and quality of his religion the more rational the inference) —— we infer, that his family is a *christian family*; and that each member of it, that is not an *opposer*, is entitled to those privileges he himself enjoys, according as it is capable: I say not an *opposer*, for to compel any, who are *sui juris*, would be impious, since christianity, in this important particular, does not interfere with the rights of nature. And the matter of *right* standing thus, it would be *uncharitable* and *unreasonable* to suppose the matter of *fact* to be otherwise, especially in the apostolic age. We may therefore conclude, when we read — " her HOUSEHOLD — his HOUSEHOLD — ALL HIS" — were baptized, that these things are spoken of *households* or families *as such*, or *collectively*; and that we should not understand the terms distributively, but with the proviso of *pro captu singulorum*. For, if a man's children be equally capable of baptism with himself, and believing or repenting is a qualification not at all essential to the ordinance, as belonging to its *nature*, but only necessary to those who are capable of them, there remains no ground of exception against infants; that is, if there were any children or infants in any of the families referred to, we *ought* to conclude they *were* baptized. The parent, or head of the family, would *of course*, according to all the sources of information he could consult, if a *heathen*, the light of nature, if a *Jew*,

the

the Old Teſtament, and more eſpecially in either caſe from the *genius* of chriſtianity, conſider his dependants, particularly his children, being at his diſpoſal for their benefit, as entitled to the *ſame privileges*, or means of grace and religion, as himſelf—*if not* EXPRESSLY PROHIBITED.

Mr. B. availing himſelf of LIMBORCH's conceſſion, that the argument from the account of *houſeholds* being baptized, amounts to no more than a *bare probability* that there were any *infants* baptized as well as adults in thoſe families; ſeems to forget that a *bare probability (cæt. par.)* is *very ſufficient* to influence an impartial mind. For if one ſide of a queſtion be only *barely* PROBABLE, all things conſidered, the other ſide ſurely is *ſo far* IMPROBABLE. " It may admit of a query," ſays Mr. B. " whether, in this metropolis, a *majority* of houſeholds have any mere infants in them." Granted: but will it admit of a query, whether *three families* for *one* in the metropolis, or in any city, town, or pariſh in the kingdom; or, more properly, in thoſe parts of the world, and that age, which theſe paſſages refer to, had any? Our argument fairly reſts not on ONE family *ſeparately* conſidered, but on the THREE unitedly. Otherwiſe, could we produce a *thouſand* inſtances out of the ſacred records of a perſon's *houſehold*, or *all his*, being baptized, Mr. B.'s mode of arguing would leave the *probability* the *very ſame*; which is abſurd.

As to what is urged from theſe phraſes—". *Elkanah and* ALL HIS HOUSE *went up to offer unto*
the

the Lord the yearly sacrifice. A nobleman at Capernaum *believed, and his* WHOLE HOUSE. *Cornelius feared God with* ALL HIS HOUSE. *Unruly talkers subvert* WHOLE HOUSES. Paul and his companion *spake the word of the Lord* to the Philippian jailor, *and to* ALL *that were in his house. He, believing in God, rejoiced,* WITH ALL HIS HOUSE. *Ye know the* HOUSE *of Stephanas, that* IT *is the* FIRST FRUITS OF ACHAIA, *and that they have addicted themselves to the ministry of the saints**—and the like; let any unprejudiced mind reflect, whether such phrases be not *perfectly consistent* with our account of households; nay, whether they do not directly tend to *establish* it. For is not this an idea most naturally suggested,—that religion, according to the *sacred oracles,* as well as from the reasonableness of the thing, is, tho' *internally* considered a *personal* concern, yet as *externally* professed a *family* concern. Do not such passages intimate, and more than barely intimate, that no surer do the means of grace belong to a person, than they belong to *his household as such?*—" In all which examples," says Mr. B. " infants must be excepted ∥." If by *examples* he intends the *actions* connected with the universal terms, " whole house, all his house, &c." such as, " all his house *went up to offer*, his whole house *believed,* all his house *feared God,* unruly talkers *subvert whole*

---

* 1 Sam. i. 21. John iv. 53. Acts x. 2. Tit. i. 11, 12. Acts xvi. 32, 34. and xviii. 8. 1 Cor. xvi. 15.

∥ Pædob. Exam. p. 369.

whole houses, Paul *spake the word* to all in a house," and so on; it is manifest such examples are nothing to the purpose. For our arguments do not *imply*, what such a remark seems alone calculated to shew, that we ascribe to infants what they are *naturally incapable* of. But if by " examples " he means the universal terms, "all, whole, &c." as being the *subjects* of those actions, and therefore there could be *no infants* in those families; our author confutes himself: for he owns " it is not uncommon for the sacred writers " to assert this, or the other, concerning a house- " hold, without any express limitation; which " is manifestly meant of only the *greater part* *." His "examples," therefore, neither tend to shew that there were *no infants* in the households in question, nor, supposing there were any, that they were *not baptized*. Not the *former*; for in the very examples he produces, there might have been infants, from his own *concession*, provided the *greater part* be adults. Not the *latter*; for that an infant should be *baptized* implies no *impossibility*, as the *actions* in the "examples" produced do; nor any thing *improbable* without begging the question in debate. What the objection really proves, is what no one ever denied, — that there *may* be families *without* infants! To which we beg leave to make a reply suitable to its importance — there *may* be families *with* infants. But is it not *probable* that in *three families*

* Ibid.

lies there was an infant or a young child? And is it not *very probable*, if infants were *capable* of the rite of baptism as well as the parents, that they were *baptized?*—But what do I say? will not the following objection marr the whole?

"If our opposers would be true to their "argument, by acting consistently with it, they "must, when called to baptize the *master* of a "family, administer the same ordinance to his "*wife*, his *children*, and his *domesticks*, without "exception, if not baptized before, whether "they profess repentance towards God, and "faith in Christ, or not*." No, this is not a legitimate consequence. For

1. Tho' a master has a right over his children, and in some measure his other domesticks, for their good and benefit, this does not imply that he ought to act the tyrant, to force the conscience, or to use compulsion in religious matters.

2. Our argument, and our acting consistently with it, require no such promiscuous and unreasonable proceedings as the objection insinuates. The law by which we suppose a parent or a master ought to be ruled in those cases is this— that he benefit his children, and *all his*, as they are *capable*. And accordingly we insist,

3. That *infancy* is no greater objection to baptism, than to proselytism or circumcision, that is, is no just plea of exclusion at all; whereas an *opposition* to Christ, his gospel, and the means of

---

* Pædob. Exam. p. 370, 371.

of grace, is a reasonable and scriptural ground of exclusion. No man has a right to *force* another, in matters of judgment and conscience, in proportion as that other has a right to judge for himself, even in the most advantageous and momentous concerns. And that there may be adult persons in a family, whose unalienable right of private judgment overbalances the authority and right of the domestick head, I suppose none will deny. Hence we conclude, that

4. Tho' the promise and its initiatory seal may be *rejected* by some of a man's domesticks, yet that these were *intended* and directed to him and to ALL HIS *as such*; and consequently that this is a sufficient reason for us to conclude, that ALL of them are entitled thereto, œconomically, who do not *reject* the counsel of God against themselves, as the Pharisees and lawyers did, Luke vii. 29, 30*.

§ 52. AMONG

---

* " When Zaccheus, who was not by birth a son of Abraham, but a sinner, a Gentile, was thus converted, Christ enlargeth his COVENANT to his *family* also — *This day is salvation come to this* HOUSE, *in as much as he also is a son of Abraham*, Luke xix. 9.— " He makes [his believing in Christ] the reason why his HOUSE " should be saved also, and so the *covenant* stuck with them of his " *family* likewise, *because the father of the family was now a believer.* " — And let me add this, that as Christ once before in the conver- " sion of the Centurion, the first-fruits of the Gentiles, (Matt. viii) " did first break open the treasury of the Gentiles' conversion; so " upon occasion of this man's conversion afterwards, he shews the " *privilege* of the Gentiles *when* converted — shewing how their *cove-* " *nant* was to run by HOUSEHOLDS, in a conformity to Abraham's " family at first.—Thus in like manner, when the apostles came to " preach the gospel to a Gentile *housholder*, master or father of a
" *family*

§ 52. AMONG those passages which tend to shew in what sense the apostles understood their commission with respect to the Jewish and Gentile nations, is Rom. xi. 11—31. on which I would offer the following reflections.

1. NOTHING

" *family*, they carried the offer of it in *this tenour*, and in the way of
" *this privilege*, as a MOTIVE to conversion.—In the New Testament
" we find in the *event* (which still answers to *promises*) that the
" gospel spread itself thro' *whole* HOUSEHOLDS, this being the tenure
" of our *covenant*—Now then, when the covenant thus runs with
" the *heads of houses* for the *families* themselves, I argue thus from
" thence for their *children*, That *they* must needs be included and
" intended in a more *special* manner; for they are the *natural* branches,
" and servants but *engrafted*, as was said of the Jews and Gentiles in
" the like case.—The *house* of Aaron and his *children*, are put for
" one and the same, Ps. cxv. 12, 15. In like phrase of speech Leah
" and Rachel in bringing forth children, are said to build up the *house*
" of Israel, Ruth iv. 11. And so the word HOUSE is used for
" *posterity* in all languages. And for the further confirmation of this,
" namely, that this tenure of the Gentiles' covenant in a conformity
" to Abraham's, should run thus *by families* from the *heads* there-
" of, this doth fully suit with the original promise made to Abraham
" himself, when the scripture foresaw (as Paul's phrase is) that the
" Gentiles should be justified—*as his seed*. The promise (Gen. xii.
" 3.) runs in these terms, *In thee shall all the* FAMILIES *of the*
" *earth be blessed*; as elsewhere (Gen. xviii. 18. and xxii. 18.) it runs
" in these terms, *All the* NATIONS *of the earth shall be blessed*.
" These expressions are both used;—to shew, the seed should be of
" all *nations and people*; yet so, as withal, the covenant was to run
" *by families* in those nations. Therefore the New Testament quotes
" it in both senses. Gal. iii. 8. says παντα τα εθνη, *all nations*,
" —Acts iii 25. αι πατζαι, *fatherhoods* of the earth.

" And further:—this was the *primitive and natural church way*,
" under the *Law of nature* alone Moses; unto which therefore for
" ever God hath suited this *family covenant*, and in Abraham ratified
" and sanctified it to the end of the world.—And the reason why God
" chose this of a *family* to convey the covenant by, was, that this soci-
" ety was the only *natural society* of all others, and therefore God did
" always

Ch. 3. *Subjects of Baptism.*

1. NOTHING less seems implied by the apostle, than that the conversion of the Gentiles was intended to be *national*, as appears from the whole of his reasoning. That is, he considers them as a *people*, or as a *body*, in the same sense as the Jews were so. All must allow his idea is a *collective* one; and we further insist, that the *individuals* or members of the gentile or gospel church here described cannot be adults *exclusively*. His idea of the gentile church is such as *cannot agree* to a company of adult believers, or the Antipœdobaptist notion of the gospel church. And if this assertion be made good, either they or Paul must be wrong. Let us briefly analyze and investigate the apostle's reasoning.

(1) HE

" always choose it throughout all states of the church.—God herein
" engrafting (as he uses to do grace on nature in our spirits, when
" he converts us, so) his covenant of grace upon this covenant of
" nature to run in the channel of it." See Dr. THOMAS GOON-
WIN's Works, Vol. ii. p. 391, 3c*, 393.—But let the less informed
reader carefully distinguish, in judging of God's covenant to man, to
families, &c. between the *exhibition made* and the *grace possessed*. The
present controversy has to do immediately only with the *former*; which
is *alone*, strictly speaking, the foundation of a sinner's encouragement to
draw near to God for mercy, grace, and every needful blessing. As
to the notion of hereditary *grace possessed*, as if *this* descended from
father to son, it is equally unscriptural and absurd. That the Lord
should condescend to declare, that he *will be* A GOD *unto me, and
mine*, is one thing (and how unspeakable the privilege!); but for me
to conclude from thence that I am *possessed* of grace, or a person
actually justified, would be highly presumptuous. He is my God, *that
I may* BELIEVE, &c ; but not that I may conclude upon my *state*
as if it proved my *justification*, &c. And yet, when from just premises
I infer my *justified state*, I may safely call the Lord " my God " in
the *more peculiar* and discriminating sense.

(1) He employs such *general terms*, in contrasting the gospel church with the Jewish, as, we apprehend, would be very improper to express any other church state, than that which agrees to a body of people, comprehending old and young. Thus he uses the terms *Gentiles*, or *nations*; the *world*; *Israel*; &c.

(2) The manner in which he *contrasts* the *partial fall*, and the *compleat restoration* of the Jews; as also the different states of the Jews and the Gentiles; is *incompatible* with that hypotheses which we oppose.

(3) His *figurative illustration* of the Jewish and gospel churches, affords another argument in favour of our view of the subject. He speaks of the two churches as the *root* and *branches* of a tree; and the *lopping off* answers to the *grafting in*.

(4) The *assignable cause* of the Jews' rejection, *unbelief*, and the *remedial means* of their reinstatement, *believing*, are mentioned in such a connection and light, as cannot be understood of their subjects as *individuals*, but as a *body of people*, consisting of old and young, parents and children. Their unbelief consisted in the general and *national rejection* of the Messiah; and their faith, the only mean of their desirable reinstatement, must consist in a *general reception* of Christ.

(5) The *universality* of their *future conversion* is represented in such a manner as totally disagrees with the Antipædobaptist view of gospel privileges

privileges in general, and church-memberſhip in particular.

(6) As their *ſtanding* before their renunciation of the Meſſiah was *compleat*, like a perfect olive tree conſiſting of root and branch,. or like the vine which God brought out of Egypt, planted in Canaan; and which covered the whole land with its luxuriant ramifications; ſo their having *quitted* that ſtanding is repreſented by the apoſtle in ſuch a manner as to ſhew them highly *blameable* and *criminal*. That *ſtanding*, then, was what they *ought* to have maintained; therefore it was not any *peculiarity* of covenant relation deſigned to ceaſe and to be annihilated under the Meſſiah. Whatever they were *before* their national unbelief, their *ſtumbling*, and *diminiſhing*; whatever that *fulneſs* was they *fell from*, on account of which they are here repreſented as *faulty* and *ſinful*; it inevitably follows, that it was ſuch a *ſtanding* and *fulneſs* as the goſpel was not *intended* to aboliſh, but was calculated to eſtabliſh and promote. But what could ſuch a *ſtanding* and compleat *fulneſs* or abundance be ? Was it their *ſtanding* faſt in *perſonal piety?* Was it their abounding in *adult believers*, when it was attempted to prevent their downfall? Was it any *peculiar privilege* deſigned to laſt until the Meſſiah came, and no longer? No: neither of theſe ſuppoſitions can poſſibly be true. Not the *two firſt*,—for they are contradicted by plain matter of fact; nor the *laſt*,—for it is incontrovertibly *implied*, that if they left their

ſtanding,

standing, and loft their fulnefs, it was owing to their fin, their *blindnefs*, &c. and on the other hand, if they, as a nation or body of people, received the Redeemer, their fall and diminution would be *prevented*.

In fhort, from the very dawn of gofpel light nothing elfe was intended than their *national falvation*, or continued *church-relation* to God as a body at large. To this tended the flaming zeal of John the Baptift; to this tended the venerable miniftry of the Son of God, and the conftant efforts of his miniftring difciples, under his direction; to this tended the unwearied labours, fervent prayers, and affectionate exhortations of his infpired apoftles; and efpecially after this Paul ardently purfued; to accomplifh this he could *wifh himfelf accurfed from Chrift*, and for non-fuccefs herein he had *great heavinefs and continual forrow in his heart*. (Rom. ix. 2, 3.)

But, if this was the real avowed *intendment* of the gofpel miniftry, which Mr. B. neither does, nor, I prefume, can deny, relative to all the inhabitants of Judea; it follows from the *whole drift* of the apoftle's argumentation — from the *general terms* he employs — from the *contraft* he draws — and from his *figurative illuftrations* and comparifons, — that the real avowed intendment of the gofpel miniftry among the Gentiles or *all the nations* of the world, is nothing lefs extenfive than their *national falvation*, that is, their external church-relation to God as bodies

Ch. 3. *Subjects of Baptism.* 361

at large, comprehensive of all ages and descriptions of mankind *.

MOREOVER: the *future fulness* of the Jews, to be accomplished by their embracing Jesus Christ as their Messiah, will *reinstate* them in their former position, ver. 23. *And they also, if they abide not still in unbelief, shall be* GRAFTED IN AGAIN. " Grafted in again!"—how? *reinstate* them! in what? No solid answer but one can be assigned, viz. In all those *church-privileges* which they enjoyed, as a general body of people, excepting what was merely typical and ceremonial. But the *church-membership* of infants and children was *not such*; it was before Moses, before Abraham, more ancient than the flood, yes, coeval with the first family in the world. Therefore, *this* will be a part of the restored privilege. While they continue to renounce all connection with Christ the Life of the tree, his church, they must needs be withered branches; but, receiving

R

---

* The inspired prophets " extol not merely the inherent ex-
" cellence, but *wide extent*, of the heavenly kingdom. When-
" ever the prospect rises before them, and it was often presented to
" their view, their heart glows with instant rapture at the splendid
" scene; the powers of language are exhausted to convey their lofty
" conceptions of those days of gladness, when all nations whom the
" Lord hath made shall turn unto him, and walk in the light of
" his holy word. We do not assert, that in order to warrant the
" expressions used on this occasion, it is necessary that every indi-
" vidual of the human species should serve God with a pure heart
" and faith unfeigned : but if the *whole race* shall not hereafter be,
" what they have not yet been, VISIBLE MEMBERS OF THE
" CHURCH OF CHRIST, language is useless, and words have no
" meaning." CHURTON's Bampton's Lectures. Serm. vii. p. 223.

ceiving him, both the branches and their *buds* shall vegetate again in the visible universal church.

Mr. B. in his *Reflection* on ver. 16. says: "Here it may be observed, that baptism is not the subject of Paul's discourse." Granted: but he must grant also in his turn, that *church-membership* and *church-privileges* are the subject of Paul's discourse. And he will find it too difficult to shew, that baptism is not *included* therein; which leads me to another reflection, viz.

§ 52. 2. THAT the apostle's reasoning *necessarily includes infant baptism*. It has been I think demonstrated, in the last section, that infant church-membership and privileges are included in his reasoning; that the christian church both of Gentiles and Jews, must, according to him, be made up in a great measure of infants and children. That is to say, the gospel ministry or dispensation *designs* and *intends*, in its own nature, nothing short of this. But if so, the consequence is evident, that they are *intitled* thereto by the very nature of the gospel church, and a *divine grant*. According to Paul, that is, according to the genuine spirit and native tendency of the gospel; according to the *Will of God*; according to the last will and testament of Jesus, which he sealed with his own blood; and according to the witness of the spirit of truth, by whose infallible direction Paul reasoned and wrote,—infants have a *right* of church-membership with their parents. But who sees not, that if they have that right, they have, of course, a right to *baptism*, the ceremony of *initiation*. To deny this

this would be as ridiculous as to fay, that a man and his family have a legal right to a houfe, but dare not enter it thro' the door, the only door, that leads to it; or, that he has a legal right to certain premifes, but has nothing to do with the ways and avenues leading thereto.

THE apoftle fays (Rom. xi. 16.) *For if the firſt fruit be* HOLY, *the lump is alſo* HOLY: *and if the root be* HOLY, *ſo are the branches.* On which Mr. B. reflects, that the word *holy* is mentioned, " in reference to the *ancient patriarchs*, " efpecially Abraham: in reference to thoſe con- " verted Jews, that were the *firſt fruits* of a " chriftian miniftry: and in reference to the *fu-* " *ture converſion* of Abraham's pofterity, in the " latter day." And immediately infers, " that " the paſſage has no regard to any chriftian pa- " rent, as a *root*; or to his infant offspring, as " *branches* ariſing from it†." But how do the premifes, fuppofing them unexceptionable, fup- port his concluſion? For fuppofe the *firſt fruit* be the *ancient patriarchs*, were not thofe their de- fcendants who *received* the Meſſiah a part of the *Lump* or confecrated maſs? Or, muſt we fay, that their reception of him, and fubmiſſion to his righteous government, made them an *unholy*, or *leſs* holy, part of that Lump? It cannot be denied, that what is here called the *lump* intends the *deſcendants* of theſe patriarchs as fuch, with- out any exception of infants; the *infants*, there- fore, of their defcendants, who had not as yet embraced the Meſſiah, were of the *holy* lump, and ſhall thoſe parts of the fame maſs be pro-

nounced

† Pædob. Exam. p. 373.

nounced *unholy*, BECAUSE of their parents' obedient faith? While *to-day* the parent *rejects* the Meffiah, he and his children are parts of the *holy lump* alike; but *to-morrow* the parent *embraces* the fame invaluable bleffing, and HE *continues* in his privilege, and has it greatly *increafed*, but his CHILDREN — ftill the *defcendants* of Abraham, and, were it not for their parents' *faith!* would ftill be *holy* — his *children* become *unholy.* While they were *holy*, it was their *privilege*, for in that view the apoftle fpeaks of it. But lo! on Antipœdobaptift principles, the parents' *faith*, makes the child *unholy!* The parent's *promotion*, *degrades* the child! " He that *can* believe it let him believe it."

AGAIN: fuppofing the *firft fruit* to intend the firft Jewifh converts to chriftianity; it ftill follows that the *whole mafs*, of which they are a part, is *holy:* and it appears from the fcope of the paffage, that this holinefs of the lump is not what *fhall hereafter* take place, as the *effect* of gofpel preaching; but is reprefented as the encouraging reafon why the gofpel *ought* to be preached to them. The apoftle's argument, it feems, is not, Inafmuch as fome Jews *do* now believe, this is a token and pledge that Abraham's pofterity at large *fhall* believe hereafter: but rather, — becaufe the *other* parts of the lump are *no lefs* holy than that which received the Meffiah; *therefore* there was an encouraging profpect of their converfion alfo. But if this be denied, the cafe is ftill worfe. For if it be faid, that the Jewifh converts to chriftianity were the *firft fruit*

in

in reference to the future church state of *all Israel*; and that the confecration of the *part* sanctified the *whole*: it then follows, contrary to what our opponents are willing to allow, that the unconverted are *sanctified*, or made *holy*, by being only related to christians; and if so, for the same reason children may be said to be sanctified or holy by their relation to christian parents. For to say, that the *remote* posterity of any is holy on account of its relation to him, but not his *immediate* descendants who are more nearly and closely related to him, is, I suppose, sufficiently absurd. I now appeal to the intelligent and impartial reader, whether this is not a fair and full reply to Mr. B's objection.

But as it is my professed design not only to confute error, but also to investigate truth, it may be proper to inquire, what is the real import of the term HOLY, here used by St. Paul? "By *holy* is here meant," says Mr. LOCKE, "that relative holiness whereby any thing hath an *appropriation* to God†." Or, more particularly, we may say, A *holy* person, in the relative sense of that word, is one to whom God gives a covenant grant of mercy and the means of grace, and in virtue of which grant he is *appropriated* to God. This appears to me to be the leading idea of the term, and its precise import in the present connection; tho' sometimes used in a different sense. For if the whole nation of the Jews was *holy* in the apostolic age, the *whole mass*

† *Note* on Rom. xi. 16.

as well as the *first fruit*, the *natural branches* as well as the *root*, as the apostle asserts; if the *future* descendants of Abraham and the patriarchs are to be regarded as *holy*, as Mr. B. allows, and for which reason they are not to be despised and insulted by the Gentiles; then the *present* Jews are so in the like sense: except we hold that the *both ends* of a genealogical chain has an *appropriation* to God, while the *intermediate* links are *unclean*. Which is the same thing as to say, that this genealogical chain is at once, and in the same respect, a *conductor* and a *non-conductor* of this relative holiness.

BUT what is deserving of particular notice is, that there are several *degrees* of relative holiness; and that, in scripture estimation, a person may be, relatively, *holy* in one sense, while *unclean* in another. Accordingly, in a very general sense, *no man* is to be deemed unclean under the gospel dispensation (Acts x. 28.), but *every man*, whether Jew or Gentile, is deemed *holy*; i. e. in virtue of the gospel *grant* of mercy and the means of grace to the Gentiles as well as the Jews, *all mankind* without distinction of nation, or tribe, are *appropriated* to God, or pointed out by him as the intended objects of such a grant. When the command was given to preach the gospel to *every creature*, to propose the means of grace to *all mankind*, they were virtually declared *holy*, and not *dogs* as before reckoned. The *promise*, or covenant grant, is now not only to the Jews and their children, but to *all that are afar off*; for

all

Ch. 3. *Subjects of Baptism.* 367

all the nations are as much the *designed* objects of the call, as the inhabitants of Judea were when the apostle wrote; and when any are actually among *the called*, that design is in them accomplished. — Now, when incorporated with the visible church, they are termed *holy* in a more particular sense. They are then more particularly appropriated to God; the promise is to them more directly; they are more expressly intitled to all the means of grace and salvation, according to their capacity. And, compared with this degree of relative holiness, those who are *holy* in the former sense, are yet *unclean*. Thus an idolater and his family in the one sense, that is, in reference to any divine *prohibition*, or any *exclusive* clause in the covenant, promise, or grant of mercy, is no longer common or unclean, but relatively *holy*. Yet in reference to the *called*, the incorporated members of the visible church, the same idolater and his family are *not* holy but *unclean*. The one is *holy* because he *may partake*, in virtue of a divine appointment; the other is *more holy* (and in *comparison* ot whom the former is unclean) because he actually *does partake* of general church-membership and privileges, and therefore baptism.

I say *general* church-membership, to distinguish it from that which belongs to any *particular* congregation; or even denomination of christians. For tho' we contend that baptism is the rite of admission into the *universal* church of
R 4   Christ

Chrift, or *general body* of chriftians, of which all denominations of chriftian people are parts; yet this is perfectly confiftent with congregational worfhip and difcipline, with diffenting churches, and the independent form in particular. And this indeed the practice of independents abundantly confirms, for when they admit any into *fpecial* memberfhip, it is immaterial whether the parties were baptized in Ruffia or Italy, in Holland or England; in the eftablifhment or among diffenters, or by what denomination of diffenters; it is fufficient in that refpect, that they have been recognized *general* church-members by baptifm. The *other* memberfhip is not to conftitute them profeffed chriftians, but is intended for the better promoting of their edification, in a manner as near as poffible to the intention of the infpired rubrick.

§ 53. WE now proceed to examine another paffage, from whence we may gather, in what light the apoftles viewed the children of believing, or chriftian parents; and that is 1 Cor. vii. 14. *For the unbelieving hufband is fanctified by the wife, and the unbelieving wife is fanctified by the hufband: elfe were your children unclean; but now are they holy.* " On the *matureft* and moft *impartial*
" confideration of this text," fays Dr. DODDRIDGE, " I muft judge it to refer to *infant*
" *baptifm*. Nothing can be more apparent, than
" that the word *holy*, fignifies perfons, who *might*
" *be admitted* to partake of the *diftinguifhing rites*
" of God's people. Compare Exod. xix. 6.
                                        " Deut.

" Deut. vii. 6. chap. xiv. 2. chap. xxvi. 19.
" chap. xxxiii. 3. Ezra ix. 2. with Ifai. xxxv.
" 8. chap. lii. 1. Acts x. 28. &c. And as
" for the interpretation, which *so many* of our
" brethren the Baptifts have contended for, that
" *holy* fignifies *legitimate*, and *unclean illegitimate*;
" (not to urge that this feems an *unfcriptural*
" fenfe of the word) nothing can be more evi-
" dent, than that the argument will by no means
" bear it*." It was not without reafon that
the Doctor expreffed himfelf with fome limitation refpecting the interpretation he oppofes, thus,
" which *so many* of our brethren the Baptifts;"
for they are by no means agreed, how to com-
pafs the wrefting of this text from the Pœdobaptifts. Dr. S. for inftance, is of opinion
" that legitimacy is not here intended †." And
thus he affigns his reafons for diffenting herein
from fome of his brethren: " If one party's
" being a believer makes cohabitation lawful,
" it fhould feem to follow as a natural confe-
" quence, that when neither is a believer co-
" habitation is unlawful; which is a propofi-
" tion no one will maintain. But (fays he,) let
" us examine the queftion refpecting *legitimacy*
" a little more attentively. The apoftle's object
" in this context was, no doubt, to diffuade
" thofe chriftians who were married to unbe-
" lievers from any thoughts of a feparation. And
" the confideration of their having been law-
" fully married, was moft certainly a good
" argument to enforce fuch advice; and the
rather:

* Fam. Expof. in *loc*, † Anf. to Dr. A. p. 3.

" rather, as a divorce would be likely to bring
" diſhonour on their offspring, in the opinion
" of thoſe who might not know the true cauſe
" of it. But if he meant to urge this argu-
" ment, it is ſcarce imaginable he would de-
" ſcribe the lawfulneſs of the marriage contract
" by the phraſe of *the unbelieving huſband's being
" ſanctified by the wife, and the unbelieving wife
" by the huſband*; ſince the validity of the
" marriage did not, could not, in the nature of
" the thing, depend upon one party's being a
" *believer*. Whether he or ſhe were or were
" not a believer, the marriage would have been
" good; nor would a ſeparation, upon pretence
" of their not being of the ſame faith, have
" made the children *illegitimate* ‖." Mr. BOOTH,
however, warmly pleads for what Dr. STEN-
NETT ſtrenuouſly oppoſes.

But as the real meaning of the text very
much depends on the exact import of certain
terms, it will be neceſſary to pay our principal
attention to them; and thence to deduce the
apoſtle's meaning.

1. THE terms ακαθαρτος and αγιος ſhould be
aſcertained. Theſe " are uſed here by the apoſ-
" tle in the Jewiſh ſenſe. The Jews called all
" that were Jews, *holy*; and all others they cal-
" led *unclean*. Thus *proles genita* EXTRA *ſanc-
" titatem*, was a child begot by parents whilſt
" they were yet heathens; *genita* INTRA *ſanc-
" titatem*, was a child begot by parents after
" they were proſelytes. This way of ſpeaking
" St.

‖ Ibid. p. 85.

"St. Paul transfers from the Jewish into the christian church, calling *all* that are of the christian church *saints*, or holy, by which reason all that were out of it were *unclean*[*]." The same author elsewhere observes: "The heathen world had revolted from the true God, to the service of idols and false gods, Rom. i. 18—25. The Jews being *separated* from this corrupted mass, to be the *peculiar people* of God, were called *holy*, Exod. xix. 5, 6. Numb. xv. 40. They being cast off, the professors of christianity were *separated* to be the people of God, and so became *holy*, 1 Pet. ii. 9, 10[‡]." Thus Mr. BAXTER: "The common and I doubt not true exposition is, That it is meant of a state of *separation to God*, as a peculiar people from the world, as the church is separated.——It is generally agreed, that the *most common* use of the word *holy*, if not the *only*, both in scripture and prophane writers, is, to signify *a thing separated* TO GOD: and to *sanctify* any thing, is to *separate it* TO GOD. *Omne sanctum est* DEO *sanctum*; whatsoever is holy, is holy *to God*. This therefore being the *proper* sense and *ordinary* use of the word, I take myself bound to receive it as the meaning here, till I know more reason to the contrary. —Now as *holiness* thus signifieth *a separation to God*, so it may be distinguished thus; a person or thing may be holy, or separated " to

---

[*] LOCKE's Paraphr. *in loc. Note.* [‡] Id. chap. i. 2. *Note.*
[‖] Plain Script. Proof, p. 80.

"to God, either in state and *standing relation*; or else only for some particular *act* or *use*, whether for shorter time or longer*." When contending with his redoubtable antagonist, Mr. TOMBES, and bearing hard on him by urging the constant use of the word *holy*, he gives him a syllogistick overthrow thus: "If the constant meaning of the word *holy* be for a *separation to God*, then we must so understand it here, except there be a palpable necessity of understanding it otherwise; but the constant sense of the word *holy* is for a separation to God, and here is no palpable necessity of understanding it otherwise: Therefore we must so understand it here*." And here it is observable, that Mr. TOMBES denied not that the *constant* meaning of the word *holy* was as Mr. BAXTER said. The latter had also urged, that the sense of the term *holy*, for which he pleaded, was used in scripture near SIX HUNDRED TIMES, and the other sense NO WHERE used. " Here," ——says the keen disputant, conscious of the truth on his side, and somewhat touched with indignation; and is it to be much wondered at, when his side of the question was illuminated with near *six hundred* rays of evidence, and the other confessedly *all dark?*—" here Mr. TOMBES denied not but that the word was taken *so oft* in *my* sense, and *never* in *his*; and yet "——and yet!——" denied the consequence. I do therefore (says the good man) here require all men that are not of desperate resolu-
"tions,

* Ibid. p. 82,

" tions, and proſtituted conſciences, to conſider
" faithfully; whether he be likely to make a
" more comfortable anſwer before the bar of
" Chriſt, who ſaith, Lord, I ſearched after thy
" will in thy word as far as I was able, and I
" durſt not raſhly venture on my ſingular fancy,
" but in my admitting or bringing infants into
" thy viſible church, I grounded my judgment and
" practice on thy word, in the ſame ſenſe as
" it is uſed near *ſix hundred* times in the ſcrip-
" ture — I ſay, will not this man have a bet-
" ter plea than he that ſhutteth infants out of
" the church upon the expoſition of ſcripture in a
" ſenſe as it is *never* elſe uſed in, but near *ſix*
" *hundred* times otherwiſe?" — Again: " If the
" apoſtle by *holy* ſhould have meant, *that they*
" *were not baſtards*, then he ſhould have ſpoke
" in a phraſe which they were unlikely to
" underſtand; and ſo his ſpeech might tend to
" draw them into miſtakes, and not to edify
" them. For if the word *holy* were *conſtantly*
" uſed (even near ſix hundred times in the bi-
" ble) for a *ſeparation to God*, and NEVER uſed
" for legitimacy (all which Mr. TOMBES de-
" nieth not), then what likelihood was there
" that the apoſtle ſhould mean it for legitimacy,
" or the people ſo underſtand him? If I ſhould
" write an epiſtle to a chriſtian congregation
" now, and therein tell them, that their chil-
" dren are all by nature *unholy*, would they
" ever conjecture that I meant that they were
" all *baſtards**?"

BUT

* *Ut ſupra*, p. 83.

But here, were we difposed to retort on the ufe of terms, with what propriety may we afk, " Is *illegitimate* in one cafe, and *legitimate* in the other, the NATURAL and PRIMARY fignification of thofe Greek words (ἀκάθαρτος and ἅγιος)? Are thefe the fenfes that would naturally *firſt* occur to the mind of a wife and impartial perfon, on reading or hearing the apoftolick obfervation ‖ ?" The inquifitive and learned Mr. BAXTER replies,—" *Six hundred to one* it is not." And Dr. GUYSE obferves : " The terms (ἀκάθαρτος)
" *unclean*, and (ἅγιος) *holy*, occur almoft num-
" berlefs times in the *Seventy* and in the New
" Teftament; but I don't find that they are *ever*
" ONCE ufed to fignify *illegitimate* and *legiti-*
" *mate*, which is the fenfe that fome would
" here put upon them. And as the apoftle
" was fpeaking of perfons already married, and
" marriage is a civil ordinance of the God of
" nature, there was *no room to doubt*, whether
" the children of fuch unbelieving and believ-
" ing parents were *legitimate*, or not, fince *that*
" depends intirely on the legitimacy of the
" *marriage* and not at all on the *religious* cha-
" racter of the hufband and wife, whether one,
" or both, or neither of them, were chriftians
" or no*." To this I will add the following remarks of Dr. WHITBY : " He doth not fay,
" Elfe were your children *baftards*, but now
" they are *legitimate*; but, elfe were they *un-*
" *clean*, i. e. heathen children, not to be owned
" as an holy feed.—That this is the true import
" of the words ἀκαθαρσία and ἁγία, will be ap-
                                               " parent

‖ Pædob. Exam. 322.   * Paraphr. in lx. Note.

" parent from the scriptures, in which the Hea-
" thens are styled *the unclean*, in opposition to
" the Jews in covenant with God, and there-
" fore styled *an holy people.* So Isa. xxxv. 8.
" ακαθαρῖος, the UNCLEAN, *shall not pass over it.*
" —Chap. lii. i. There shall no more come
" unto thee ακαθαρῖος, *the* UNCLEAN. So Acts
" x. 28. *God hath shewed me that I should call no*
" *man common,* or, ακαθαρῖον, UNCLEAN. Whence
" it is evident, that the Jews looked upon
" themselves as δύλοι Θιῦ καθαροὶ, *the clean servants*
" *of God,* Neh. ii. 20. and upon all Heathens,
" and their offspring, as unclean, by reason of
" their want of circumcision, the sign of the
" covenant. Hence whereas it is said, that
" Joshua *circumcised* the people, chap. v. 4. the
" septuagint say, περικαθαριν, he *cleansed* them.
" Moreover, of Heathen children, and such as
" are not circumcised, they say, *They are not*
" *born in holiness*; but 'they on the contrary are
" styled σπερμα αγιον, *an holy seed,* Isa. vi. 13.
" Ezra ix. 2. and 'the offspring from them,
" and from those proselytes which had embraced
" their religion, are said to be born *in holiness*,
" and so thought fit to be admitted to circum-
" cision, or baptism, or whatsoever might initiate
" them into the Jewish church. And therefore
" to this sense of the words *holy* and *unclean*,
" the apostle may be here *most rationally* supposed
" to allude, declaring that the seed of holy per-
" sons, the offspring born ἐκ τῶν ἁγιασμένων, *of*
" *saints,* as christians are still called in the New
" Testament

"Testament, are also *holy*. (See note on chap.
"i. 2.) And though one of the parents be still
"an Heathen, yet is the denomination to be
"taken from the *better*, and so their offspring
"are to be esteemed not as Heathens, i. e.
"*unclean*, but *holy*, as all christians by denomi-
"nation are. So CLEMENS ALEXANDRINUS
"(Strom. L. iii. p. 445. D.) infers, saying,
"*I suppose the seed of those that are holy is* HOLY,
"*according to that saying of the apostle Paul, The
"unbelieving wife is sanctified by the husband,*
"&c.—The word used for a *bastard* by this
"apostle being νόθος, Heb. xii. 8. and the word
"γνήσιος being the proper word for a *legitimate*
"offspring, had the apostle *intended* such a sense,
"[as our opponents plead for] he would have
"used the words, which in the greek writers
"are generally used in that sense, and not such
"words as in the septuagint, and in the Jewish
"language, ALWAYS have a relation to fœderal
"[or relative] holiness, or the want of it; but
"NONE AT ALL to the legitimacy or spuriousness
"of the birth*."

THESE quotations are inserted, not so much
to shew what were the *opinions* of these learned
writers (for the general current of expositors
runs in the same channel) but for the sake of
the *reasons* and *grounds* by which their interpretation is supported. A gentleman well known
to my opponent, on a certain occasion borrows
the following passage, which, because it is common

*. Comment. in loc.

mon property, I here infert: "We are not "to forfake the *genuine* and *natural* fignification "of words, unlefs there be the HIGHEST EVI- "DENCE that the author did otherwife intend "them, faith the Civil Law. And as AUSTIN "fays, The proper fignification of words is al- "ways to be retained, unlefs NECESSITY inforce "us to expound them otherwife.—What better "evidence can we have of the fenfe of a place, "than that, had an author *intended* fuch a "meaning, he could have ufed no plainer "expreffion to declare it*."

BUT fays Mr. B. "Whatever the apoftle intends by the word *holy*, as here applied to children, one of whofe parents is a believer; it is not confined to the *infants* of fuch perfons, but belongs to *all* their offspring, whether younger or older; whether born *before* the converfion of either parent, or after that happy event had taken place: for the *children*, without any diftinction are pronounced holy ‡." And what then? Does the afpect of the gofpel difpenfation, or God's *grant* of mercy to the Heathen, who were not *a people*, appear *lefs* amiable becaufe it fmiles on *all* the children of a chriftian, and not on fome only? Or, what inconvenience is there in allowing, what impropriety in maintaining, that the relative holinefs for which we plead, while granted to the parent, fhould

* Pædob. Exam. p. 324. From FERGUSON's Intereft of Reafon in Religion. p. 328, 333, 354, 462.
‡ Pædob. Exam. p. 389.

should be also granted to *all his*?—But will not this be the fearful consequence? " If it be lawful to baptize them on the ground of this holiness, while infants, it must be equally so when grown up ‖." Very true—and what harm can this blunted arrow do? Is not this the very thing we plead for; provided you grant that this reasonable postulate should be taken into the account; viz. That whatever *right* an adult has, in virtue of a divine *grant*, to any religious privileges, Christianity will justify no *compulsive* measures for the purpose of intruding on him these privileges against his good will and liking. Christianity does not annihilate, nay in this instance does not suspend, the *natural rights* of parents and children. And what can be more plain than this, that the natural authoritative right of parents over their children, for their good, is in a great degree absolute, while *infants*; and that *in proportion* as they grow up to reason and manhood, this authoritative right is *lessened*? Nor is there any more difficulty in ascertaining these degrees, than in transacting the common concerns of life, where any degree of wisdom and prudence are required. At least, a christian minister could not, in the nature of the thing, be more at a loss how to act in this case, than in determining the *degrees* of teaching, and the kind of profession, requisite in adults. We will suppose, therefore, that God by his apostle pronounces *the children*

‖ Ibid.

dren of a chriftian without exception *holy*, and let us further fuppofe fome of them are *infants*, and others *grown up*. If God pronounce them *holy*, that is, direct his grant of mercy to them, declaring *the promife* is to them, and that they are all alike, in common with their parents, welcome to his vifible church; it is manifeft there lies no objectionable ground to their baptifm, but their own *diffent* from the chriftian connection, their perverfe *oppofition* to its humbling doctrines and holy laws. Are they *compliable?* willing to enter into the fchool; that is, the church of Chrift? or, in other words, do they believe with all the heart, that Jefus Chrift is the true Meffiah? Who can *forbid* water? On the other hand, do they *oppofe?* are they unwilling to enter the fchool, to embrace its doctrines and to be governed by its laws? Who has power to *conftrain?* . For, in the nature of the cafe, in proportion as the oppofition is criminal or morally evil, the authority of the parent is weakened.

It is again objected: " That *holinefs* of which the infpired author fpeaks, is not inferred from the *faith* of the believing parent, but from the *fanctification* of the unbelieving party, *by*, or *to*, the believer†." But does not this involve a contradiction? For, furely, if the fanctification of the unbelieving party is *by* the *believer*, as fuch, it muft be inferred from his *faith*. And again, if the fanctification be *by* the believer, how can

it

† Pædob. Exam. p. 389.

it be *to* him? Are not the two renderings of the prepofition ιν, *by* and *to*, of which the objector gives us our choice, effentially different and contradictory? If we fay *to* him; the effect, fanctification, muft be caufed by another, that it may terminate on him. But if we fay *by* him; he muft be the caufe, that the effect may terminate on another.—This diverfity of rendering, and the importance of the term *fanctified*, make it neceffary that we fhould,

§ 54. 2. ATTEMPT to afcertain the import of the phrafe ηγιασται εν. "On this term " *fanctified*, fays Mr. B. the infpired writer ma-
" nifeftly lays a peculiar emphafis; *fuch* an
" emphafis, that it feems to be the governing
" word of the whole fentence, and a *key* to
" its true meaning. For it is twice mentioned
" as containing the *grand reafon*, why the be-
" lieving party fhould neither defert, nor divorce,
" the unconverted companion; and alfo as ex-
" preffing *the ground* of that holinefs which is
" afcribed to their children†." This, then, being the *key* to unlock the text, and difcover its contents, let us examine the *wards*, and fee whether they fit Mr. B.'s interpretation. "BENGELIUS, fays our author, con-
" fiders the holinefs of the *children*, and of the
" *unbelieving* parent, as *the fame*; becaufe ηγιασται,
" and αγια εστιν, differ only as, to be *made holy*,
" from to *be holy*." On which he reflects: "If
" then, that fanctification of the unbelieving huf-
" band

† Ibid. p. 400.

"band, gives him no claim to baptism; the holiness thence arising cannot invest his *children* with such a right ‡." This our author seems to consider as an insurmountable objection. And in the same light, we suppose Dr. S. views it. "Now I readily admit," says he, "that the children of believers, or of parents, one of whom only is a believer, are here stiled *holy*. But then I insist, that such children are in no other sense *holy*, than is the unbelieving parent also. For the apostle as expresly asserts that the unbelieving husband is sanctified or made holy (ηγιασται) by the wife, and the unbelieving wife sanctified or made holy by the husband, as that the children of such parents are holy (αγια). And, thus considered, it will follow, that if the holiness of the children, whatever be the sense of the word here, is to be admitted as a proof that they are included in the christian covenant, the holiness of the unbelieving parent is to be admitted as a proof that such parent is included in the christian covenant also. And, if upon this ground the former have a right to the positive institutions of Christ, upon the same ground the latter has also §." But this objection has been sufficiently replied to, virtually, in the last section; when treating of *adult* children, who are relatively *holy* though unbelievers, or opposers to

the

‡ p. 390.   § Anf. to Dr. A. p. 81, 82.

the chriftian faith. And were we to grant, according to our opponents' wifhes, that the children are holy in no higher fenfe than the *unbelieving* parent is, it would ftill follow, on the principle already ftated, that the *children* ought to be baptized, but not the parent. The one and the others have the grant of a privilege, the covenant and its initiatory feal; and the believing parent has a divine right and rubrick for having the feal applied to the *children*, who are at his difpofal for their good, and who do not *oppofe* the faith; but this cannot extend to the *unbelieving* partner, his unbelief counteracting his relative fanctification.

Thus we may obferve, thefe two refpectable authors, though widely differing in their interpretations of the text, are equally confident that *relative holinefs*, which intitles to chriftian ordinances, is not intended. " It may be diffi-
" cult, fays Dr. S. to fix his [the Apoftle's]
" precife meaning; but if we will make reafon,
" fcripture, and fact our guide, it cannot be
" difficult to determine upon fome of the fenfes
" given, that they are not his meaning. Per-
" fonal *internal holinefs*, for inftance, cannot be
" here intended*." In *this* decifion, I believe the generality of Pœdobaptifts will readily concur; though fome divines have pleaded for *real* holinefs, as here afcribed to the *children*, and particularly Dr. Thomas Goodwin‡. On this head

* Ibid.   ‡ Works, Vol. ii. p. 400, &c.

head Mr. B. is sufficiently explicit: "Neither "have we any reason to think, that the chil- "dren of believers are denominated holy, in ".reference to *internal sanctification* ‖." What, then, does this gentleman think was the *holi- ness* referred to, whereby the unbelieving party was *sanctified* by the believer? That which you have seen confuted by Dr. STETNETT in the last section—*marriage!* Take his own words: "The public and voluntary act of taking the "woman for a wife, and the man for a huſ- "band. By this transaction, according to the "legal custom of their country, they mutually "*gave up*, or *set apart*, themselves one to ano- "ther*." Well, reader, what say you to this? Here is, ——*one infidel* SANCTIFYING *another!* Or, if you had rather, *each infidel* SANCTIFYING *himself!*

IF ηγιαςαι signify no more than *to be married*, or to be *given up* in marriage, the one party to the other, it had no influence to satisfy their scruples. For the Israelites, who had married idolatrous wives, could say the same; yet it was no sufficient plea that one of them had been ηγιαςαι, in Mr. B.'s sense, *set apart* to the other. The question would still return, How shall I know that this party that has been *given up* to me, is not to be discarded, or put away, as in Ezra x. 3, &c.? If our author's explanation be admitted, it is to make the Apostle to solve a case of conscience in a manner totally unworthy

‖ Pædob. Exam. p. 392.   * Ibid. p. 400.

thy of him; for he muſt do it by aſſerting a *fact*, that they were once married, of which they were as well aſſured before it was aſſerted: while he ſays nothing of the *lawfulneſs* of that fact, which could be the only ground of ſcruple. The doubts of theſe Corinthian queriſts were raiſed by reflecting on the *quality* of the relation contracted, and not the *fact*; whereas the apoſtle, if our author be right, ſolves the difficulty by paſſing by the *quality*, and aſſerting the fact; that is to ſay, by ſaying ſomething wide of the point, but nothing at all to the purpoſe. Whereas, had it been his deſign to prove the *validity* of their marriage, would he not naturally have done it by ſuggeſting ſome middle term or conſideration, beſides barely referring them to the fact? Was it not neceſſary for them, that they ſhould be certified of the *lawfulneſs* and *propriety* of their marriage relation? On Mr. B.'s hypotheſis this *is not* done; on ours *fully*. If the queſtion be propoſed to him, Why ſhould the believer cohabit with the unbeliever? he muſt reply, Becauſe they were formerly married. Or rather, Not becauſe you, believer, have been devoted to your partner, and are bound to fulfil your engagement; but becauſe your infidel partner has formerly given himſelf to you. But was this a remedy ſuited to the diſeaſe? Or ſhould it be ſaid, This is a ſatisfactory conſideration why the parties ſhould continue, not merely becauſe there has been a mutual *dedication*, but becauſe there has been a divine appointment

pointment of marriage as the bafis of it. But the duty of marriage was from the beginning; yet thofe in the time of Ezra were obliged to put off each man his wife, to which neverthelefs he had been *wedded*. Nor is it available to fay, That thofe in Ezra offended againſt a *pofitive* divine law, but not thefe; for that is the very point in which they defire fatisfaction, viz. Whether the chriftian law does or does not require a *feparation?* His anfwer is not, The law of nature is binding, and chriftianity has nothing againſt it. This would have been his idea if *nothing more* was intended than the *validity* of marriage. But he fays more; the unbeliever *has been* (from the moment of the partner's converfion to chriftianity) or, by an ennalage of time, *is,* made holy or fanctified by the believer, in virtue of a *divine grant,* which divine grant is much in favour of infants. The grant of the parent's covenant and its feals being always intended for them and their children, according to their capacity, be it known, as if Paul had faid, That tho' God hath been difpleafed with mixed marriages, and tho' he ſtill fays, " Be not unequally yoked with unbelievers," yet the idolatry and unbelief, that is, the heathenifm, of the one parent, ſhall be no prejudice to their children. They are not debarred from any privileges given by divine grant to other children *both* whofe parents are chriftians. The faith, or chriftianity, of the one ſhall avail more

S   to

to infure thofe privileges, than the unbelief of the other to prevent them.

THIS is a medium of proof calculated to fatisfy their fcruples. To the pure, all things are pure; the unbelief of your partner fhall not pafs over to you, as if you were involved in his unbelief and guilt; or as if the precept " touch not, tafte not, handle not," affected you. God will gracioufly deal with *you and your children* without any reference to your partner's unbelief. He fhall ftand or fall alone; his obftinacy fhall be *perfonal*, centering in himfelf; but *mercy* herein *rejoicing againft judgment*, the promife is *to you*, chriftian party, and to your children, tho' your partner oppofe.—Nature dictates that a *father*, who is king in his own family, fhould exercife his authority to the benefit of all his domefticks; but by a *gracious exprefs-appointment*, the children common to both fhall be deemed *holy*, on account of the *mother* as well as the father, fo as to be treated as if both parents believed. The feed of mixed marriages were not deemed *holy*, Ezra ix. 2. Neh. ix. 2. it might be objected. True, fays the Apoftle, and to anfwer your fcruples I am authorifed to fay, That under *this* difpenfation there is the difference I have mentioned; and let this quiet your minds. Your continuance together, rather than thofe you refer to, is owing to a *fpecial grant* in their favour, as more agreeable to this difpenfation.

God

God does not now infist on a divorce as he did heretofore, for wife reasons, and among others, because he designs hereby *more speedily to christianize all nations*. For if the unbelief of one party were sufficient to denominate and regard their common offspring in the class of heathens rather than christians, how slow must be the progress of christianity! but now, if one believes in the Messiah, all the family is christian, and is treated accordingly. Otherwise, were not this God's plan and our practice, your children and the whole family but yourself must be deemed *unclean*, or *heathenish*, and visibly related to Satan's interest. But as an unbelieving son, daughter, or servant, is not sufficient to class the family of which either is a part among heathen families, so neither shall the unbelief of your partner, even a husband, have that influence.

AGAIN: If my opponent be right, " the epithet *unbelieving*, as BEZA well observes, would be quite superfluous, as also the *implied* epithet *believing*; *believing* wife, and *believing* husband*."

" For

---

* " *In uxore*, εν τη γυναικι, Vulg *Per mulierem* FIDELEM, " εν τη γυναικι πιςη: quam lectionem in Claromontano et alio " præterea manuscripto Græco codice invenimus: et rursum paulo " post εν τω ανδρω πιςω, *per virum fidelem.*—AUGUSTINUS l. i. " quo exponit sermonem in monte habitum, legit, *In fratre fideli*, " εν αδελφω τω πιςω. Vetus autem interpres habet, *Per mulie-* " *rem fidelem*, et, *per virum fidelem*; et nos in uno VETUSTO " CODICE reperimus ad marginem annotatum πιςη priore loco,
" et

"For we should consider, what is the subject
"matter in dispute; namely, Whether matri-
"mony contracted between two persons, one an
"infidel and the other a believer, is holy, and
"for that cause the believer is bound to con-
"tinue in it? Were it not so, why should Paul,
"in the other member, add the epithet *unbe-*
"*lieving?* Nor can any one truly say, that the
"marriage between two infidels is *holy*, and that
"their *children* are *holy*.—I grant that the mar-
"riage of infidels is valid in a civil sense, nor
"is their matrimonial commerce to be re-
"garded *coram Deo pro scortatione.* But what
"has this to do with Paul's design, who treats
"of a case of conscience, or a religious scru-
"ple†?" The *unbelieving* husband is sanctified
by the *believing* wife, and *vice versa.* Whereas,
if Mr. B.'s hypothesis be true, the *sanctification*
was neither *by* nor *to* the believer, as a *believer,*
but was possessed of it while an infidel. But if
the *sanctification* does not respect the party *as
believing,* it seems inserted for no other use than
to mislead us. If the apostle only meant simply, " you have been *married,*" or, " you have
been *devoted* to each other by marriage," why
introduce and *interchange* the expressions and
ideas—" the *unbelieving* by the *believing* party?"
                                                    Mr.

"et πιςω posteriore. Claromontanus autem codex habet, ιν.ανδρι
"αδελφω, In viro fratre, id est, qui sit frater sive fidelis. Et
"certe etiamsi hæc epitheta non addas, tamen NECESSARIO *subau-*
"*dienda sunt.* BEZA *in loc.*

† BEZA *ut supra.*

Mr. B. seems to be aware of this objection, and observes: "The *unbeliever only* could en- "tertain a doubt, concerning the *lawfulness* of "cohabiting with an unbeliever." Very well; but the question still returns, If the apostle meant, as our author would have it, That the unconcerned party was *married* to the *scrupulous*; is it not reasonable to suppose, that the idea would be *differently* expressed? Is it not confessedly an *unprecedented mode* of expressing a *common idea?* Whereas, if he intended to shew —that the christianity of the one party was more prevalent, in virtue of the more merciful and extensive grant of God, and the genius of the gospel dispensation, towards classing the children among the christians; than the *infidelity* of the other party towards the classing them among *idolaters*—what expressions could he use better adapted to express the sentiment?

Moreover: be it observed, that the very existence of the other opinion depends on rendering the preposition εν, TO, which rendering ought not to be adopted without manifest necessity, if on any consideration whatever, in that sense of *to,* which denotes a *dative* case. It is well known that the most common acceptations of εν are *in, by, among, with,* and sometimes it is used for, *because of, for,* or *for the sake of, by reason of*; and the like ‖." EN imports

‖ "Ει τη γυναικι, *by the wife, Uxoris gratia,* BECAUSE OF the "wife; i. e. he is to be reputed as sanctified, because he is one "flesh

" imports the *state* and *disposition*, the *abode* and
" *situation*; *habitum et situm*, says VERGARA;
" corresponding to the Latin *in**." And " it
commonly marks the term of rest, or the state
in which a thing is; wherefore it *only* governs
an *ablative*†." But what has Mr. B. to say
in vindication of his rendering? " The unbe-
" lieving husband is sanctified TO the wife.—
" So Dr. DODDRIDGE and others render the par-
" ticle εν; and I think more properly in *this*
" passage than in our common version. *So* the
" preposition is translated in the very next verse;
" as also in Luke i. 17. 1 Thess. iv. 7. and six
" or seven times over in 2 Pet. i. 5, 6, 7‡."
But *why* is the rendering *to*, more proper in *this*
passage than in our common version? This
answer we have still to learn. We hear a language somewhat different whenever it is found
in connection with *water*, and especially a
river. Thus, we may be sure, were we to
meet with εν ποταμω, in connection with baptism, it would be IN, and not *at* or *by* the
river. However, let us a little more narrowly
inspect

" flesh with her who is holy. So *Israel served* εν γυναικι, *for*
" *a wife, and,* εν γυναικι, *for a wife* he kept sheep. Hos. xii. 12.
" *I desire that you faint not,* εν ταις θλιψεσι μου, BY REASON OF
" *my tribulations*, Eph. iii. 13, and, *that no man be shaken* εν ταις
" θλιψεσι ταυταις, BY REASON OF *my tribulations.* See NALDIUS
" in the 23d signification of the particle *Bath.*" WHITBY *in loc.*

* *Messieurs* DE PORT ROYAL's New Method. p. 195.

† Ibid. p. 334. and their *Greek Primitives*, by NUGENT, p. 297.

‡ Pædob. Exam. p. 395.

inspect the authorities produced, and I am very much mistaken if *any one* of these instances answer the purpose for which they are adduced: for if they do not answer the idea of a *dative*, which implies that something is GIVEN TO the object, they are useless. And I believe the best Criticks and masters of the Greek language unanimously maintain, that the preposition εν never conveys that idea §." The *dative* case is so called, " quia per eum alicui aliquid nos " dare demonstramus †." This the particle in question *never* signifies, any more than the latin *in*; and yet without that use of it Mr. B.'s interpretation is a baseless fabrick.

WE are referred to " the very next verse" following the controverted text (1 Cor. vii. 15.) *God hath called us*, εν ειρηνη, TO *peace*, according to our version; whereas Dr. HAMMOND justly observes,

§ " Εν τη γυναικι, *by* or *thro'* the wife. This the preposition, " εν, so ordinarily signifies, that it cannot need to be further testified " (and in this notion it is, that we here take it); whereas the " notion, which by opposers is here affixt to it, that it should " signify *to* (that *to*, which is a sign of the *dative* case)—is " never once found to belong to it in the New Testament; nor " *can* with any tolerable *congruity* or *grammatical* analogy, be affixt " to it. All the places that are produced for this sense are com- " monly mistaken —And so still the rendering it *to the wife* [in " the *dative* sense] will be without any one example, and the " turning it into quite *another* phrase, as if it were γυναικι with- " out εν; which to do without any *necessity* or *reason*, save only " — to serve the opposer's turn upon the place, and support his " false opinion, must needs be very unreasonable," HAM- MOND's Six Quer. Q. 2. iv. § 32.

† LITTLETON, sub voce *dativus*.

observes, "It is not *to* as the note of a *dative* "case, but UNTO *peace*, as εν is taken for εἰς ‡." Again we are referred to Luke i. 17. *To turn —the disobedient* TO *the wisdom of the just.* But this is by no means the sign of a *dative.* There is nothing *given to* wisdom. " ELSNER would render it, as Dr. DODDRIDGE observes, BY *the wisdom of the just**." And thus Sir NORTON KNATCHBULL: " *Et infideles instruat* IN *sapientia justorum* ‖." And so other literal versions; " IN *prudentiam justorum* §." " AD *scientiam rectorum* §§." " AD *scientiam justorum* ‡‡." " AD *prudentiam justorum***." " *Ad intelligentiam justorum* ‖‖," &c. In like manner, 1 Thess. iv. 7. For God hath not called us unto (επι) uncleanness, but εν αγιασμω, UNTO *holiness.* That is, in the phrase of Dr. DODDRIDGE, "to the love and practice of universal holiness." But what has this to do with *giving to* a recipient? As to 2 Pet. i. 5, 6, 7. it seems still less to his purpose. *Add to your faith virtue, and to virtue knowledge*, &c. επιχορηγησατε εν τη πιςει ὑμων την αρετην, εν δε τη αρετη την γνωσιν, &c. i. e. bring forward, *with* your faith, virtue, and, *with* virtue, knowledge. " The word επι- " χορηγησαι. properly signifies to *lead up*, as in " a dance, one of these virtues after another in " a beautiful and majestic order †." " Respexisse " videtur

‡ Dr. HAMMOND *ut supra.* * Fam. Expos. *in loc.* ‖ Animadver. *in loc.* § MONTAN. §§ SYR. INTERPRET.
‡‡ ARAB. INTERPRET. ** Vulg. ‖‖ ÆTHIOP. INTERPRET.
† DODDR. Fam. Expos. *in loc.*

"videtur Apostolus ad antiquum morem ducendi "choros; vox enim επιχορηγειν proprie significat "chorum ducere †." Accordingly the same Author renders the passage, "Jungite invicem *cum* "fide virtutem, *cum* virtute scientiam, &c." I repeat the question, What has this to do with *giving to* a recipient? Or what similarity has it to Mr. B.'s *dative* sense?—Who knows not that the article *to* has *various* acceptations, beside what Mr. B. would force upon it? For instance, we say, *appointing to* an office, *going to* a place, *calling to* enjoy, *turning to* wisdom, &c. yet such an acceptation of the particle *to* will not serve him.

Nor will Dr. DODDRIDGE's version answer his purpose in sense, tho' in sound. For tho' he renders ηγιασαι *is sanctified to*, yet the particle has not the *dative* signification. He evidently gives the original particle the acceptation of the Greek εις or Latin *in*, signifying *towards*, *in respect of*, *for*, &c. It is but fair the Doctor should explain himself: "For in such a case as "this, the unbelieving husband is so *sanctified to* "the wife [*in uxorem*], and the unbelieving wife "is so *sanctified to* the husband [*in maritem*], that "their matrimonial converse is as lawful AS IF "THEY WERE BOTH OF THE SAME FAITH: "*Otherwise their children* in these mixed cases "*were unclean*, and must be looked upon, as "unfit to be admitted to those peculiar ordi- "nances, by which the seed of God's people "are distinguished; *but now they are* confessedly "*holy*

† Sir NORTON KNATCHBULL, *ut supra.*

" *holy*, and are as readily admitted to baptifm
" in all our churches, as if BOTH the parents
" were chriftians: So that the cafe you fee,
" is in effect decided by this prevailing prac-
" tice*." In a *note* the Doctor oppofes the
idea of legitimacy; by fhewing " that the argument will by no means bear it." But is it
not furprizing that perfons of difcernment, that
Mr. BOOTH in particular, fhould fuppofe this
rendering, *fanctified to*, gives the leaft countenance to his *dative* notion? Is this any thing
better than a play upon the various acceptations
of an englifh particle? Is it not taking, or at-
tempting to take, an advantage of found againft
fenfe? And is it not ftill more furprizing that
Dr. S. fhould exprefs himfelf thus: " Indeed
" Dr. DODDRIDGE, to whofe character for learn-
" ing, candour, and piety I pay great deference,
" has fo expreffed himfelf in his *paraphrafe* on
" this paffage, as *very naturally to convey this*
" *idea* [of legitimacy], tho' in his note he op-
" pofes the fentiment. How to reconcile him
" with himfelf I am at a lofs†."—*The paraphrafe very naturally conveys this idea.* And I
am quite at a lofs to know, by what medium
the Dr. views it. Whereas it appears to me
" very naturally to convey the *contrary* idea."
Does it not evidently refolve the *lawfulnefs* of
matrimonial converfe, in fuch a mixed cafe, to
a *divine grant*, declaration and appointment, that
is, to the party's being *fo fanctified*, in virtue of
a gra-

* Fam. Expof. *in loc.* † Anfwer to Dr. A. p. 83.

a gracious privilege conferred under the gospel, *as if they were both of the* SAME FAITH? And does not this clearly imply, that what *sanctified* the unbeliever was (not his *giving* himself *to* the other in marriage, but) God's favourable *appointment* in such a case? Had they been of the *same faith*, no scruple could have existed; the PRIVILEGE therefore consists in the *opposing* party's being *so sanctified* for the use of the other, *as if both believed* alike; otherwise, their having " mutually *given up*, or *set apart* themselves one to another," would have been no security against a *divorce*, which was the point in question, if the Lord were equally strict against infidel and idolatrous connections under the present, as he was under the preceding œconomy *(Deut.* vii. 3, 4, &c.)': and the PRIVILEGE moreover is expressly extended to the *children*; which would have been reckoned (according to Ezra ix. 2. Nehem. ix. 2.) not among the relatively *holy* seed, in such a mixed case. Such a grant of special privileges, therefore, the text and the paraphrase imply; and *nothing short* of this could tend to satisfy the scrupulous querist.

But tho' Dr. DODDRIDGE appears to me perfectly consistent with himself, while he opposes the idea of *legitimacy*; yet I cannot help thinking but he is more reserved than he had need to be, if he had meant to confine the *sanctification* to the matrimonial converse. For, tho' we should allow that the *sanctification* of the unbelieving partner and of the children is *the same*; and that the terms *sanctified* and *holy* imply a qualification, as far as a divine grant can qualify, or a declarative permission and liberty, " to partake of the distinguishing rites of God's people;" yet, as before shewn, the *opposer* of the gospel should not be *forced*; for violent measures are no weapons of the gospel, and should not be employed in its propagation, or in administering its initiatory seal. To which we may add, that such an opposing infidel or idolater, being an *avowed enemy* to the head of the church, does not possess a subjective *suitableness* to enter upon a visible relation to him and his subjects. He may, therefore, possess a *right*, in virtue of his relative sanctification or holiness, a right founded on a divine grant, and yet no minister has a right, or lawful authority, to *impose* upon him what he *rejects*, however beneficial it might be to him if accepted. But this is only a *circumstance*, that takes its rise solely in adults from the perverse exercise of human liberty, the sacred rights of conscience in religious matters, and a subjective unsuitableness to answer the design of the ordinance. The *sanctified* unbeliever is *entitled* to the covenant and its seal, unconditionally; which *title* he derives, independent of his choice, from his relation to his christian partner, and as the Gift of God: but the actual *application* of the external privilege ministerially, is suspended on a *condition*, viz.

viz. his accepting of it in a manner suitable to his condition and circumstances.—On the contrary, supposing the children to be *holy* only in the same sense, still the rule holds, that infant ones ought to be baptized; because they are capable subjects, and have not forfeited the grant, nor failed in any *condition* required of them.

It may not be improper to remark, that, notwithstanding we have, for argument' sake, admitted Mr. B.'s idea of *sameness* in having been *sanctified* and being *holy*, there seems to be a *difference*: As if the Apostle intended to shew, that the unbelieving partner was sanctified, not *merely* for his own sake, but as also having a *further* influence on the children, and without which they would have been *unclean*. The influence of the unbelief and heathenism of the one party, as if he had said, is annihilated, by the counter influence of the other party's faith or christianity, with respect to their offspring. The faith of the one party, by the merciful tenour of the gospel dispensation, is more efficacious towards classing the children among the christians, than the unbelief of the other towards classing them among heathens. The unbeliever is *sanctified*, i. e. his professed unbelief is *overpowered by the professed holiness* of the other, in reference to their respective influence upon their children, which were to be ranked either among heathens or christians. But as to the *children*, their holiness appears in stronger and more expressive terms, alluding, it should seem, to a well known *fact* that they were

were treated as *holy*; were deemed members of the christian church, and made partakers of its privileges according to their capacity. (Επει αρα,) *Otherwise* were your children unclean, (νυν δε) *but now* are they holy. " Nam particula νῦν hoc " in loco, says BEZA, non est temporis adver- " bium, sed est conjunctio quæ adhiberi solet in " argumentorum assumptionibus, ut alibi ostendi- " mus*." Therefore the phrase νῦν δὲ ἅγια ἐςιν, is tantamount to, " *sancti sunt autem.*"

THUS we see that the interpretation for which Mr. B. contends, is in every view indefensible. It directly tends to make the apostle Paul, with all his superior abilities and supernatural endowments,—an unskilful casuist, a very abstruse, if not an inconclusive, reasoner, and a blunderer in

* Annot. *in loc.*—The following exposition of this part of the text, and the reflections, by a masterly critick, are worthy of insertion here.—" Επει ἄρα — Alioquin [nisi parentum alteruter esset fidelis] " *liberi vestri essent immundi,* i. e. manerent Ethnici: νῦν δὲ, nunc " *vero* [quoniam parentum alter est fidelis] ἅγιά ἐςιν, *sancti* " *sunt,* i. e. reputantur membra Ecclesiæ Christianæ. Et in hac " notione credo Apostolum sæpius usurpare vocem ἅγιος, ut in " initio hujus epistolæ, &c. Ecclesia enim et sancti sunt sæpius apud " Aposto'um Synonyma, ut apparet etiam alibi, manifest ssime vero " 2 Cor. i 1, &c.—Non quod omnes, qui essent in Ecclesia Corinthi " vel Ephesi, erant revera sancti, sed quia membra erant visibilia eccle- " siæ, ideo vocabantur *sancti,* & ob eam causam liberi eorum ex alte- " rutro parente fideli, qui fuit vocatus sanctus, participes facti " sunt BAPTISMI, quomodo filius ex selytæ lotus est particeps " circumcisionis, etiam infans octiduanus. E si liberi eorum qui " vocantur *sancti,* cum sint etiam ipsi *sancti,* non capaces sint " baptismi, 'n quo præcellunt *sancti* immunos? quid inde habent " commodi, eo quod vocentur vel reputentur *sancti?*" Animadv. *in loc.* a NORTONO KNATCHBULL.

in the language in which he wrote. Whereas ours regards him, as indeed he was, a skilful casuist, a masterly reasoner, and a good writer.

But we must not quit this subject without attending for a few moments to Dr. S.'s compromising plan. Having discarded the intention of personal internal holiness, legitimacy, &c. from the text, he observes: "If Mr. A. will but give
" up his general proposition [that the children of
" pious parents are included with them in the
" christian covenant] in those exceptionable sen-
" ses of it to which I have all along objected,
" we shall perhaps be able to *compromise* the
" matter upon this text without much diffi-
" culty. I agree then, that there is a sense in
" which every good man may be said to SANC-
" TIFY *his wife and his children*. He DEVOTES
" them by faith and prayer to God, he *sepa-*
" *rates* them, as far as his influence reaches,
" to the fear and service of heaven.—Thus
" Job is said to have *sanctified* his children, ch.
" i. 5‡." But instead of *compromising* the matter, the Dr. seems to me to *give up* the point. And one would think he is apprehensive of it himself; for, after having endeavoured to support his notion by a full paraphrase, he observes:
" This paraphrase may perhaps not satisfy, nor
" do I lay any great stress upon it*" But seeing this notion is hardly expected to give satisfaction, he flies to the *dernier* resort of Antipœdobaptists, I mean, their peculiar notion about
positive

‡ Ans. to Dr. A. p. 87.   * *Ut supra*, p. 89.

positive institutions: " Could it be proved that
" the children of christian parents are included
" with them in the christian covenant, and on
" that account *holy:* it would not follow that
" therefore they should be baptized: their right
" to baptism must depend, and depend alone,
" upon the direct express command of the In-
" stitutor; for it is *absurd* to talk of *analogy*
" and *consequence* in the matter of positive in-
" stitution†." And yet *this* fort is untenable;
yes, I am bold to affirm, it is a vain and useless refuge in the present cause. (See Chap. i.)
If the reasoning contained in the preceding
pages be just, I say it again, " Instead of compromising the matter, the point is *given up.*"
For, if every good man, as priest in his own
house, may SANCTIFY *his wife and children,*
may DEVOTE them *by faith* and prayer to God,
and SEPARATE them to the fear and service
of heaven; if those who are thus treated may
be termed *holy,* and are so termed by the apostle, as the Dr. supposes—the very nature of the
case shews, that the *holiness* spoken of is *relative*; and the nature and design of christian
baptism shew, that he may with *equal* propriety,
set apart all of them, *as* HIS, for that ordinance; and it appears from what has been said,
that none in such a family should be left unbaptized, except those who *reject* the counsel of
God, or are manifestly *disaffected* to the christian church and its divine Founder.

§ 55. FROM

† Ibid.

§ 55. From what has been said in this chapter we may draw the following obvious corollaries.

1. *Coroll.* Thofe *principles* whereby infant children are debarred from their parents' privileges, from a vifible ftanding in the church of Chrift, and particularly from baptifm, which is itfelf a privilege, and the only introductory rite to that vifible ftanding among God's people, are *unreafonable*, *unfcriptural*, and highly *uncharitable*.

(1) *Unreafonable*—becaufe " infants are *capable* of the OBLIGATIONS of baptifm; for the *obligation* arifeth from the EQUITY *of the thing*, not from the underftanding and capacity of the perfon*." And " if we confider baptifm as an ordinance of *dedication*—it is the indifpenfible duty of believers to devote themfelves, and *all they have*, to God; which is *founded in the law of nature*, and is the refult of God's right to us *and ours.*" And if it be objected : " Since infants cannot *devote themfelves* to God in this ordinance, therefore it is not to be applied to them; to this it may be replied, That as there is no other *medium* which can be made ufe of to prove that the folemn act of confecration, or dedication to God in baptifm, is to be made *only* by ourfelves, but what is taken from a fuppofition of the matter in controverfy, by thofe who affert that infants are not to be baptized : fo if this method of reafoning be allowed of, we might as well fay, on the other hand

---

* Poole's Annot. on Matt. xxviii. 19.

hand; Infants are to be baptized; therefore baptism is not an ordinance of self dedication, since they cannot devote themselves to God; and that would militate against what is allowed of by all, that baptism, when applied to the adult, is an ordinance of self-dedication.—When I do, as it were, pass over my right to another, there is nothing required in order hereunto, but that I can lawfully do it, considering it as *my property*; and this is no less to be doubted concerning the *infant seed* of believers than I can question, whether an adult person has a right to *himself* when he gives up himself to God in this ordinance.— And from hence it may be inferred—that infants descending from parents, either both, or but one of them professing faith in Christ, are to be baptized: since *one* parent has as much a right to the child as the *other**." To these reflections of the judicious Dr. RIDGLEY, I will add the following from the justly celebrated Dr. OWEN: " All children in their infancy are reckoned unto the covenant of their parents, by virtue of *the law of their creation.*—Those who by God's appointment, and by virtue of the law of their creation, are and *must of necessity* be included in the covenant of their parents, have the same right with them unto the privileges of that covenant, no *express exception* being put in against them. This right it is in the power of none to deprive them of, *unless they can change the*

---

* RIDGLEY's Body of Div. vol. ii. p. 408, 409.

the law of their creation†." To attempt which, it is hardly neceſſary to remark, that it is ſufficiently *unreaſonable*.

(2) *Unſcriptural*. In addition to what has been ſaid on the various diſpenſations of the covenant of grace, or the grant of mercy to men; the declarations of prophecy; and the records of the New Teſtament; let the following remarks from the author laſt referred to, be impartially weighed. " Believers under the New Teſtament, have loſt nothing, no privilege that was enjoyed by them under the old. Many things they have *gained*, and thoſe of unſpeakable excellency, but they have loſt nothing at all. Whatever they had of *privilege* in any ordinance, that is continued; and whatever was of *burden* or bondage, that is taken away: all that they had of old was on this account, that they were the *people of God.*—Into this great *fountain privilege* believers under the goſpel have now ſuccceeded.—This I ſuppoſe is unqueſtionable; that God making them to be *his people* who were *not a people*, would not cut them ſhort of any privilege which belonged before to *his people* as ſuch.—Let men but give *one inſtance* to this purpoſe, and not beg the matter in queſtion, and it ſhall ſuffice.—And is it poſſible that any man ſhould be a loſer by the *coming of Chriſt*, or by his *own coming* unto Chriſt? It is againſt the whole goſpel once to imagine it in the leaſt inſtance. Let it now be inquired, whether it were not a great

---

† Tract of Inf. Bapt. ap. Collect. of Serm. p. 577.

great *privilege* of the *people of God* of old, that their *infant seed* were taken into covenant with them, and were made partakers of the *initial seal* thereof? Doubtlefs it was the greateft they enjoyed, next to the grace they received for the faving of their own fouls.—Without this, whatever they were, they were not *a people*. Believers * under the gofpel are, as we have fpoken, the *people of God*; and that with all forts of advantages annexed unto that condition, above what were enjoyed by them who of old were fo. How is it then that this *people of God*, made fo by Jefus Chrift in the gofpel, fhould have their *charter* upon its *renewal razed* with a deprivation of one of their choiceft rights and privileges? Affuredly it is not fo. And therefore, if believers are now, as the apoftle fays they are, the *people of God* (Heb. iv. 9.) their children have a right to the *initial seal* of the covenant†."

(3) *Uncharitable.* Is it not uncharitable (to fay nothing worfe) to conclude, that all the infants in the chriftian world are as unqualified for a vifible memberfhip in the church of God, as the moft hardened infidel? Nay, much further from the gofpel kingdom; fince the latter *may* come to be a member in a few days, while the former *muft*, on this plan, be fhut out for years; and this exclufion muft continue for ever,

if

---

* UNDERSTAND by *Believers* and the *people of God*, CHRISTIANS; that is, thofe who are fuch by *denomination*; which remarks are ftill more forcible with refpect to the truly pious.

† Dr. OWEN, On the Hebr. vol. ii. p. 256.

if the party do not *submit* to such terms of communion, as nine godly persons out of ten judge and sincerely believe are *unreasonable* and *unscriptural,* viz. a *renunciation* of the baptism and church-membership of infants, and of every mode of receiving and administering the ordinance, except a total immersion of the body. Our opponents, indeed, extend their charity as far as we could wish, to *dying* infants, while they are so sparing of it to the *living*. The dying are numbered with the *saints*, the living, as to church relation and privileges, are classed with *infidels*. And is it not strange to astonishment, that the *excellency* and *spirituality* of the gospel dispensation should be considered as an argument by men of sense, for excluding infants from a visible relation to Christ and his people! But if this be a just plea of exclusion, why so freely allow them a standing in a state far *more* excellent and spiritual? How can these things hang together? Does it not involve an *absurdity*, as well as uncharitableness, to say, that a person may be very well admitted to heaven, *without* believing and repenting, but not to be a member of the visible church? The church, it is allowed, is the common nursery from whence paradise is planted; and yet infants must not be taken into this nursery, but heaven must have them from the wild waste!—Dr. JOHN OWEN was a man whom no modest person would venture to pronounce either a shallow divine or a superficial reasoner; he was a person much conversant with the controversial parts of divinity

nity, eminently versed in the *rationale* of the divine dispensations, well acquainted with the nature of positive institutions in general; and the subjects and mode of baptism in particular, possessed a share of his investigations. Thus qualified to instruct us, let us hear his words: " Why is it the will of God, that *unbelievers* " and *impenitent* sinners should not be baptized? " It is because, not granting them the *grace*, he " will not grant them the *sign*. If therefore " God *denies* the *sign* to the infant seed of be- " lievers, it must be *because* he denies them the " grace of it; and then *all* the children of be- " lieving parents, dying in their infancy, must " without hope be eternally damned. I do not " say, that all must be so, who *are not* baptized; " but *all must be so whom God* WOULD HAVE " NOT BAPTIZED*." Infants being not *naturally incapable* of baptism, as before shewn, any more than of circumcision, and scripture evidence affording no express exception against them, but on the contrary contains much in their favour as members of the christian church, and their right to baptism, may we not ask, if Dr. OWEN's reasoning be just (and we may safely challenge the whole *corps* of Antipœdobaptists to refute it) must not *our denying* baptism to our infant children be a conduct towards them highly *uncharitable*, as well as unscriptural and unreasonable? We impeach not the tenderness and affection of our brethren to their children in *other* respects, and readily suppose that there is a sense
in

* Dr. OWEN of Inf. Bapt. *ut supra.*

in which every *good man* among them " *devotes* them (as Dr. STENNETT expresses it) by faith [tho' in this respect *weak*] and prayer to God —*separates* them as far as his influence reaches [*except* in the case of church-membership and baptism] to the fear and service of heaven, and they derive from their connection with him such external advantages of a religious kind [tho' in an *irregular* way, if it be irregular to separate what God hath joined, the *charter* and the *seal*; and to tear away the stamp and signature of the only charter whereby they enjoy those external advantages] as often prove the happy means of their conversion and salvation †." The *uncharitableness* we are speaking of consists, not in restraining prayer before God for them, or in neglecting moral parental duties (except what arises naturally and necessarily from their distinguishing tenet); but in acting the part of the disciples over again, who *forbad* infants and children to be brought to Christ in all the *external ways* they are capable of being brought.

2. *Coroll.* From what has been said it may evidently appear, what that *church membership* is which we claim for infants, and what those different *relations* are in which they stand to Christ and his people before and after baptism. The term itself, *church-membership*, being expressive of relation and comparison, admits of different *degrees*; so that the same person may be a church-member in one sense, but not in another. The gospel church is a select body of people of which Christ

† Anf. to Dr. A. p. 87.

Chrift is the head, and each perfon of which it is compofed is a member. But this body may be *felect* in a manner lefs or more ftrict; and confequently the *relation* of the members to the head and to each other muft be proportionally remote or intimate. Accordingly we may obferve,

(1) That perfons are often called *church-members* in this controverfy, when they are fo only *de jure*, or *quoad debitum*. And in this fenfe we regard all adults *before* baptifm, who neverthelefs *may* be lawfully baptized. The infant children of profefling chriftians, thofe of our opponents not excepted, we alfo regard as church-members in the fame fenfe, tho' not baptized. And we cannot but confider this circumftance with pleafure and gratitude, on behalf of children, that there is *one degree* of church-memberfhip, that which is *quoad debitum*, which it is out of the power of men to deprive them of. The propriety of their being denominated *members* of the church, antecedent to their being minifterially recognized fuch, arifes hence, That they actually poffefs the qualifications of members, and therefore *are fo* in the *divine eftimation*, and *ought* to be fo in ours, tho', *quoad eventum*, they may never be baptized, thro' the miftakes and faults of others. This relation to Chrift is appointed and determined by himfelf, and ftands abfolutely independent on the will of others.

(2) Persons are called *church-members* in a *ftricter* fenfe, when they have been regularly admitted

Ch. 3.   *Subjects of Baptism.*   409

mitted by baptifm, the ordinance of admiffion, into the number of thofe who are profeffed *chriftians*, in contradiftinction to Jews, Heathens, &c. And it is evident from the nature of the cafe, that *this* degree of memberfhip depends on the will and miniftry of man, *quoad eventum*. The *right* of memberfhip, being a divine gift, muft needs be *abfolute*; but the publick avowal and recognition of that right by an ordinance inftituted for that purpofe, muft needs depend on the judgment, volition, and agency of men. If any abufe this difcretionary truft, they are accountable to the Judge of all; neverthelefs, with regard to the validity of *minifterial* acts, in admitting perfons into *this* memberfhip, or fhutting them out, we may fay, that what is bound on earth is bound in heaven, and what is loofed on earth is loofed in heaven. Therefore, the firft relation is to be fought from the determination of God, but the laft from the determination of man. And then alone is the latter right, when it coincides with, and is expreffive of, the former. And in reference to baptifm we may fay, it *belongs* to the firft, but *makes* the fecond.

(3) AGAIN: Perfons are called *church-members* in the *ftricteft* fenfe, when they have confented to affociate together for divine worfhip and chriftian fellowfhip, for promoting their mutual edification, the converfion of fouls, &c. But fuch a body is not, ftrictly fpeaking, *the church* of Chrift, but *a part* of it. Chrift has

T   but

but *one* body, the church, myftically; and but *one*, vifibly; and as to congregational churches, fo called, they are but collective parts of that one vifible church. Or if we borrow an illuftration from the ftarry heaven, we may fay, That a *particular* church is a *conftellation* of ftars, which makes but a fmall *part* of the general catalogue.

But what particularly deferves our notice is, That the *firft* relation *entitles* to baptifm; that the *fecond* relation fuppofes the *application* of baptifm; and the *third alone* is what infants and young children are to be debarred from. And this exclufion is no arbitrary proceeding, but refults from the very nature and defign of fuch a fociety. The only *pofitive* qualification requifite for this laft memberfhip, is, that a perfon be baptized; and in that refpect every baptized perfon may be faid to have a legal right to it. But again, feeing the nature and defign of fuch a fociety, as may be gathered from nature and revelation, does not comprehend infants and children, and adults evidently difqualified by error and wickednefs; the one not poffeffing natural, the other not moral qualifications; the not admitting baptized infants to the Lord's Supper; which is *peculiar* to church-members in this ftricteft fenfe, is founded on the jufteft principles; for when laws and rights *pofitive* and *moral interfere*, the former muft yield to the latter.

If our opponents wilfully overlook thefe plain and neceffary diftinctions, it is no wonder, if

fo

so disposed, that they should be able to represent the Pædobaptists in an inconsistent and ridiculous light: for what armour is proof against such weapons? At this rate, the sacredness and dignity of truth itself are no defence. Mr. B. having made some remarks on the word "covenant" as used by Mr. MATTHEW HENRY (as if *that* term also had not *various* acceptations), adds: "The conduct of Mr. HENRY is quite
" similar, in regard to *church-membership*. For
" in one place he tells us, that baptism is an
" ordinance of Christ, *whereby* the person bap-
" tized is *solemnly* ADMITTED a member of the
" visible church: yet in the same treatise, he af-
" sures us, that baptism is an ordinance of the
" visible church, and pertains therefore to those
" that ARE *visible members* of the church. — Their
" covenant right and their *church-membership*, in-
" titleth them to baptism — Baptism doth not
" *give* the title, but *recognize* it, and compleat
" that church-membership which before was im-
" perfect†." But does this passage deserve all the ridicule Mr. B. affects to treat it with? Is there any thing here deserving of "the sarcastic reflection of a profane poet?" Mr. B.'s *ironies* in the present case, affect — not Mr. HENRY's *cause*, nor the *sentiments* here advanced, but — the defect of language, or at most an omission in *defining* terms and making distinctions, to prevent the cavils of those who seek occasion.

† Pædob. Exam. p. 322, and Mr. *Henry's* Treatise on Baptism, p. 25, 66, 107.

sion.—Having examined as proposed, Who are the proper *Subjects* of baptism; particularly, whether it is the WILL OF CHRIST that the infants of believing or christian parents should be baptized? we proceed to consider next the *mode* of administering the ordinance.

END OF VOL. I.

www.ingramcontent.com/pod-product-compliance
Lightning Source LLC
Chambersburg PA
CBHW030543300426
44111CB00009B/845